Praise fo

In a fast-changing culture that seems alien to many Christians (just as Christians seem alien to many in the culture!), it is easy for Christians to throw up their hands in despair and adopt a purely defensive mode. In this important book, Tim Keller unpacks the gospel and gently but firmly reminds us that it is nonnegotiable. At the same time, he enables us to think through how we can responsibly interact with the culture, how we can — indeed, must — appreciate good things within it, and how we can firmly and faithfully apply the gospel to it. But this is not a mechanical how-to book; rather, it is a reflective meditation on some hugely important themes in Scripture written by someone who has exercised faithful pastoral ministry in a major city for two decades.

> D. A. CARSON, research professor of
> New Testament, Trinity Evangelical Divinity School

No one has listened more closely to the harmonies of city, culture, church, and Scripture than Tim Keller. In *Center Church*, he not only describes the different strains of music but also tells us how he has orchestrated the results for the sake of ministry outreach and renewal. Now it's our turn to listen, as Tim practically yet powerfully prepares us to participate in this great symphony of the gospel.

> BRYAN CHAPELL, president, Covenant Theological Seminary

Center Church is an immensely helpful resource for the next generation of church leaders. It is theologically profound, thought provoking, and energizing, and it will make you uncomfortable in measure. Once again, Tim Keller has hit the bull's-eye!

> ALISTAIR BEGG, senior pastor,
> Parkside Church, Cleveland, Ohio

We don't need another "do ministry like my church does ministry" book. Nor do we need another book that critiques other church models. We need a book that helps us think critically and biblically as we structure our churches. *Center Church* is packed with Tim Keller's experience, humility, and wisdom. This book will help you if you are serious about seeing your city transformed by the gospel of grace.

DARRIN PATRICK, lead pastor,
The Journey, St. Louis, Missouri

Church leaders abandon their unique calling if they merely think theologically to the exclusion of seeing the world in light of the gospel and helping their churches live in the world with gospel wisdom. No one makes this case more clearly today than Tim Keller. He resists the all-too-easy pattern of selling a simple model of what it means to be the church that fits every setting. Instead he brings to life the myriad ways churches are called to be faithful and fruitful in their own unique cultural context. Read this book if you want to learn how to ask the really important (and difficult) questions by which the gospel confronts our ecclesial identity.

RICHARD LINTS, Andrew Mutch distinguished professor
of theology, Gordon-Conwell Theological Seminary

Cities are challenging and complex but also important and strategic. And those who are called to minister in cities need encouragement and resources that fuel hope and effectiveness. That's why I'm so glad that Tim Keller has written this book. His passion for the gospel, heart for the city, and vision of a movement of the Holy Spirit that will transform lives and bring hope and peace to our cities has compelled him to share his insights and thinking with us. What's more, the church he serves speaks to the integrity of his heart and the possibility of the reality of this vision. Be prepared. Your thinking will be sharpened, and your heart will be moved.

DR. CRAWFORD W. LORITTS JR., senior pastor,
Fellowship Bible Church, Roswell, Georgia

This outstanding book, like the Manhattan ministry out of which it has come, shows how Reformed theological acumen and wise pastoral intelligence may combine to achieve spiritual fruitfulness in urban contexts everywhere. Every page illuminates. Keller is a huge gift to today's church.

J. I. PACKER, professor emeritus, Regent College

Most of us observe and see the obvious. Tim Keller observes and sees that which is unseen by others—especially when it comes to the truth of God's Word and the culture of the day. Once again, he has given us deeper insights—this time regarding the church and how she can experience her healthiest potential. How foolish to know of this book and not read it!

RANDY POPE, pastor, Perimeter Church, Atlanta, Georgia

Tim Keller has given us the must-read book on gospel-shaped ministry. Robustly theological and profoundly practical, it is a top-to-bottom survey of gospel implications for the life and ministry of the church. The gap between biblical and practical theology is masterfully bridged. Having worked with Tim and Redeemer City to City, I have benefited from the content of this book and can also attest to its profound influence on ministers and churches throughout the world. This is not simply curriculum content; it is exactly the kind of life-giving, generative gospel theology our churches need. No thoughtful Christian's bookshelf should be without it.

STEPHEN T. UM, senior minister,
Citylife Presbyterian Church, Boston, Massachusetts

In *Center Church*, one of the great missionary statesmen of our time lays out a vision of the church vigorous enough to transform entire cities through its agency of the gospel. Tim Keller is a gifted teacher, an outstanding leader, and an exemplary disciple of Jesus. A worthy read!

ALAN HIRSCH, founder of 100Movements
and the Forge Mission Training Network

We live in a day of remarkable church leaders and wonderful Christian thinkers, but I'm not sure there's a more thoughtful church leader in our day than Tim Keller. *Center Church* is his call for church ministry formed by deep theological reflection and sensitive cultural exegesis executed by courageous leaders so that the city may once more flourish under the gospel.

JOHN ORTBERG, senior pastor,
Menlo Park Presbyterian Church, Menlo Park, California

Tim Keller's church in New York City serves as one of the world's best models for gospel-centered ministry that wisely, biblically, and fruitfully connects with its community. This is mainly due to Dr. Keller's deep understanding of the gospel and his exceptional gift for interpreting culture. His latest book will be immensely helpful to anyone doing ministry anywhere. *Center Church* is not a manual for replicating Keller's ministry, but something much more important: a theological vision for how the gospel of Jesus Christ relates to culture, ministry, and the Christian life.

PHILIP RYKEN, president, Wheaton College

I'm not exaggerating when I say that *Center Church* is my favorite book Tim Keller has written thus far. Perhaps this book simply represents the distillation of Tim's wisdom — the synthesis of years of marinating in the gospel, exegeting the text of Scripture, and engaging the soul of our culture; his willingness to dialogue without diatribe; his ongoing commitment to think through the radical implications of God's grace; his great love for Jesus' bride, God's kingdom, and the history of redemption. It's all refreshingly here. What an awesome and practical read! I cannot wait to use this book with emerging leaders and churches willing to dream.

SCOTTY SMITH, founding pastor,
Christ Community Church, Franklin, Tennessee

LOVING THE CITY

DOING BALANCED, GOSPEL-CENTERED MINISTRY IN YOUR CITY

A New Edition of
Section Two
of Center Church

TIMOTHY KELLER

WITH NEW CONTRIBUTIONS BY
**DANIEL STRANGE, GABRIEL SALGUERO,
AND ANDY CROUCH**

ZONDERVAN

Loving the City
Copyright © 2016 by Redeemer City to City, Timothy J. Keller, and Zondervan

This title is also available as a Zondervan ebook.

Requests for information should be addressed to:
Zondervan, 3900 *Sparks Dr. SE, Grand Rapids, Michigan* 49546

Library of Congress Cataloging-in-Publication Data

Names: Keller, Timothy, 1950- author. | Keller, Timothy, 1950- Center church.
Title: Loving the city : doing balanced, Gospel-centered ministry in your city / Timothy
    Keller with new contributions by Daniel Strange, Gabriel Salguero, and Andy Crouch.
Description: Grand Rapids, MI : Zondervan, [2015] | "A new edition of section 2". |
    Revised edition of: Section 2 of Center church. Grand Rapids, MI : Zondervan, c2012.
    | Includes bibliographical references.
Identifiers: LCCN 2015041229 | ISBN 9780310514084 (softcover)
Subjects: LCSH: City missions. | City churches. | Church work. | Evangelistic work.
Classification: LCC BV2653 .K452 2015b | DDC 266/.022—dc23 LC record available at
    http://lccn.loc.gov/2015041229

Cover design: *Lucas Art and Design*
Interior design: *Kait Lamphere*

Printed in the United States of America

HB 03.23.2021

CONTENTS

Part 3: Cultural Engagement

SERIES INTRODUCTION

Two kinds of books are ordinarily written for pastors and church leaders. One kind lays out general biblical principles for all churches. These books start with scriptural exegesis and biblical theology and list the characteristics and functions of a true biblical church. The most important characteristic is that a ministry be faithful to the Word and sound in doctrine, but these books also rightly call for biblical standards of evangelism, church leadership, community and membership, worship, and service.

Another category of book operates at the opposite end of the spectrum. These books do not spend much time laying biblical theological foundations, though virtually all of them cite biblical passages. Instead, they are practical "how-to" books that describe specific mind-sets, programs, and ways to do church. This genre of book exploded onto the scene during the church growth movement of the 1970s and 1980s through the writing of authors such as C. Peter Wagner and Robert Schuller. A second generation of books in a similar vein appeared with personal accounts of successful churches, authored by senior pastors, distilling practical principles for others to use. A third generation of practical church books began more than ten years ago. These are volumes that directly criticize the church growth how-to books. Nevertheless, they also consist largely of case studies and pictures of what a good church looks like on the ground, with practical advice on how to organize and conduct ministry.

From these latter volumes I have almost always profited, coming away from each book with at least one good idea I could use. But by and large, I found the books less helpful than I hoped they would be. Implicitly or explicitly, they made near-absolutes out of techniques and models that had worked in a certain place at a certain time. I was fairly certain that many of these methods would not work in my context in New York and were not as universally applicable as the authors implied. In particular, church leaders outside of the United States found these books irritating because the authors assumed that what worked in a suburb of a U.S. city would work almost anywhere.

As people pressed me to speak and write about our experience at Redeemer, I realized that most were urging me to write my own version of the second type of book. Pastors did not want me to recapitulate biblical doctrine and principles of church life they had gotten in seminary. Instead, they were looking for a "secrets of success" book. They wanted instructions for specific programs and techniques that appealed to urban people. One pastor said, "I've tried the Willow Creek model. Now I'm ready to try the Redeemer model." People came to us because they knew we were thriving in one of the least churched, most secular cities in the U.S. But when visitors first started coming to Redeemer in the early and mid-1990s, they were disappointed because they did not discern a new "model" — at least not in the form of unique, new programs. That's because the real "secret" of Redeemer's fruitfulness does not lie in its ministry programs but in something that functions at a deeper level.

Hardware, Middleware, Software

What was this deeper level, exactly? As time went on, I began to realize it was a middle space between these two more obvious dimensions of ministry. All of us have a *doctrinal foundation* — a set of theological beliefs — and all of us conduct particular *forms of ministry*. But many ministers take up programs and practices of ministry that fit well with neither their doctrinal beliefs nor their cultural context. They adopt popular methods that are essentially "glued on" from the outside — alien to the church's theology or setting (sometimes both!). And when this happens, we find a lack of fruitfulness. These ministers don't change people's lives within the church and don't reach people in their city. Why not? Because the programs do not grow naturally out of reflection on both the gospel and the distinctness of their surrounding culture.

If you think of your doctrinal foundation as "hardware" and of ministry programs as "software," it is important to understand the existence of something called "middleware." I am no computer expert, but my computer-savvy friends tell me that middleware is a software layer that lies between the hardware and the operating system and the various software applications being deployed by the computer's user. In the same way, between one's doctrinal beliefs and ministry practices should be a well-conceived vision for how to bring the gospel to bear on the particular cultural setting and historical moment. This is something more practical than just doctrinal beliefs but much more theological than how-to steps for carrying out a particular ministry. Once this vision is in place, with its emphases and values, it leads church leaders to make good decisions on how to worship, disciple, evangelize, serve, and engage culture in their field of ministry—whether in a city, suburb, or small town.

Theological Vision

This middleware is similar to what Richard Lints, professor of theology at Gordon-Conwell Theological Seminary, calls a "theological vision."[1] According to Lints, our doctrinal foundation, drawn from Scripture, is the starting point for everything:

> Theology must first be about a conversation with God ... God speaks and we listen ... The Christian theological framework is primarily about listening—listening to God. One of the great dangers we face in doing theology is our desire to do all the talking ... We most often capitulate to this temptation by placing alien conceptual boundaries on what God can and has said in the Word ... We force the message of redemption into a cultural package that distorts its actual intentions. Or we attempt to view the gospel solely from the perspective of a tradition that has little living connection to the redemptive work of Christ on the cross. Or we place rational restrictions on the very notion of God instead of allowing God to define the notions of rationality.[2]

However, the doctrinal foundation is not enough. Before you choose specific ministry methods, you must first ask how your doctrinal beliefs "might relate to the modern world." The result of that question "thereby form[s] a theological vision."[3] In other words, a theological vision is a vision for what you are going to *do* with your doctrine in a particular time and place. And what does a theological vision develop from? Lints shows that it comes, of course, from deep reflection on the Bible itself, but it also depends a great deal on what you think of the culture around you. Lints offers this important observation:

> A theological vision allows [people] to see their culture in a way different than they had ever been able to see it before ... Those who are empowered by the theological vision do not simply stand against the mainstream impulses of the culture but take the initiative both to understand and speak to that culture from the framework of the Scriptures ... The modern theological vision must seek to bring the entire counsel of God into the world of its time in order that its time might be transformed.[4]

In light of this, I propose a set of questions that can guide us in the development of a theological vision. As we answer questions like these, a theological vision will emerge:

- What is the gospel, and how do we bring it to bear on the hearts of people today?
- What is this culture like, and how can we both connect to it and challenge it in our communication?
- Where are we located — city, suburb, town, rural area — and how does this affect our ministry?
- To what degree and how should Christians be involved in civic life and cultural production?
- How do the various ministries in a church — word and deed, community and instruction — relate to one another?
- How innovative will our church be and how traditional?
- How will our church relate to other churches in our city and region?

- How will we make our case to the culture about the truth of Christianity?

Our theological vision, growing out of our doctrinal foundation but including implicit or explicit readings of culture, is the most immediate cause of our decisions and choices regarding ministry expression. It is a faithful restatement of the gospel with rich implications for life, ministry, and mission in a type of culture at a moment in history. Perhaps we can diagram it like this (see figure).

Center Church

This book was originally published in 2012 as one of three sections of a longer work called *Center Church*. In that book, I presented the theological vision that has guided our ministry at Redeemer. But what did we mean by the term *center church*? We chose this term for several reasons.

1. The gospel is at its center. It is one thing to have a ministry that is gospel-believing and even gospel-proclaiming but quite another to have one that is gospel-centered.

WHAT TO DO

How the gospel is expressed in a particular church in one community at a point in time

- *Local cultural adaptation*
- *Worship style & programming*
- *Discipleship & outreach processes*
- *Church governance & management*

↑

HOW TO SEE

A faithful restatement of the gospel with rich implications for life, ministry, and mission in a type of culture at a moment in history

- *Vision and values*
- *Ministry "DNA"*
- *Emphases, stances*
- *Philosophy of ministry*

THEOLOGICAL VISION

↑

WHAT TO BELIEVE

Timeless truths from the Bible about God, our relationship to him, and his purposes in the world

- *Theological tradition*
- *Denominational affiliation*
- *Systematic & biblical theology*

2. The center is the place of balance. We need to strike balances as Scripture does: of word *and* deed ministries; of challenging *and* affirming human culture; of cultural engagement *and* countercultural distinctiveness; of commitment to truth *and* generosity to others who don't share the same beliefs; of tradition *and* innovation in practice.

3. Our theological vision must be shaped by and for urban and cultural centers. Ministry in the center of global cities is the highest priority for the church in the twenty-first century. While our theological vision is widely applicable, it must be distinctly flavored by the urban experience.

4. The theological vision is at the center of ministry. A theological vision creates a bridge between doctrine and expression. It is central to how all ministry happens. Two churches can have different doctrinal frameworks and ministry expressions but the same theological vision — and they will feel like sister ministries. On the other hand, two churches can have similar doctrinal frameworks and ministry expressions but different theological visions — and they will feel distinct.

The Center Church theological vision can be expressed most simply in three basic commitments: Gospel, City, and Movement.[5] Each book in the Center Church series covers one of these three commitments.

Gospel. Both the Bible and church history show us that it is possible to hold all the correct individual biblical doctrines and yet functionally lose our grasp on the gospel. It is critical, therefore, in every new generation and setting to find ways to *communicate the gospel clearly and strikingly*, distinguishing it from its opposites and counterfeits.

City. All churches must understand, love, and identify with their local community and social setting, and yet at the same time be able and willing to critique and challenge it. Every church, whether located in a city, suburb, or rural area (and there are many permutations and combinations of these settings), must become wise about and conversant with the distinctives of human life in those places. But we must also think about how Christianity and the church engage and interact with culture in general. This has become an acute issue as Western culture has become increasingly post-Christian.

Movement. The last area of theological vision has to do with your church's *relationships*—with its community, with its recent and deeper past, and with other churches and ministries. Some churches are highly institutional, with a strong emphasis on their own past, while others are anti-institutional, fluid, and marked by constant innovation and change. Some churches see themselves as being loyal to a particular ecclesiastical tradition—and so they cherish historical and traditional liturgy and ministry practices. Those that identify very strongly with a particular denomination or newer tradition often resist change. At the other end of the spectrum are churches with little sense of a theological and ecclesiastical past that tend to relate easily to a wide variety of other churches and ministries. All of these different perspectives have an enormous impact on how we actually do ministry.

The Balance of Three Axes

One of the simplest ways to convey the need for wisdom and balance in formulating principles of theological vision is to think of three axes.

legalism
religion

GOSPEL

relativism
irreligion

1. The Gospel axis. At one end of the axis is legalism, the teaching that asserts or the spirit that implies we can save ourselves by how we live. At the other end is antinomianism or, in popular parlance, relativism—the view that it doesn't matter how we live; that God, if he exists, loves everyone the same. But the gospel is neither legalism nor relativism. We are saved by faith and grace alone, but not by a faith that remains alone. True grace always results in changed lives of holiness and justice. It is, of course, possible to lose the gospel because of heterodoxy. That is, if we no longer believe in the deity of Christ or the doctrine of justification, we will necessarily slide toward relativism. But it is also possible to hold sound doctrine and yet be marked by dead orthodoxy (a spirit of self-righteousness), imbalanced orthodoxy (overemphasis on some doctrines that obscure the gospel call), or even "clueless orthodoxy," which results when doctrines are expounded as in a theology class but aren't brought together to penetrate people's hearts so they experience conviction of sin and the beauty of grace. Our communication and practices must not tend toward either law or license. To the degree that they do, they lose life-changing power.[6]

underadapted
only challenge

CITY

overadapted
only appreciate

2. The City axis (which could also be called a Culture axis). We will show that to reach people we must appreciate and adapt to their culture, but we must also challenge and confront it. This is based on the biblical teaching that all cultures have God's grace and natural revelation in them, yet they are also in rebellious idolatry. If we overadapt to a culture, we have accepted the culture's idols. If, however, we underadapt to a culture, we may have turned our own culture into an idol, an absolute. If we overadapt to a culture, we aren't able to change people because we are not calling them to change. If we underadapt to a culture, no one will be changed because no one will listen to us; we will be confusing, offensive, or simply unpersuasive. To the degree a ministry is overadapted or underadapted to a culture, it loses life-changing power.

structured organization
tradition and authority

MOVEMENT

fluid organism
cooperation and unity

3. The Movement axis. Some churches identify so strongly with their own theological tradition that they cannot make common cause with other evangelical churches or other institutions to reach a city or work for the common good. They also tend to cling strongly to forms of ministry from the past and are highly structured and institutional. Other churches are strongly anti-institutional. They have almost no identification with a particular heritage or denomination, nor do they have much of a relationship to a Christian past. Sometimes they have virtually no institutional character, being completely fluid and informal. A church at either extreme will stifle the development of leadership and strangle the health of the church as a corporate body, as a community. To the degree that it commits either of these errors, it loses its life-giving power.

The more that ministry comes "from the center" of all the axes, the more dynamism and fruitfulness it will have. Ministry that is toward the end of any of the spectrums or axes will drain a ministry of life-changing power with the people in and around it.

As with the original publication of *Center Church*, my hope is that each of these smaller volumes will be useful and provoke discussion. The three volumes of the paperback series each correspond to one of the three axes.

Shaped by the Gospel looks at the need to recover a biblical view of the gospel. Our churches must be characterized by our gospel-theological depth rather than by our doctrinal shallowness, pragmatism, nonreflectiveness, and method-driven philosophy. In addition, we need to experience renewal so that a constant note of grace is applied to everything and our ministry is not marked by legalism or cold intellectualism.

Loving the City highlights the need to be sensitive to culture rather than choosing to ignore our cultural moment or being oblivious to cultural differences among groups. It looks at how we can develop a vision for our city by adopting city-loving ways of ministry rather than approaches that are hostile or indifferent to the city. We also look at how to engage the culture in such a way that we avoid being either too triumphalistic or too withdrawn and subcultural in our attitude.

Serving a Movement shows why every ministry of the church should be outward facing, expecting the presence of nonbelievers and supporting laypeople in their ministry in the world. We also look at the need for integrative ministry where we minister in word *and* deed, helping to meet the spiritual and physical needs of the poor as well as those who live and work in cultural centers. Finally, we look at the need for a mind-set of willing cooperation with other believers, not being turf conscious and suspicious but eagerly promoting a vision for the whole city.

The purpose of these three volumes, then, is not to lay out a "Redeemer model." This is not a "church in a box." Instead, we are laying out a particular theological vision for ministry that we believe will enable many churches to reach people in our day and time, particularly where late-modern Western globalization is influencing the culture. This is especially true in the great cities of the world, but these cultural shifts are being felt everywhere, and so we trust that this book will be found useful to church leaders in a great variety of social settings. We will be recommending a vision for using the gospel in the lives of contemporary people, doing contextualization, understanding cities, doing cultural engagement, discipling for mission, integrating various ministries, and fostering movement dynamics in your congregation and in the world. This set of emphases and values—a Center Church theological vision—can empower all kinds of church models and methods in all kinds of settings. We believe that if you embrace the process of making your theological vision visible, you will make far better choices of model and method.

A NOTE FROM
TIMOTHY KELLER

Center Church is a textbook for church leaders working at ministry today, especially for those in urban or urbanized areas. The volume in your hands is the second of three. It consists of material from the middle three parts of *Center Church*, namely, Gospel Contextualization, City Vision, and Cultural Engagement, together with three essays by other authors giving their reflections on the content, followed by my responses to their reflections. The three authors are Daniel Strange, Gabriel Salguero, and Andy Crouch.

I think it is fair to say that these represent the most unique parts of the *Center Church* textbook. There is a great deal of talk about contextualization but little in the way of practical instruction that is accessible for most church leaders. There is, I'm glad to say, more interest in ministry to the city today than ever before, but there is still a dearth of theological reflection on cities by evangelicals. And while there has been an explosion of proposals on how Christians should relate to culture, *Center Church* tries to survey and assess them all rather than making a proposal designed to compete with all the others.

My three conversation partners have written excellent papers that make genuine contributions to these topics in their own right. Dan Strange is a British theologian who both confirms and challenges my theory and practice of contextualization but who is in such fundamental sympathy with the basic approach that he ends up strengthening the theological underpinnings of the model and gives us some new tools to use.

Gabriel Salguero brings a crucial non-Anglo voice and perspective.

His essay convicts this older white minister that the *Center Church* equipping community needs not merely the occasional input of non-Anglo and non-Western leaders but their shared leadership as well.

Andy Crouch's essay is unique among all the reflection papers written about *Center Church*. Rather than writing a typical review containing appreciation and critique, Andy rolls up his sleeves and produces a constructive rewrite of one of the Cultural Renewal chapters. Using the biblical theme, metaphor, and story of *the image of God*, he builds a framework that not only positively conveys our responsibility as Christian culture makers but also explains and holds together the wisdom of each of the classic models of cultural engagement.

I have learned much from these essays, as well as from those found in *Shaped by the Gospel* and *Serving a Movement*—the other two volumes reflecting on other parts of *Center Church*. Let me briefly mention my two top-level lessons.

One is that *Center Church* cannot stand alone. Most essayists argue that there are missing arguments, biblical cases or rationales, or balancing emphases and practices that should have been mentioned at particular points in the material but are missing. One of the primary missing pieces is much more help on what preaching should look like. Originally I was going to include an entire section in *Center Church* on the topic of preaching, but we determined that this would lengthen an already intimidatingly thick book. This content has become *Preaching: Communicating Faith in an Age of Skepticism*. I've come to see that especially the first three parts of *Center Church*—Gospel Theology, Gospel Renewal, and Gospel Contextualization—need to be read in tandem with my book on preaching. It is just as true that the chapters on City Vision (part 4 of *Center Church*), as well as some later chapters on Integrative Ministry (part 7), should be read along with my book *Generous Justice: How God's Grace Makes Us Just*.

The second major lesson I've learned is that I am more of a practitioner than a theologian. I have not theorized a way to do preaching, evangelism, and ministry—and then proceeded to put the theorized model into practice. Rather, I have been involved directly in years of heavy preaching and evangelism in the city—and then tried to sit down and put on paper what I learned. As I've reread my own material and interacted with my often brilliant conversation partners, I've come to see that my practice is more complete than my descriptions of those practices. But this is helping me become a better teacher of ministry.

I hope readers of this volume will be just as challenged and changed by the accumulated wisdom within these pages as I have.

Part 1

GOSPEL
CONTEXTUALIZATION

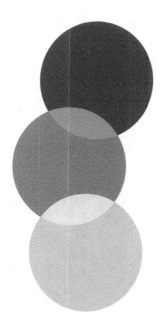

Chapter 1

INTENTIONAL CONTEXTUALIZATION

Redeemer City to City is an agency that promotes church planting and gospel movements in the great city centers of the world (see www.redeemercitytocity.com). As part of our global ministry, we have had opportunities to talk with Chinese house church leaders. God is blessing the church in China with extraordinary growth. However, when Chinese churches and ministers who had experienced God's blessing in their rural ministries entered the mushrooming cities of China and tried to minister and communicate the gospel in the same ways that had been blessed in the countryside, they saw less fruitfulness.

More than a decade ago, several Dutch denominations approached us. While they were thriving outside of urban areas, they had not been able to start new, vital churches in Amsterdam in years—and most of the existing ones had died out. These leaders knew the gospel; they had financial resources; they had the desire for Christian mission. But they couldn't get anything off the ground in the biggest city of their country.[1]

In both cases, ministry that was thriving in the heartland of the country was unable to make much of a dent in the city. It would have been easy to say, "The people of the city are too spiritually proud and hardened." But the church leaders we met chose to respond humbly and took responsibility for the problem. They concluded that the gospel ministry that had fit nonurban areas well would need to be adapted to the culture of urban life. And they were right. This necessary adaptation to the culture is an example of what we call "contextualization."

Sound Contextualization

Contextualization is not—as is often argued—"giving people what they want to hear."[2] Rather, it is giving people *the Bible's answers*, which they may not at all want to hear, *to questions about life* that people in their particular time and place are asking, *in language and forms* they can comprehend, and *through appeals and arguments* with force they can feel, even if they reject them.

Sound contextualization means translating and adapting the communication and ministry of the gospel to a particular culture without compromising the essence and particulars of the gospel itself. The great missionary task is to express the gospel message to a new culture in a way that avoids making the message unnecessarily alien to that culture, yet without removing or obscuring the scandal and offense of biblical truth. A contextualized gospel is marked by clarity and attractiveness, and yet it still challenges sinners' self-sufficiency and calls them to repentance. It adapts and connects to the culture, yet at the same time challenges and confronts it. If we fail to adapt to the culture or if we fail to challenge the culture—if we under- or overcontextualize—our ministry will be unfruitful because we have failed to contextualize well.

Perhaps the easiest way to quickly grasp the concept is to think about a common phenomenon. Have you ever sat through a sermon that was biblically sound and doctrinally accurate—yet so boring that it made you want to cry? What made it tedious? Sometimes it's the mechanics (e.g., a monotone delivery), but more often a boring sermon is doctrinally accurate but utterly irrelevant. The listener says to himself or herself, *You've shown me something that may be true, but in any case I don't care. I don't see how it would actually change how I think, feel, and act.* A boring sermon is boring because it fails to bring the truth into the listeners' daily life and world. It does not connect biblical truth to the hopes, narratives, fears, and errors of people in that particular time and place. It does not help the listener to even *want* Christianity to be true. In other words, the sermon fails at contextualizing the biblical truth for the hearers.

When we contextualize faithfully and skillfully, we show people how the baseline "cultural narratives" of their society and the hopes of their hearts can only find resolution and fulfillment in Jesus. What do I mean by this? Some cultures are pragmatic and prod their members to acquire possessions and power. Some are individualistic and urge their members to seek personal freedom above all. Others are "honor and shame" cultures, with emphasis on respect, reputation, duty, and bringing honor to your family. Some cultures are discursive and put the highest value on art, philosophy, and learning.[3] These are called "cultural narratives" because they are stories that a people tell about themselves to make sense out of their shared existence. But whatever these personal and cultural narratives may be, sound contextualization shows people how the plotlines of the stories of their lives can only find a happy ending in Christ.[4]

So contextualization has to do with culture, but what exactly is culture? Effective contextualization addresses culture in the broadest sense of the word, along the maximum surface area. Culture is popularly conceived narrowly—as language, music and art, food and folk customs—but properly understood, it touches every aspect of how we live in the world. Culture takes the raw materials of nature and creates an environment. When we take the raw material of the earth to build a building or use sounds and rhythms to compose a song or fashion our personal experiences into a story, we are creating an environment we call a culture. We do all this, however, with a goal: to bring the natural order into the service of particular "commanding truths," core beliefs, and assumptions about reality and the world we live in.

Missionary G. Linwood Barney speaks of culture as resembling an onion. The inmost core is a worldview—a set of normative beliefs about the world, cosmology, and human nature. Growing immediately out of that layer is a set of values—what is considered good, true, and beautiful. The third layer is a set of human institutions that carry on jurisprudence, education, family life, and governance on the basis of the values and worldview. Finally comes the most observable part of culture—human customs and behavior, material products, the built environment, and so on.[5] Some have rightly criticized this model—of an onion or a ladder—as not sufficient to show how much all these "layers" interact with and shape one another.[6] For example, institutions can produce something new like the United States interstate highway system, which created "car culture" behavior, which has in turn undermined older forms of communities and therefore many institutions. So the interactions are neither linear nor one-way.

But the main point here is that contextualizing the gospel in a culture must account for all these aspects. It does not mean merely changing someone's behavior, but someone's worldview. It does not mean adapting superficially—for example, in music and clothing. Culture affects every part of human life. It determines how decisions are made, how emotions are expressed, what is considered private and public, how the individual relates to the group, how social power is used, and how relationships, particularly between genders, generations, classes, and races, are conducted. Our culture gives distinct understandings of time, conflict resolution, problem solving, and even the way in which we reason. All these factors must be addressed when we seek to do gospel ministry. David Wells writes, "Contextualization is not merely a practical application of biblical doctrine but a translation of that doctrine into a conceptuality that meshes with the reality of the social structures and patterns of life dominant in our contemporary life."[7]

Skill in contextualization is one of the keys to effective ministry today. In particular, churches in urban and cultural centers must be exceptionally sensitive to issues of contextualization, because it is largely there that a society's culture is being forged and is taking new directions. It is also a place where multiple human cultures live together in uneasy tension, so cultural compounds are more complex and blended there.

A Brief History of the Term

The term *contextualization* may have first been used in 1972 by Shoki Coe, a Taiwanese-born man who was one of the key figures in the formation of the World Council of Churches.[8] Coe questioned the adequacy of the older "indigenous church movement" model identified with Henry Venn and Rufus Anderson. Venn and Anderson directed Western missionaries to plant churches in new cultures that were "self-supporting, self-governing, and self-propagating." Older missionaries had planted churches in foreign cultures and maintained control of them indefinitely, using native Christians only in assisting roles. They also explicitly directed national Christians to adopt Western ways wholesale. The indigenous church movement, however, called missionaries to see themselves as temporary workers whose job was to do initial evangelism and then, as quickly as possible, to turn the churches over to indigenous, national leadership so the Christian churches could worship and minister in native languages, music, and culture.

This was a good and important step forward in our understanding of how Christian mission is conducted. But Coe, who served as principal of Tainan Theological College, argued that something more than just empowering national leaders was needed. He observed that the missionaries still gave national leaders *forms* of church ministry—ways of expressing and formulating the gospel and structuring churches—that were unalterably Western. National Christians were not being encouraged to think creatively about how to communicate the gospel message to their own culture.[9]

The Theological Education Fund of the World Council of Churches was the first agency to use this new term and pursue it within its mission. The earliest work under this name, however, caused grave concerns. Following the existential theological thinking of Rudolf Bultmann, who was still highly influential in the 1970s, and Ernst Käsemann, theologians connected to the WCC insisted that the New Testament was itself largely adapted to a Hellenistic worldview that did not have abiding validity. Therefore, it was argued, Christians were free to determine, in whatever way that fit their particular culture, the "inner thrust of Christian [biblical] revelation" and discard or adapt the rest.[10]

This approach to contextualization assumes that both the text (Bible) and context (culture) are relative and equally authoritative. Through a dialectical process in which the two are brought into relationship to one another, we search for the particular form of Christian truth (with a small *t*) that fits a culture for the time being. Virtually any part of the Christian faith, then—the deity of Christ, the triunity of God, the gracious basis of the gospel—can be jettisoned or filled with radically new content, depending on the particular cultural setting. In the name of contextualizing to its culture, a church has the potential to make radical changes to historical Christian doctrine.

The irony is deep. The original call for contextualization intended to allow national churches to do theological reflection without having extrabiblical, Western thought forms imposed on them. However, much of what the ecumenical WCC Theological Education Fund propagated was nonetheless deeply shaped by Western thinking. contextualization based on the idea of a nonauthoritative Bible stems from the views of modern Western theologians who themselves accepted the European Enlightenment's skepticism about the miraculous and supernatural. The result was that, yet again, the Christian faith was overadapted to culture. This time it was not the older, more conservative Western culture of nineteenth-century missionaries, but the liberal culture of twentieth-century Western academia.

The Danger of Contextualizing

Because of this history, the word *contextualization* makes many people in conservative theological circles nervous, as indeed it should. As Craig Blomberg points out in an essay on contextualization, "Many who have embraced universalism began life as evangelicals ... In the Spanish-speaking world, the same is true of many liberation theologians."[11] In all these cases, the values of a culture were given preference over the authority of Scripture.

Although the word *contextualization* was not around at the time, this was the same issue J. Gresham Machen faced in the Presbyterian Church in the early twentieth century. In his book *Christianity and Liberalism*, Machen states that liberal Christianity was trying to solve a problem:

> What is the relation between Christianity and modern culture; may Christianity be maintained in a scientific age?
>
> It is this problem which modern liberalism attempts to solve. Admitting that scientific objections may arise against the particularities of the Christian religion—against the Christian doctrines of the person of Christ, and of redemption through His death and

resurrection—the liberal theologian seeks to rescue certain of the general principles of religion, of which these particularities are thought to be mere temporary symbols, and these general principles he regards as constituting "the essence of Christianity."

As a matter of fact ... what the liberal theologian has retained after abandoning to the enemy one Christian doctrine after another is not Christianity at all, but a religion which is so entirely different from Christianity as to belong in a distinct category.[12]

Machen, speaking from the early twentieth century, declared that his culture had become "naturalistic"—it had completely rejected any account of supernatural intervention by God. Everything, in this view, must have a natural, scientific explanation. The problem with the liberal Christianity of Machen's day is that it granted this cultural belief, even though it clearly contradicted Scripture. Liberal Christianity adapted to the culture when it should have been confronting it.[13] In order (they thought) to make Christianity palatable to modern people, liberal Christian leaders redefined all doctrine in naturalistic terms. The reformulated version of Christianity looked (and still looks) like this:

- The Bible is filled with divine wisdom, but this doesn't mean it is inerrant—it is a human document that has errors and contradictions.
- Jesus is the Son of God, but this doesn't mean he was the preexisting, divine Son of God. He was a great man infused with God's Spirit.
- Jesus' death is not a cosmic event that propitiates the wrath of God—it is an example of sacrificial love that changes us by moving us through his example.
- Becoming a Christian, then, doesn't entail the supernatural act of the new birth. It means to follow the example of Jesus, follow the teaching of the Sermon on the Mount, and live a life of love and justice in the world.

Machen goes on to argue forcefully and persuasively that the effort to reconcile Christianity to a naturalistic philosophy results not in an adapted version of biblical faith but an entirely new religion, one that directly contradicts classic Christianity at nearly every important point. Perhaps the most telling and devastating example is given in Machen's chapter titled "Salvation." There he points out that if Jesus' atonement is now just an example of how to live, and if being a Christian is not to be born again but to live like Jesus, we have replaced the Christian gospel of salvation by grace with a religion of salvation by good works. "Such teaching is just a sublimated form of legalism," he concludes.[14]

The call to contextualize the gospel has been—and still often is—used as a cover for religious syncretism. This means not *adapting* the gospel to a particular culture, but rather *surrendering* the gospel entirely and morphing Christianity into a different religion by overadapting it to an alien worldview. But how do we judge when we have moved from legitimate contextualization into fatal syncretism? In a helpful essay, Natee Tanchanpongs states that evangelicals usually try to defend contextualization by arguing that it is simply adapting the *less essential* parts of Christianity and that syncretism occurs when "the critical and basic elements" of the gospel are lost.[15] In this view, contextualization involves keeping the essentials while flexing on the nonessentials.

Tanchanpongs argues, however, that it is wrong to look at Scripture and imagine that some core, essential teachings are more important than other, more tangential ones. In fact, Harvie Conn argued that syncretism is most likely to occur when (in the name of culture) we forbid the *whole* of Scripture to speak. Every culture will find some parts of Scripture more attractive and other parts more offensive. It will be natural, then, for those in that culture to consider the inoffensive parts more "important" and "essential" than the offensive parts. This is exactly what the liberal Christianity of Machen's day did in rejecting the "offensive" supernatural elements of the Bible. Syncretism is, in fact, a rejection of the full authority of the Bible, a picking and choosing among its various teachings to create a Christianity that does not confront or offend.[16] Faithful contextualization, then, should adapt the communication and practice of *all* scriptural teaching to a culture (see below on the dangers of having a "canon within a canon" when contextualizing).

The Inevitability of Contextualizing

Here is a beautiful paradox that is easy to miss: the fact that we must express universal truth in a particular cultural context does not mean that the truth itself is somehow lost or less universal. D. A. Carson writes, "[While] no truth which human beings may articulate can ever be articulated in a culture-transcending way ... that does not mean that the truth thus articulated does not transcend culture."[17]

It is important to seek to maintain the balance of this careful and important statement. First, this means there is no one, single way to express the Christian faith that is universal for everyone in all cultures. As soon as you express the gospel, you are unavoidably doing it in a way that is more understandable and accessible for people in some cultures and less so for others. On the other hand, while there is no culture-transcending way to express the truths of the gospel, there is nonetheless only one true gospel. The truths of the gospel are not the products of any culture, and they stand in judgment over all human cultures. If you forget the first truth — that there is no cultureless presentation of the gospel — you will think there is only one true way to communicate it, and you are on your way to a rigid, culturally bound conservatism. If you forget the second truth — that there is only one true gospel — you may fall into relativism, which will lead to a rudderless liberalism. Either way, you will be less faithful and less fruitful in ministry.

What should we conclude from this? If there is no single, context-free way to express the gospel, then contextualization is inevitable. As soon as you choose a language to speak in and particular words to use within that language, the culture-laden nature of words comes into play. We often think that translating words from one language to another is simple — it's just a matter of locating the synonym in the other language. But there are few true synonyms. The word *God* is translated into German as *Gott* — simple enough. But the cultural history of German speakers is such that the word *Gott* strikes German ears differently than the English word *God* strikes the ears of English speakers. *It means something different to them.* You may need to do more explanation if you are to give German speakers the same biblical concept of God that the word conveys to English speakers. Or maybe a different word will have to be used to have the same effect. As soon as you choose words, you are contextualizing, and you become more accessible to some people and less so to others. There is no universal presentation of the gospel for all people.[18]

However, even within the field of one language, numerous other factors unavoidably involve us in the work of contextualization. Let's think back for a moment to the boring sermon. Sometimes the sermon we hear is boring because it went on for too long (or it was not long enough) to engage the listeners. One of the most culturally sensitive areas of human life is this area of time. What various people and cultures consider "late" and "too long" varies widely. In the United States, African-American and Hispanic Christians have services in which singing, prayer, and preaching go on at least 50 percent longer than the attention spans and comfort zones of most Anglo people. Anyone who leads worship services will, then, unavoidably be contextualizing toward some people and away from others.

A sermon can also lose listeners because of the types of metaphors and illustrations that are chosen. When Jesus tells those who preach the gospel to hostile people to avoid throwing pearls to pigs (Matt 7:6), he is uniting two fields of discourse. He is connecting preaching the gospel to the concrete world of raising pigs. By doing so, he is conveying meaning in a far more riveting and illuminating way than if he had simply said, "Don't preach the gospel indefinitely to people who are hostile to it." Jesus used an illustration, but every illustration by definition must use some concrete life experience. And so, as soon as we choose an illustration, we move toward some people (who share those life experiences) and become more remote and less accessible to others (who do not).

I once spoke to a mature British Christian believer from a working-class background. For a time, he attended a solidly evangelical church, but all the leaders and ministers were from the upper classes and the elite schools. The preaching referred to life situations and concepts that the speakers knew, which meant frequent illustrations drawn from the sports of cricket and rugby. This man shared, "People in my world know very little of these sports, and the constant references to them reminded me that I did not go to their schools or have their privileges. That was distracting, but not insurmountable, because we are all one in Christ now. But I realized that I could not bring to that church the working-class folks to whom I was ministering. The continual reminders that the leaders were from the upper crust would make it very hard for my friends to listen to the Word. You might say to them, 'Why so touchy?'—but you can't expect people to be sanctified before they are justified. You can't expect people who are not yet believers to shed all their cultural sensitivities." Eventually he went to another church.

Does this example mean that the church in this situation failed in some way? It is possible that the church could have consulted with this man and others to discuss ways that it could have been less culturally strange and remote to working-class people. But there is always a limit to this flexibility. The preachers must choose *some* particular illustrations and concepts that will inevitably be more meaningful to some cultural groups than others. We need to stretch as much as we can to be as inclusive as possible. But we must also be aware of our limits. We should not live in the illusion that we can share the gospel so as to make it all things to all people at once.

Another reason a sermon can be accurate but still have little impact is that the level of emotional expressiveness is not calibrated to the culture of the person listening. I once had a Hispanic member of my church tell me, a bit sheepishly, that when he brought other Hispanic people to hear me preach at Redeemer, he had to tell them, "He really *does* believe what he is saying with all his heart, in spite of what it looks like." He had to do that because so many people from his culture felt that my level of emotional expression signaled indifference to my subject matter. "In our culture, if you *really* believe something and are committed to it, you express more *feeling*." I was struck by the fact that if I adapted to a certain type of culture and expressed my emotions more fervently, it would look to people from another culture like a rant and be completely unpersuasive to them. There is no universal presentation. We *cannot* avoid contextualization.

We have talked about the manner and mode of preaching, but contextualization also has much to do with the content. A sermon could be unengaging to a person because, though expressing accurate biblical truth, it does not connect biblical teaching to the main objections and questions people in that culture have about faith. A few years ago, I participated in a consultation on evangelism for several churches in London. One of the dilemmas we discussed was the two very different groups of non-Christians in a particular area of the city. On one side were millions of Hindus and Muslims who believed that Christianity was not moralistic enough; on the other side were secular British people who thought that Christianity was far too rigidly moralistic. Of course, the gospel is neither legalism nor antinomianism, and so it is possible to preach a single sermon on the gospel that engages listeners from both groups, but if we are ministering in a neighborhood or area dominated by one of these groups, we must preach each passage with the particular objections of that people group firmly in mind. No one single gospel presentation will be equally engaging and compelling to both sides.

Finally, as we will see below, contextualization doesn't simply include language and vocabulary, emotional expressiveness and illustrations. It goes even deeper. contextualization affects the way we reason because people in one culture find one way of appealing persuasive, while those of another may not. Some people are more logical; some are more intuitive. When we choose a particular way to persuade and argue, we will unavoidably be adapting more to some kinds of people than to others.

As soon as we seek to communicate, we will automatically be making all sorts of cultural moves.

The Danger of Not Contextualizing (or of Thinking You Aren't)

All gospel ministry and communication are already heavily adapted to a particular culture. So it is important to do contextualization *consciously*. If we never deliberately think through ways to rightly contextualize gospel ministry to a new culture, we will unconsciously be deeply contextualized to some other culture. Our gospel ministry will be both overadapted to our own culture and underadapted to new cultures at once, which ultimately leads to a distortion of the Christian message.[19]

The subject of contextualization is particularly hard to grasp for members of socially dominant groups. Because ethnic minorities must live in two cultures—the dominant culture and their own subculture—they frequently become aware of how deeply culture affects the way we perceive things. In the movie *Gran Torino*, an older blue-collar American named Walt Kowalski (Clint Eastwood) lives alongside an Asian family in a deteriorating Detroit neighborhood. He finds it impossible to understand the cultural forms of the Hmongs, just as the elderly Hmongs (who cannot speak English and live completely within their ethnic enclave) find Walt strange and inexplicable. But the teenage Hmong girl, Sue, is bicultural—she lives in both worlds at once. So she understands and appreciates both Walt and her own parents and grandparents. As a result, she is able to communicate persuasively to both about the other. Isn't this the very thing we are doing whenever we present the truth of the gospel to a culture that has alienated itself from it?

In the United States, Anglo-Americans' public and private lives are lived in the same culture. As a result, they are often culturally clueless. They relate to their own culture in the same way a fish that, when asked about water, said, "What's water?" If you have never been out of water, you don't know you are *in* it. Anglo Christians sometimes find talk of contextualization troubling. They don't see any part of how they express or live the gospel to be "Anglo"—it is just the way things are. They feel that any change in how they preach, worship, or minister is somehow a compromise of the gospel. In this they may be doing what Jesus warns against—elevating the "traditions of men" to the same level as biblical truth (Mark 7:8). This happens when one's cultural approach to time or emotional expressiveness or way to communicate becomes enshrined as *the* Christian way to act and live. Bruce Nicholls writes the following:

> A contemporary example of cultural syncretism is the unconscious identification of biblical Christianity with "the American way of life." This form of syncretism is often found in both Western and Third World, middle-class, suburban, conservative, evangelical

congregations who seem unaware that their lifestyle has more affinity to the consumer principles of capitalistic society than to the realities of the New Testament, and whose enthusiasm for evangelism and overseas missions is used to justify [lives of materialism and complacency].[20]

Lack of cultural awareness leads to distorted Christian living and ministry. Believers who live in individualistic cultures such as the United States are blind to the importance of being in deep community and placing themselves under spiritual accountability and discipline. This is why many church hoppers attend a variety of churches and don't join or fully enter any of them. American Christians see church membership as optional. They take a nonbiblical feature of American culture and bring it into their Christian life. On the other hand, Christians in more authoritarian and patriarchal cultures often are blind to what the Bible says about freedom of conscience and the grace-related aspects of Christianity. Instead, their leaders stress duty and are heavy-handed rather than eager to follow Jesus' words that "anyone who wants to be first must be the very last, and the servant of all" (Mark 9:35).

An inability to see one's own enculturation has other results. One of the most basic mistakes ministers make is to regurgitate the methods and programs that have personally influenced them. After experiencing the impact of a ministry in one part of the world, they take up the programs and methods of that ministry and reproduce them elsewhere virtually unchanged. If they have been moved by a ministry that has forty-five-minute verse-by-verse expository sermons, a particular kind of singing, or a specific order and length to the services, they reproduce it down to the smallest detail. Without realizing it, they become method driven and program driven rather than theologically driven. They are contextualizing their ministry expression to themselves, not to the people they want to reach.

I have been moved to see how churches and ministries around the world have looked at what we do at Redeemer Presbyterian Church and how they have expressed their appreciation and have sought to learn from this ministry. But I have been disappointed to visit some congregations that have imitated our programs—even our bulletins—and haven't grasped the underlying theological principles that animate us. In other words, they haven't done the hard work of contextualization, reflecting on their own cultural situation and perspective to seek to better communicate the gospel to their own context. They have also failed to spend time reflecting on what they see in Redeemer and how *we* have adapted our ministry to an urban U.S. culture.

Everyone contextualizes—but few think much about how they are doing it. We should not only contextualize but also think about *how* we do it. We must make our contextualization processes visible, and then intentional, to ourselves and to others.

DISCUSSION QUESTIONS

1. This chapter defines contextualization as "giving people *the Bible's answers*, which they may not at all want to hear, *to questions about life* that people in their particular time and place are asking, *in language and forms* they can comprehend, and *through appeals and arguments* with force they can feel, even if they reject them." Unpack the four parts of this definition. Which of these elements of contextualization do you tend to do best? Which do you tend to skip or overlook?

2. Evangelicals often try to defend contextualization by arguing that it is about adapting the less essential parts of Christianity and that syncretism and compromise occur when "the critical and basic elements" of the gospel are lost. In this view, contextualization involves keeping the essentials while flexing on the nonessentials. What is the danger of this approach, according to this chapter?

3. Keller writes, "There is no universal presentation of the gospel for all people." What do you think is meant by this statement? Do you agree or disagree?

4. D. A. Carson is quoted as stating that "no truth which human beings may articulate can ever be articulated in a culture-transcending way."

What distinctive values or biases have you learned through your own cultural formation (family, hometown, nation, race, church, etc.) that affect your communication of truth? Which biblical themes are you most tempted to edit out? How did you become aware of these biases?

5. Keller writes, "One of the most basic mistakes ministers make is to regurgitate the methods and programs that have personally influenced them. After experiencing the impact of a ministry in one part of the world, they take up the programs and methods of that ministry and reproduce them elsewhere virtually unchanged ... They are contextualizing their ministry expression to themselves, not to the people they want to reach." How have you seen this mistake made in ministry? What do you need to do to begin intentionally contextualizing?

Chapter 2

BALANCED CONTEXTUALIZATION

John Stott's book on preaching, *Between Two Worlds*, likens Christian communication to building a bridge from the Scriptures to the contemporary world.[1] Some sermons are like "a bridge to nowhere." They are grounded in solid study of the biblical text but never come down to earth on the other side. That is, they fail to connect the biblical truth to people's hearts and the issues of their lives. Other sermons are like bridges *from* nowhere. They reflect on contemporary issues, but the insights they bring to bear on modern problems and felt needs don't actually arise out of the biblical text. Proper contextualization is the act of bringing sound biblical doctrine all the way over the bridge by reexpressing it in terms coherent to a particular culture.

How do we do this? Scholars point out that any reader of the Bible who wants to understand it must go back and forth between two different horizons, between the two banks of the river in Stott's analogy—the biblical text and the reader's cultural context. Scripture has supreme authority, and so it cannot be wrong and does not need to be corrected. But a Christian communicator's understanding of the Bible may definitely be wrong—indeed, is always partly so—and therefore must always be open to being corrected. The same goes for the gospel communicator's understanding of the hearer's context, which can also benefit from more insight and correction.

Many Christians seeking to preach the gospel to a new culture are simply unwilling or unable to deal with this issue; they believe their task is simply to carry biblical doctrine over the bridge into the new culture. In other words, they see gospel communication as a one-way bridge.

They do not like the idea that information must come over the bridge in the other direction. They don't see its importance, or they see this as a threat to the authority of Scripture. The problem with this idea of mission is that it assumes we who are on one side of the bridge already have an undistorted grasp of the gospel, and that our knowledge of the culture on the other side is not important. This view is blind to the truth that we are not only sinful but also finite, and therefore we cannot have clear and exhaustive knowledge of anything. We are largely oblivious to the power of culture to shape our understanding of things.[2]

So how can we guard the authority and integrity of Scripture and remain open to being corrected in our understanding of it? How can our message to the new culture be both faithful and fruitful? The answer is to allow some two-way traffic on the bridge.

When we approach the biblical text, we come with a "pre-understanding," a set of already established beliefs about the subjects addressed in the Bible. These beliefs are strong and deep, and many are tacit—that is, they are difficult to verbalize, formulate, or even recognize in oneself.[3] They come from a variety of voices we have listened to within our own culture. This does not mean we cannot or have not arrived at a sufficient and true understanding of biblical teaching. But it does mean the process is not a simple one, for our existing beliefs—many of them virtually unconscious—make it difficult for us to read Scripture rightly, to let it correct our thinking, and to carry it faithfully over the bridge to someone who needs it.

Because of our cultural blinders, we must not only *speak* to the people over the bridge; we must *listen* to them as well. We need to listen to what they are saying and take seriously their questions, their objections to what we are saying, and their hopes and aspirations. More often than not, this interaction with a new culture shows us many things taught in the Bible—things we either missed altogether or thought unimportant, possibly even ways in which we misread the Bible through the lens of our own cultural assumptions.

When I was a professor at Westminster Seminary in Philadelphia, many of my students had traveled from Korea to study in our school. I often led case study seminars that discussed real-life ministry situations with both Korean and Anglo-American students. Despite the fact that all of the students shared the same conservative Reformed theology, they approached ministry in very different ways. One of the key differences had to do with how my Asian students wielded and regarded human authority. Koreans cede far more power to pastors and fathers, while American culture is much more egalitarian and democratic. The Korean students were able to point out to American students that there is quite a lot in the Bible about the authority of civil magistrates, parents, elders, and ministers, which Americans tend to ignore or screen out because our culture is deeply suspicious of institutions and authority. But while Korean students could point to texts such as Romans 13 and Hebrews 13:17, American students could point Asian colleagues to passages such as Matthew 20:24–28 and 1 Peter 5:1–4 (warning against leaders "lording it over" others) or Acts 4:19 and 5:29 (telling us we must not let human authority usurp God's) or the book of Revelation (in which human authority overreaches and becomes demonic).[4]

What was happening? Information was going back and forth over the bridge. Our interaction with a different culture leads us to ask the text questions we may never have asked it before and to see many things we didn't see clearly before. Entering into the text from a different perspective provides a point of triangulation that can help us to identify our own culturally bound presuppositions about the gospel. As a result we begin to see truths and insights in the Bible that were there all along, yet we had simply been blind to them. The questions of the new culture reveal to us as communicators that we have our own unique cultural blind spots.

To provide another example, secular people in Western culture are highly individualistic, which makes them sensitive to violations of human dignity on the basis of race. Their commitment to individual freedom leads to sensitivity to racial prejudice wherever it exists. Many Christians who have interacted with secularists have gone back to the Scriptures and found that the Bible speaks far more about the evil of racism than they had thought. Christians are not correcting the Bible, but they are correcting their understanding of the Bible through humble interaction with nonbiblical philosophies. We know that God in his mercy sometimes gives pagans morally informed consciences (Rom 2) that sense real evil and truth even if their overall worldview has no basis for their insights.

One of the main ways our understanding of the Bible remains distorted is through what has been called "the canon within the canon." That is, we treat some parts of Scripture as more important and ignore or discard other parts of it. All Christians fall victim to some form of this, depending on our temperament, experience, and culture. D. A. Carson notes many instances of this. For example, the Bible tells us that God loves everyone in the world with his providential love, and yet it also teaches us that he loves the saved with his gracious love and is angry at the wicked.[5] Different cultures will respond to these biblical aspects of God's love differently. Members of Western cultures love the concept of God's love for all and recoil from the doctrine of God's wrath on evil. More traditional tribal cultures will have no problem with a God of judgment but will bristle at the idea that he loves all people groups equally. Each culture, then, will tend to highlight certain biblical teachings and downplay others, creating a mini-canon within the canon of Scripture. But if we stress the first biblical teaching (about God's universal, providential love) and play down the second (about God's judgment)—or vice versa—we have distorted the faith. Interactions with different cultures help us lose our blinders and slowly but surely move to a more rounded biblical Christianity.

Other examples abound. The Bible has much to say about wealth and poverty, and what it says is enormously varied and nuanced. In some places it is very positive about private property and riches—such as when God blesses Abraham, Job, and others with great wealth. Other Bible passages contain severe warnings about the dangers of money and make strong statements about the responsibility of God's people to promote justice and care for the poor. People typically ignore much of the teaching on one side and latch on to other parts, largely dependent on whether they live in prosperous conditions or in poor ones. Carson summarizes: "The name of the game is reductionism," that is, taming Scripture by not letting all of it speak to us.[6] Our sociocultural location makes us prone to flatten the teachings of Scripture, ignoring some parts and exaggerating others. When we interact with people from other cultures and social settings, we find our particular distortions being challenged. So while gospel communicators should seek to correct their *hearers'* cultural beliefs with the gospel, it is inevitable that contact with a new culture will also end up correcting the *communicators'* understanding of the gospel.

The bridge, then, must run in both directions. While the Bible itself cannot be corrected by non-Christian cultures, individual Christians—and their culturally conditioned understanding of the Bible—can and should be. There should be heavy traffic back and forth across the bridge. We speak and listen, and speak and listen, and speak again, each time doing so more biblically *and* more compellingly to the culture.

The Bridge and the Spiral

The two-way bridge image is important. In hindsight, we now recognize that the original call for contextualization in the 1970s was essentially a call for a two-way bridge rather than the older, one-way bridge of the "indigenous church" model. The older model did not encourage national Christian leaders to engage in deep theological reflection on how profoundly the gospel challenges culture. It assumed Western Christianity was the true, undistorted, universal expression of the faith. Transporting it across the bridge required only a few minor adaptations, such as language translation and appropriating native music and dress. Harvie Conn argued that the indigenous model was based on a "functionalist" view of culture, which saw culture as a set of unrelated practices that helped a people group adapt to its environment. In this view of culture, you can slip out one piece of a culture (say, by replacing Hinduism with Christianity) and not expect the rest of the culture to change (such as the music, art, family structures, relationships between classes, and so on). This encouraged national Christians to engage in wholesale adoption of much of their indigenous culture, uncritically embracing it without examining it in light of the Scriptures. The indigenous church movement also failed by not challenging Western missionaries to recognize the culturally adapted nature of their own theology and practices.

But for all its benefits, the two-way bridge has limitations as a metaphor for explaining contextualization. In the end, evangelicals believe the two sides of the bridge do not have equal authority—the Bible is supreme. Yes, our interaction with culture helps us adjust and change our understanding of the Bible for the better, but in the final analysis, the Bible must be seen as the ultimate authority over both the culture and our consciousness.[7]

If the Bible is instead seen as a fallible product of human culture, then we are locked in an endless interpretive circle that goes back and forth between our culture and the Bible. In this view, the Bible and culture are equally authoritative, which is to say equally relative. Thus we may use the Bible to correct a culture, but we can also use the culture to argue that parts of the Bible are now obsolete. This is why, for example, some mainline denominations use the Bible to denounce various forms of economic injustice in the United States, but at the same time they insist that what the Bible teaches about sex and gender is oppressive and dated. Following this pattern, in every generation and culture Christianity will be changing radically, often contradicting the teaching of the church in other centuries and lands. There is no way for us to increasingly come to grasp the truth.

But the deeper flaw in this "hermeneutical circle" approach is that it cannot exist in real life. Though we may say we make the Bible and culture equally authoritative, in the end we really are not doing so. If we state that what the Bible says here is true but what the Bible says over here is regressive and outdated, we have absolutized our culture and given it final authority over the Bible. Either the Bible has final authority and determines what in the culture is acceptable or unacceptable, or the culture has final authority over the Bible and determines what in the text is acceptable or unacceptable. So the image of the circle (or of a completely symmetrical two-way bridge) falls short. In the end the circle must be broken, and fallen creatures that we are, we will always break it by privileging our own cultural biases.

For these reasons evangelicals have insisted that while contextualization must be a two-way process, the final authority of the Bible must be maintained.[8] This is why many have come now to speak of contextualization as a hermeneutical *spiral* rather than a circle.[9] If Scripture and culture are equally authoritative, the movement back and forth between text and context is an endless circle of change. But if Scripture is the supreme authority and the interaction with culture is for the purpose of understanding the text more accurately (not to bring it into line with the culture), then the text-context movement is a spiral, moving us toward better and better understanding of the Word of God and how it can be brought to bear on and communicated to a particular culture.[10]

Using the hermeneutical spiral, evangelicals have been seeking to avoid either extreme on a spectrum described by Richard Lints in his book *The Fabric of Theology*.[11] At one end of his spectrum is a cultural fundamentalism that believes we can read the Bible and express its theology in culture-free, universal terms; at the other end is a cultural relativism that holds "that the Scripture can have no other meaning than that which is permitted by the conceptuality of the present-day situation."[12] Evangelicals seek to work in the middle of this spectrum, insisting that while there are no universal, culture-free *expressions* of biblical teachings, the Bible nonetheless expresses absolute and universal truths. I would call this approach "balanced contextualization" because it avoids these two extremes as it rests, ultimately and firmly, on the fulcrum of scriptural authority.

Lints writes that despite the effort to find this middle ground of balanced contextualization, there is still a lack of consensus about many particulars, and of course many evangelicals tend to lean toward one side of the spectrum or the other. Some are moving more toward giving the culture more say in how the gospel is communicated, and this is driving others toward the other end of the spectrum, refusing to acknowledge how culturally influenced our theological formulations are. Since this is a book for practitioners, I will not delve further into a discussion of the more theoretical issues related to contextualization other than to say how important it is to maintain the balance that Lints and many others speak of.

But it's important not only to maintain this balance, but to do so in a way that is shaped by the patterns and examples of Scripture. I want to look at three biblical foundations for doing contextualization and then use Paul's ministry to provide some examples and practical "ways and means" to go about it.

DISCUSSION QUESTIONS

1. When you err in the way you contextualize the gospel, do you tend to create a "bridge to nowhere," or a "bridge from nowhere"? What makes you suspect this is true? What factors or beliefs contribute to this tendency?

2. Keller writes, "Our interaction with a different culture leads us to ask the text questions we may never have asked it before and to see many things we didn't see clearly before ... As a result we begin to see truths and insights in the Bible that were there all along, yet we had simply been blind to them." Have you ever experienced the benefit of interacting with another culture in this way? What blind spots has this experience revealed to you in your own understanding of the Bible and the gospel?

3. What is your "canon within the canon"? Take a few moments to jot down the themes of Scripture to which you typically give special prominence. Which parts do you notice other Christians emphasizing that you do not? Do you see a pattern? What does this tell you about your spiritual or cultural blind spots?

4. Keller writes, "Evangelicals have been seeking to avoid either extreme on a spectrum ... At one end ... is a cultural fundamentalism that believes we can read the Bible and express its theology in culture-free, universal terms; at the other end is a cultural relativism that holds 'that the Scripture can have no other meaning than that which is permitted by the conceptuality of the present-day situation.'" What dangers are associated with each of these two extremes? What examples have you seen of either extreme? On which side of the spectrum do you tend to err?

Chapter 3

BIBLICAL CONTEXTUALIZATION

The Bible has much to say about human culture and how the gospel frames our relationship to it. I'll begin by looking at three key passages that have proved helpful to me in developing a biblical view of contextualization. The first, Romans 1 and 2, provides the *basis* for contextualization, namely, that the Bible takes a mixed view of culture, and while many elements of a culture can be affirmed, we must avoid uncritically accepting aspects of culture without first examining them in light of the gospel. The second passage, 1 Corinthians 9, speaks to our *motive* for contextualization, reminding us that we need to be flexible toward culture, ready to adapt what we can to communicate the gospel message. Third, in 1 Corinthians 1, the Bible gives a basic *formula* for contextualization and shows us how to keep a balance between affirming and confronting culture.

Romans 1 – 2 and the Mixed Nature of Culture

Every culture is a mixed bag of good and bad elements, and we should avoid rejecting certain aspects of a culture simply because they differ from our own. While this idea seems true at a commonsense level, does the Bible actually give a warrant for it? A study of Romans 1 and 2 suggests it does.

Every culture assumes a set of answers to the big questions: Why are we here? What are therefore the most important things in life? What is wrong with the world? What will put things right? And every society considers something of supreme worth; accordingly, they seek to bring their environment into service to it. No culture is neutral on these matters, and in this sense all cultural work can be said to be "covenantal"—we are all committed to something, even when those presuppositions and assumptions aren't consciously identified. Romans 1 and 2 get this point across by telling us that all have sinned and fall short of God's glory—that both Jews and Gentiles alike are lost. The pagan Gentiles may make sensuality an idol, but the Jews make moral righteousness an idol—like every culture, they look to something else to justify and save them rather than God.

Yet at the same time we see in Romans 1 and 2 that all human beings possess a primordial knowledge of God. In Romans 2:14–15, Paul states that God's law is written on the heart of every human being. All people have an innate sense of the rightness of honesty, justice, love, and the Golden Rule.[1] Because we are made in the image of God (Gen 1:26–28), all people know at some deep level that there is a God, that we are his creatures, and that we should serve him and are accountable to him. There is "general revelation" or "common grace"—a nonsaving knowledge and likeness of God that he grants to all those who bear his image—present in some way in every culture. This is not saving knowledge. It does not tell us about Jesus or what he has done for us, for that can only be known through the "special revelation" of the Bible. But a general understanding of God exists, for God reveals a measure of his truth and wisdom to all.

This is why Isaiah 28:23–29 can state that anyone who is skillful in agriculture, who brings forth an advancement in farming science, has been "instructed by God." One commentator writes about this text, "What appears as a discovery (the proper season and conditions for sowing, farm management, rotation of crops, etc.) is actually the Creator opening his book of creation and revealing his truth."[2] And farming is just one aspect of human culture. The development of new music, new technologies that advance our ability to travel by air or communicate with others, wise political leadership—all of these things are the result of God's opening his book of creation and teaching us (cf. Exod 31:2–11; Jas 1:17).

Romans 1:18–25 gives a dynamic and balanced picture of how

general revelation (or common grace) actually works in people's lives. We read that the truth is being suppressed (v. 18), but it continues to bear down on us. The NIV translates verse 20 as "Since the creation of the world God's invisible qualities ... have been clearly seen, being understood from what has been made, so that people are without excuse." But the verbs *nooumena* ("are being understood") and *kathoratai* ("are being seen") are in the form of present passive participles. In other words, the reality of God's nature and our obligations to him are *continuously* present to us. General revelation is not just a set of innate ideas or static principles; it is the continuous and insistent pressure of God's truth on the consciousness of every human being.

Every human culture is an extremely complex mixture of brilliant truth, marred half-truths, and overt resistance to the truth. Every culture will have some idolatrous discourse within it. And yet every culture will have some witness to God's truth in it. God gives out good gifts of wisdom, talent, beauty, and skill completely without regard for merit. He casts them across a culture like seed, in order to enrich, brighten, and preserve the world. Without this understanding of culture, Christians will tend to think that they can live self-sufficiently, isolated from and unblessed by the contributions of those in the world. Without an appreciation for God's gracious display of his wisdom in the broader culture, Christians may struggle to understand why non-Christians often exceed Christians in moral practice, wisdom, and skill. The doctrine of sin means that as believers we are never as good as our right worldview should make us. At the same time, the doctrine of our creation in the image of God, and an understanding of common grace, remind us that nonbelievers are never as flawed as their false worldview should make them.

This suggests that our stance toward every human culture should be one of critical enjoyment and an appropriate wariness. Yes, we should enjoy the insights and the creativity of other peoples and cultures. We should recognize and celebrate expressions of justice, wisdom, truth, and beauty in every culture. But we approach every culture with awareness that it has been distorted by sin and in particular, the sin of idolatry. All cultures contain elements of darkness and light. We can't

simplistically conclude that traditional, conservative cultures are biblical and that liberal, secular cultures are immoral and evil. Traditional
cultures have their own idols, often elevating the family or ethnicity
to an absolute value—leading to the evils of racism, tribalism, patri-
archy and other forms of moralism and oppression. Liberal cultures
elevate the individual and the principle of human freedom to an absolute
value—leading to the erosion of family, community, of integrity in both
business and sexual practices. Yet both the importance of the family *and*
the worth and freedom of the individual are to be found at the center
of a biblical worldview. A coherent and biblical understanding of the
gospel (Christians are saved but sinners); of the image of God (people
are lost but indelibly reflect the nature of God); and of common grace
(all people suppress the truth about God but they nonetheless "hear"
and "know" it)—provides us with a nuanced understanding of culture.
This gives us the basis for contextualization.

First Corinthians 9 and Flexibility toward Culture

First Corinthians 9 is very likely the first Bible passage many people
think of when the topic of contextualization is considered, and it is an
important one to consider:

> Though I am free and belong to no man, I make myself a slave
> to everyone, to win as many as possible. To the Jews I became like
> a Jew, to win the Jews. To those under the law I became like one
> under the law (though I myself am not under the law), so as to win
> those under the law. To those not having the law I became like one
> not having the law (though I am not free from God's law but am
> under Christ's law), so as to win those not having the law. To the
> weak I became weak, to win the weak. I have become all things to
> all men so that by all possible means I might save some. I do all this
> for the sake of the gospel, that I may share in its blessings.
>
> *1 Corinthians 9:19–23*

Prior to this part of his letter, Paul speaks about the *skandalon*—stumbling block—and provides as a case study a conflict in the Corinthian church. Jewish Christians occasionally purchased meat after it had been used in idol ceremonies. Jews knew that idols were nonentities and therefore believed there was nothing wrong with eating the meat. Gentile Christians, however, "stumbled" at this. As former pagans, they could not eat such meat without feeling spiritually defiled (1 Cor 8:7), and to see Jewish brothers doing this distressed them and tempted some of them to do what they weren't able to do with a clear conscience.

Paul responds by saying that the Jews were right theologically—indeed the meat was harmless, and thus the Gentile believers with "weak" consciences were being controlled by a strictly cultural taboo (1 Cor 8:4–5). Nevertheless, Paul says that the Jewish believers (whom he called the "strong") should not exercise their cultural freedom in this situation. They should refrain from eating the meat to remove the merely cultural offense, the stumbling block (1 Cor 8:9–12), from their Gentile brothers and sisters. Cultural adaptation here is seen as an expression of love. Later, in 1 Corinthians 10:32–11:1, Paul lays this out in the form of a principle: "Do not cause anyone to stumble, whether Jews, Greeks or the church of God—even as I try to please everyone in every way. For I am not seeking my own good but the good of many, so that they may be saved. Follow my example, as I follow the example of Christ."

In areas where the Bible has left us free, when we carry out Christian ministry, we should be constantly engaged in cultural adaptation—refraining from certain attitudes or behaviors to remove unnecessary stumbling blocks from the paths of people with culturally framed perceptions. For example, we may need to refrain from particular music, clothing, foods, and other nonessential practices and concepts that could distract or repulse people from clearly perceiving the gospel. Similarly, where the Bible has not spoken, we must not elevate relative human cultural norms to make them absolutes. For example, we should not absolutize styles of dress or insist that rhythmic music is less pleasing to God than melodic music and must be excluded from worship.

D. A. Carson makes this observation about this section of 1 Corinthians:

When in the last century Hudson Taylor, the founder of the China Inland Mission (now the Overseas Missionary Fellowship), started to wear his hair long and braided like Chinese men of the time and to put on their clothes and to eat their food, many of his fellow missionaries derided him. But Hudson Taylor had thought through what was essential to the gospel (and was therefore non-negotiable) and what was a cultural form that was neither here nor there, and might in fact be an unnecessary barrier to the effective proclamation of the gospel ...

This is not to say that all cultural elements are morally neutral. Far from it. Every culture has good and bad elements in it ... Yet in every culture it is important for the evangelist, church planter, and witnessing Christian to flex as far as possible, so that the gospel will not be made to appear unnecessarily alien at the merely cultural level.[3]

"Every culture has good and bad elements in it," writes Carson. If some aspect of a new culture does not compromise the gospel itself and makes you more accessible to others, there is no reason not to adapt to that element out of courtesy and love — even if it is not your preference. Otherwise, the gospel may, because of you, appear "unnecessarily alien." We must avoid turning off listeners because *we* are culturally offensive rather than the gospel. Seen in this way, sound contextualization is an expression of unselfishness. It is choosing in love not to privilege yourself or to exercise your full freedom as a Christian so people can hear and follow Christ's call.

On the other hand, our message and teaching must not eliminate the offense, the *skandalon*, of the cross (1 Cor 1:23). What the Bible has clearly and absolutely taught we cannot soft-pedal or discard. If we do, we have not adapted to the culture; we have capitulated to it. If we never speak to our relatively wealthy congregation about social justice — an implication of the gospel (Jas 1–2) — we eliminate a biblical *skandalon*. Proper contextualization means causing the *right* scandal — the one the gospel poses to all sinners — and removing all unnecessary ones. This is the motive for contextualization.

First Corinthians 1 and the Biblical Balance

Though Romans 1–2 and 1 Corinthians 9 establish the basis and motive for contextualization, no single biblical text is more helpful on the subject of contextualization than 1 Corinthians 1:22–25, which provides the basic formula for doing contextualization:

> Jews demand signs and Greeks look for wisdom, but we preach Christ crucified: a stumbling block to Jews and foolishness to Gentiles, but to those whom God has called, both Jews and Greeks, Christ the power of God and the wisdom of God. For the foolishness of God is wiser than human wisdom, and the weakness of God is stronger than human strength.

Here Paul assumes the mixed nature of culture. He tells us that when he spoke to Greeks, he confronted their culture's idol of wisdom. The Greek culture put a high value on philosophy, intellectual attainment, and the arts. To the Greeks, a salvation that came not through teaching or reflection but through a crucified savior was pure foolishness. Jewish culture, on the other hand, put its highest value on something entirely different, which Paul describes with three synonyms—miraculous signs, power, and strength. Unlike the Greek culture, Jewish culture was highly practical, valuing actions and results. Rather than discursive thought, the Jewish culture valued getting things done through power and skill. To the Jews, a salvation that came through a crucifixion was weak and ineffective. A messiah should overthrow the Romans; he should *do* something. A suffering, weak savior made no sense at all to the Jews.

Notice, however, that while the gospel offended each culture in somewhat different ways, it also drew people to see Christ and his work in different ways. Greeks who were saved came to see that the cross was the ultimate *wisdom*—making it possible for God to be both just and the justifier of those who believe. And Jews who had been saved came to see that the cross was true *power*. It meant that our most powerful enemies—sin, guilt, and death itself—have been defeated.

It is striking, then, to see how Paul applies the gospel to confront and complete each society's baseline cultural narrative. He does this both negatively and positively. He confronts each culture for its idols, yet he positively highlights their aspirations and ultimate values. He uses the cross to challenge the intellectual hubris of the Greeks and the works-righteousness of the Jews. But he also affirms their most basic collective longings, showing that Christ alone is the true wisdom the Greeks have looked for and is the true righteousness that the Jews have sought. Paul's approach to culture, then, is neither completely confrontational *nor* totally affirming. He does not simply rail against Greek pride in intellect and Jewish pride in power; instead he shows them that the *ways* they are pursuing these good things are ultimately self-defeating. He reveals the fatal contradictions and underlying idolatry within their cultures and then points them to the resolution that can only be found in Christ. This is the basic formula for contextualization. We will now examine how this formula is fleshed out in Paul's actual ministry practice.

Paul's Speeches in Acts

We have looked at the need to approach contextualization with an awareness of our own cultural presuppositions, those assumptions we make about the Bible and its message that we are unable to see until we are exposed to the questions another culture is asking of the Scriptures. We have also sought to establish some necessary biblical foundations, recognizing the mixed nature of every culture—that there are good and bad elements in every culture—while still affirming the need to adapt the message of the Bible to a specific cultural context. Paul gives a basis for contextualization in Romans 1–2, a motive for contextualizing in 1 Corinthians 9, and a basic formula for contextualization in 1 Corinthians 1. Yet it is in his speeches in the book of Acts that we actually see him engaged in the *work* of contextualization, communicating the gospel to different people groups.

We immediately notice that Paul is able to adapt his message to communicate with a variety of people from very different backgrounds. In Acts 13:13–43, while in Antioch, Paul speaks to an audience of Bible believers—Jews, Gentile proselytes, and "God-fearers" (Gentiles who believed the Bible and met in synagogues but who had not been circumcised). Then, at Lystra, in Acts 14:6–16, Paul addresses a crowd of peasant polytheists, uneducated folk who still believed in the old gods. Next, while visiting Athens, in Acts 17:16–34, Paul speaks to sophisticated pagans who had largely abandoned belief in literal gods, instead holding to a variety of philosophical views (such as Stoicism and Epicureanism). In Acts 20:16–38, at Miletus, we see Paul delivering a farewell sermon to Christian elders, while in Acts 21:27–22:22, in Jerusalem, he speaks to a hostile Jewish mob. Finally in Acts 24–26, in Caesarea, Paul addresses Felix, Festus, and Herod Agrippa—governing elites with mixed cultural backgrounds and knowledge of both Judaism and paganism.

When reading these addresses, we are immediately struck by how Paul's gospel presentations differ markedly, depending on the culture of the listeners. What can we learn from them? Our conclusions must be drawn with great care. In every case, we must keep in mind that the biblical accounts of the speeches are fragmentary. In Acts 17, for example, Paul is interrupted before he finishes his message. Nevertheless, with these cautions in mind, we can still detect some patterns in his public communication in Acts.[4]

First, let's take a look at the *differences* among the speeches. Paul's citation of authority varies with changing audiences. With Bible believers, he quotes Scripture and John the Baptist; with pagans he argues from general revelation and the greatness of creation. The biblical content in his presentation varies as well, depending on the audience. He changes the order in which various truths are introduced, as well as the emphasis he gives to different points of theology. With Jews and God-fearers, Paul spends little time on the doctrine of God and gets right to Christ. But with pagans, he concentrates most of his time on developing the concept of God. With Greeks and Romans, Paul goes to Christ's resurrection first—not the cross.

When it comes to speaking about sin, Paul is clear in his message to the Jews that the law cannot justify them, that moral effort cannot save them (Acts 13:39). In effect, Paul is saying to Bible believers, "You think you are good, but you *aren't* good enough!" However, his approach with a pagan audience is to urge them to turn from "worthless things"—idols—"to the living God," who is the true source of "joy" (Acts 14:15–17). In effect, Paul says, "You think you are free, but you are enslaved to dead idols." Paul varies his use of emotion and reason, his vocabulary, his introductions and conclusions, his figures of speech and illustrations, his identification of the audience's concerns, hopes, and needs. In every case, he adapts his gospel presentation to his hearers.[5]

Despite all these profound differences, the speeches show several important commonalities as well. David Peterson observes that while there is no standard "gospel presentation," it is assumed through the book of Acts that there is only one gospel for all peoples.[6] It is called "the good news about the Lord Jesus" (11:20), "this message of salvation" (13:26), "the message of his grace" (14:3), "the message of the gospel" (15:7), "the gospel" (14:7, 21; 16:10), "the good news of God's grace" (20:24), and "the word of his grace" (20:32). What do all the presentations have in common? What is the common core that Paul shares in his preaching?

In every gospel presentation, there is an *epistemological challenge*. People are being told that their understanding of God and ultimate reality is wrong. Jews are told that though they think they understand the God of the Bible, they have seriously misunderstood the Scriptures. Gentiles are told that though they think they understand the world, they have seriously misread creation and their instincts. There is only one true God who has created all things. Both audiences are told about a God who is powerful, yet good (Acts 13:16–22; 14:17).

There is also a *personal challenge* regarding sin and a depiction of the listeners' fallen condition. Jews are trying to obey the law (Acts 13:39) and pagans are giving themselves to idols and gods that cannot satisfy (14:15). One group is trapped by works-righteousness, the other by a more conventional idolatry. Both audiences are trying to save themselves, and both are failing.

Then there is a *proclamation of Christ* as the answer and solution to their sin. As David Peterson states, "The messianic kingship of Jesus and its implications remains the core of the message to pagan audiences, though the terminology and approach are very different from the preaching to Jews or Gentiles who were familiar with the Jewish

Scriptures."[7] With pagans, Paul emphasizes the resurrection to prove that Jesus is the divine Savior come into the world, the only true King. With Jews, Paul demonstrates that the covenant promises are actually fulfilled in a suffering Messiah (cf. Luke 24:25–26). So both Jew and Gentile are told to turn from their schemes of performance because God has broken into history to accomplish our salvation.

In summary, there is truth about God ("you think you know who God is, but you do not"), truth about sin and our need for salvation ("you are trying to save yourself, but you cannot"), truth about Jesus ("he is the messianic King who comes to accomplish your salvation for you"), and a call to respond to these truths by repenting and believing in him.[8] These speeches of Paul give us a strong biblical case for engaging in careful contextualization. They remind us that there is no universal, culture-free formulation of the gospel for everyone. The Scriptures show numerous instances when gospel truths are brought out in different orders, argued for using different premises, and applied to hearts in distinctive ways. It is clear that Paul does not feel an obligation to give the whole gospel picture to his audience in one sitting. He puts the pagan Gentiles on a very gradual ramp and works to establish foundational principles without necessarily getting to the work of Christ right away. And yet, while these gospel truths are never expressed in the same way to all, it is clear they have the same content—the nature of God as just and loving, the state of our sin and lostness, the reality of Christ's accomplishment of salvation on our behalf, and the necessity of receiving that salvation by faith and through grace.

The Appeals of the Bible

Some years ago, I read a book based on Jesus' encounter with the rich young ruler. The book concluded that when we evangelize, we must always spend time "preaching the law for conviction," because Jesus in this passage takes pains to bring about a sense of guilt and need in this self-righteous, self-satisfied young man. The problem with the book's thesis is, of course, that this is not the only example of how Jesus evangelized someone. In John 4, with the woman at the well, Jesus spends very little time trying to bring her to a place of guilt and conviction of sin. He is considerably gentler and focuses not on the law but on his ability to satisfy spiritual thirst. (Jesus' behavior in John 4 can also be contrasted with his much more confrontational approach to Nicodemus in John 3.) To make any of these forms of persuasion *the* paradigm for gospel communication will lead to fruitlessness in ministry. We all tend to be blind to how much our own culture and temperament shape how we do gospel ministry, but careful attention to the remarkable diversity of gospel ministry in the Bible can broaden us.

People of a conservative temperament may want to stress judgment even more than the Bible itself does, while people of a liberal temperament may want to stress unconditional love more than the Bible does. Those of a rational bent need to see the importance of narrative, while those who love stories need to appreciate the extremely closely reasoned arguments of, say, Paul's letters. D. A. Carson has written an article that is a valuable resource for understanding the work of contextualization.[9] He argues that the biblical authors use a range of motivations when appealing to their readers to believe and obey the truth. They do not seek to persuade in just one way. As missiologists have pointed out, people of different temperaments and from different cultures reason differently. Some people are highly logical, others more intuitive, and others simply practical. In order to persuade people, you must adapt to these differences. Carson lists eight motivations to use when appealing to non-Christians to believe the gospel. I have combined and simplified his categories down to six:

1. Sometimes the appeal is to come to God out of fear of judgment and death. Hebrews 2:14–18 speaks about Christ delivering us from the bondage of the fear of death. In Hebrews 10:31, we are told it is a terrible thing to fall under the judgment of the living God.

2. Sometimes the appeal is to come to God out of a desire for release from the burdens of guilt and shame. Galatians 3:10–12 tells us we are under the curse of the law. Guilt is not only objective; it can also be a subjective inner burden on our consciences (Ps 51). If we feel we have failed others or even our own standards, we can feel a general sense of shame and low self-worth. The Bible offers relief from these weights.

3. Sometimes the appeal is to come to God out of appreciation for the "attractiveness of truth." Carson writes, "The truth can appear wonderful … [They can] see its beauty and its compelling nature." In 1 Corinthians 1:18, Paul states that the gospel is foolishness to those who are perishing, but to those who are being saved it is the power of God. Yet, immediately after this statement, Paul argues that the wisdom of the cross is the consummate wisdom. Paul is reasoning here, appealing to the mind. He is showing people the inconsistencies in their thinking (e.g., "your culture's wisdom is not wisdom by its own definition"). He holds up the truth for people to see its beauty and value, like a person holding up a diamond and calling for people to admire it.

4. Sometimes the appeal is to come to God to satisfy unfulfilled existential longings. To the woman at the well Jesus promised "living water" (John 4). This was obviously more than just eternal life — he was referring to an inner joy and satisfaction to be experienced now, something the woman had been seeking in men.

5. Sometimes the appeal is to come to God for help with a problem. There are many forms of what Carson calls "a despairing sense of need." He points to the woman with the hemorrhage (Matt 9:20–21), the two men with blindness (Matt 9:27), and many others who go to Jesus first for help with practical, immediate needs. Their heart language is, "I'm stuck; I'm out of solutions for my problems. I need help for this!" The Bible shows that Jesus does not hesitate to give that help, but he also helps them see their sin and their need for rescue from eternal judgment as well (see Mark 2:1–12; Luke 17:11–19).

6. Sometimes the appeal is to come to God simply out of a desire to be loved. The person of Christ as depicted in the Gospels is a compellingly attractive person. His humility, tenderness, wisdom, and especially his love and grace draw people like a magnet. Dick Lucas, longtime pastor at St Helen's Bishopsgate in London, has said that in the Bible God does not give us a watertight argument so much as a watertight *person* against whom, in the end, there can be no argument. There is an instinctive desire in all human beings to be loved. A clear depiction of Christ's love can attract people to want a relationship with him.

These are six ways the biblical authors use to persuade people, and notice what a motley assortment they are. Some are what we might call "sticks," while others are "carrots." One is essentially logical ("attractiveness of the truth"), relying on thinking things out. Some are intuitive (the "attractiveness of Jesus" and "fulfillment of longings"), relying on narratives and stories that compel. Sometimes the need is short term ("a despairing sense of need"), while others want to escape judgment and hell in the long term—an equally practical concern!

In conclusion, Carson argues, "We do not have the right to choose only one of these motivations in people and to appeal to it restrictively." This addresses one of the greatest dangers for us as preachers and evangelists. Most of us come to Christ through one of these motivations, or we are part of a community of people who find one of these motivations to be persuasive. It is natural for us to exclusively use this motivation in our appeals to others. When expounding a particular text, we tend to use our "pet" motivation, even though the biblical author may not. This is a failure to be fully biblical in our preaching. And yet Carson states, "On the other hand, we may have the right to emphasize one motivation more than others." Why? "In the same way that the structure and emphases of Paul's evangelistic addresses could change, depending on whether he was addressing biblically literate Jews and proselytes (Acts 13) or completely biblically illiterate pagans (Acts 17), so the particular motivations to which we appeal may vary according to our knowledge of our audience."[10] Here we see a strong biblical pattern of contextualization. In the long run, we must expose people to all that the Bible says. But, as Carson argues, it is right to lead with the passages and approaches that will be most effective in opening our audience to the message of the gospel.

The Gospel and Contextualization

I believe that faithful contextualization is a direct implication of the gospel of salvation by grace alone through faith alone. Paul used the gospel of justification on Peter in Galatians 2:14 when he criticized Peter's failure to be culturally open to Gentile believers. As we have seen, the gospel gives two impulses that lead us toward balanced, biblical contextualization. Religion ("I obey—therefore I am accepted") leads to pride if we are living up to standards, or to inferiority if we are failing to live up to standards. But the gospel ("I am accepted through Christ—therefore I obey") makes us both humble and confident at once. And these two attitudes are critical for doing faithful and sound contextualization. If we need the approval of the receiving culture too much (not enough gospel confidence), we will compromise in order to be liked. If we are too proudly rooted in any one culture (not enough gospel humility), we will be rigid and unable to adapt. Only the gospel gives us the balance we need.

A major reason the gospel is necessary for us to do contextualization is that in our default mode of self-justification we tend to turn neutral cultural traits into moral virtues. Some years ago, I performed a wedding in which the groom was from an Anglo culture and the bride from a Hispanic culture. At the hour the wedding was to begin, not only had the bride not arrived at the church; almost none of her family or friends of the family had arrived either. Not until forty-five minutes after the stated hour of the service did the bride and her family arrive at the church. The Anglo guests were filled with indignation about how rude, undisciplined, and insensitive this late arrival was. I heard some mutter, "No wonder those people can't ..." The Hispanic folks thought the Anglos were, as usual, rigid, uptight, and more oriented to goals and schedules than to relationships. What was happening? Each side was moralizing the time orientation of their particular culture.[11]

The gospel brings about great humility. A heart reoriented by a grasp of the gospel of grace does not have the same need to get a leg up on everyone. Richard Lovelace writes the following:

> [Those] who are not secure in Christ cast about for spiritual life preservers with which to support their confidence, and in their frantic search they not only cling to the shreds of ability and righteousness they find in themselves, but they fix upon their race, their membership in a party, their familiar social and ecclesiastical patterns, and their culture as means of self-recommendation. The culture is put on as though it were armor against self-doubt, but it becomes a mental straitjacket which cleaves to the flesh and can

never be removed except through comprehensive faith in the saving work of Christ. Once faith is exercised, a Christian is free to be enculturated, to wear his culture like a comfortable suit of clothes. He can shift to other cultural clothing temporarily if he wishes to do so, as Paul suggests in 1 Corinthians 9:19–23, and he is released to admire and appreciate the differing expressions of Christ shining out through other cultures.[12]

But it is not *only* the gospel that calls us to contextualization; a high view of the Bible does so as well. Why? If we believe in *sola scriptura*, that only the Bible has unquestioned authority over our lives, then at any place where the Bible leaves our consciences free we should be culturally flexible. Since the Bible never prescribes details on how to dress or on what kind of music to listen to, there is freedom to shape dress and music in such a way that both honors the biblical boundaries and themes and yet fits a culture.[13] To deny that much of our Christianity is culturally relative is to elevate human culture and tradition to a divine level and to dishonor Scripture.

Francis Schaeffer often spoke about the difference between biblically prescribed "form" and cultural "freedom": "Anything the New Testament does not command in regard to church form is a freedom to be under the leadership of the Holy Spirit for that particular time and place."[14] In the next chapter, we'll look at practical steps for engaging in active contextualization of the gospel message in a way that uses this freedom wisely. This involves a three-part process: *entering* the culture, *challenging* the culture, and *appealing* to the culture.

DISCUSSION QUESTIONS

1. According to Romans 1 and 2, what is the basis for contextualization?

2. Keller writes, "Christians may struggle to understand why non-Christians often exceed Christians in moral practice, wisdom, and skill. The doctrine of sin means that as believers we are never as good as our right worldview should make us. At the same time, the

doctrine of our creation in the image of God, and an understanding of common grace, remind us that nonbelievers are never as flawed as their false worldview should make them." What does this understanding of common grace suggest about our stance toward the culture? How does this awareness provide balance to your engagement with the culture? What types of relationships, spiritual disciplines, readings, and exercises help you employ a balance of "critical enjoyment and an appropriate wariness"?

3. The formula for contextualization, as derived from 1 Corinthians 1, is defined as applying the gospel "to confront and complete each society's baseline cultural narrative." This must be done both negatively and positively, confronting each culture for its idols, while positively highlighting its aspirations and ultimate values. Name an idol in your own culture. How might Paul have exposed the futility of that idol while also affirming the God-given desires that led people to pursue it in the first place? How might he have persuaded his listeners that the true answer to their deepest desires can be found in Jesus?

4. This chapter summarizes six ways of making a biblical appeal to people to come to God:

   - out of fear of judgment and death
   - out of a desire for a release from the burdens of guilt and shame
   - out of appreciation for the "attractiveness" of truth
   - to satisfy unfulfilled existential longings
   - for help with a problem
   - simply out of a desire to be loved

Which of the six ways of making appeals are most comfortable and natural for you? Which are most difficult? Why? What resources can help you become more adept at using all these appeals?

Chapter 4

ACTIVE CONTEXTUALIZATION

To illustrate what is needed for effective contextualization, let's turn to the world of demolition. Say you are building a highway and want to remove a giant boulder. First, you drill a small shaft down into the center of the rock. Then you put explosives down the shaft into the core of the stone and detonate them. If you drill the shaft but never ignite the blast, you obviously will never move the boulder. But the same is true if you only blast and fail to drill—putting the explosives directly against the surface of the rock. You will simply shear off the face of it, and the boulder will remain. All drilling with no blasting, or all blasting with no drilling, leads to failure. But if you do both of these, you will remove the rock.

To contextualize with balance and successfully reach people in a culture, we must *both* enter the culture sympathetically and respectfully (similar to drilling) *and* confront the culture where it contradicts biblical truth (similar to blasting). If we simply "blast" away—railing against the evils of culture—we are unlikely to gain a hearing among those we seek to reach. Nothing we say to them will gain traction; we will be written off and dismissed. We may feel virtuous for being bold, but we will have failed to honor the gospel by putting it in its most compelling form. On the other hand, if we simply "drill"—affirming and reflecting the culture and saying things that people find acceptable—we will rarely see anyone converted. In both cases, we will fail to "move the boulder." We may feel virtuous for being sensitive and open-minded, but we will have failed to honor the gospel by letting it speak pointedly and prophetically. It is only when we do our blasting on the basis of our drilling—when we challenge the culture's errors on the basis of something it (rightly) believes—that we will see the gospel having an impact on people.

For example, consider the biblical doctrine of "the priesthood of all believers." This doctrine fits well with our Western concept of the freedom and rights of the individual, and Western churches can easily "drill" into this cultural narrative by stressing the importance of lay ministry. However, it is also possible for our Western individualism to have an unhealthy influence on the church. We see this problem when church members refuse to respond to church discipline and claim that no one—not even church leaders—has the right to tell anyone else how to live *their* Christian life. This is an area where some "blasting" work must be done, confronting the individualism of contemporary Christianity with the truth of God's Word.

The need for both drilling and blasting—for both respectful affirmation of culture and confrontation of culture—makes it challenging to engage in the work of contextualization.[1] We want to avoid both *cultural captivity* (the refusal to adapt to new times and new cultures)—and *syncretism* (bringing unbiblical views and practices into our Christianity). While the danger of the former is becoming incomprehensible and irrelevant, the danger of the latter is losing our Christian identity and distinctiveness.

So how do we proceed? Most books and chapters on gospel contextualization are (to me) frustratingly impractical. Christian leaders are therefore (1) ignorant of the very idea of contextualization, (2) naively against it, or (3) for it but don't know how to do it. As a result, most contextualization happens passively, and in this way we enculturate the gospel in all sorts of unconscious and unfruitful ways. Instead we need to engage in a process I call practical, active contextualization because it requires us to be proactive, imaginative, and courageous at every step.

What are these steps? Active contextualization involves a three-part process: *entering* the culture, *challenging* the culture, and then *appealing* to the listeners. These three parts generally relate to one another as steps, but they overlap.[2] And as we proceed through these stages, we will bring to bear all we've learned about contextualization so far. We must make our assumptions and processes intentional (as discussed in ch. 1); we must stay aware of the need for balance (as discussed in ch. 2); and we must be faithful to the biblical patterns of contextualization (as discussed in ch. 3).

Entering and Adapting to the Culture

The first step in active contextualization is to understand and, as much as possible, identify with your listeners, the people you are seeking to reach. This begins with a diligent (and never-ending) effort to become as fluent in their social, linguistic, and cultural reality as possible. It involves learning to express people's hopes, objections, fears, and beliefs so well that they feel as though they could not express them better themselves. In Francis Schaeffer's address to the 1974 Lausanne Congress (published as *2 Contents, 2 Realities*), he began by stressing the importance of sound doctrine. But he immediately added that this doctrine must be communicated in the form of "honest answers to honest questions." Truth should not be simply declared into a vacuum — it must be delivered as a response to the questions of particular people, and this means understanding their culture. He writes the following: "The lordship of Christ covers the whole man. That includes his so-called spiritual things and his intellectual, his creative and cultural things ... Christianity demands that we have enough compassion to learn the questions of our generation ... Answering questions is hard work ... Begin to listen with compassion."[3]

This emphasis on listening to questions is a crucial aspect of contextualization. When a church writes a "confession of faith," it is not simply writing down what the Bible says. A confession is a series of answers from the Bible to a particular set of questions the church is asking of it. There are some questions almost everyone will ask of the Scriptures, but no one person or group will ask *all* the questions that can honestly and profitably be asked. Every church's questions depend on its experience, social location, historical period, and cultural situation.

Missions professor Harvie Conn used to point out that missionaries from the United States and Europe directed the new Presbyterian churches of Korea to adopt the Westminster Confession as their statement of faith. The Westminster standards were formulated in seventeenth-century Britain, and it should not surprise us that this confession contains very little about how to regard our ancestors, parents, and grandparents. Yet issues relating to respect for one's family and to ancestor worship are paramount in Korean culture. Koreans who want to live Christian lives need to know what the Bible says about the family, but the framers of the Westminster Confession simply did not ask the Bible much about that subject. This confession does not go into the level of detail necessary for most Asian believers.[4]

If twentieth-century Koreans had written their own confession, they would have likely asked several questions that the seventeenth-century British did not. And in doing so, they would have learned much truth from the Bible that would have been practically invisible to the British. Instead, opined Conn, Koreans never went through that exercise in contextualization and have in many cases uncritically adopted their culture's views of authority and family without examining them in light of the Bible. This does not mean that Korean and Hispanic confessions, by being different, would contradict British and older confessions. There would certainly be significant areas of overlap because many of the questions human beings ask of the Bible are common questions we all ask. Nevertheless, different times and cultures will lead to a different range of questions. You can have different contextual confessions that are not contradictory—all of them being quite biblically sound.

How to Enter a Culture

So the first task of contextualization is to immerse yourself in the questions, hopes, and beliefs of the culture so you can give a biblical, gospel-centered response to its questions. When Paul began to speak to the philosophers in Athens, he began by saying he had carefully studied their objects of worship (Acts 17:23). We should do the same. There are several ways to become familiar with the questions and beliefs of a particular culture. One way is to get the point of view of outside experts, often academicians. Because I was "from the north," when I went to

Hopewell, Virginia, to serve as a minister, it was important for me to read up on their cultural history, particularly the history of the Civil War and of the civil rights movement. Again, when I moved to New York City, I spent time reading several studies of the city's demographics, as well as novels such as *The Bonfire of the Vanities*, which captured the spirit of the age of Manhattan in the 1980s.

Ultimately, the most important source for learning will be the hours and hours spent in close relationships with people, listening to them carefully. In the earliest days of my ministry in New York City, I preached at both morning and evening services. New Yorkers are gregarious, and after each sermon many people came up to give frank opinions about what they had heard. I made appointments to see them to discuss things at greater length, and I would often talk to fifteen or twenty people a week who bombarded me with feedback about my preaching. Christians were bringing a lot of non-Christian friends, and I was able to hear reactions to my preaching from people across the spectrum, from mature Christians to skeptics.

As I listened, I heard four categories of responses. Some told me about things I had said that *confused* them; some shared something that had *moved and helped* them; some related things that had *offended* them. This last category I divided into two. I came to see that some of the things that bothered people were simple, irreducible, biblical, gospel truths. But I also realized that some of my statements upset people because I had assumed beliefs listeners did not have and failed to clarify or qualify statements at crucial points. In other words, I had not known enough about the beliefs, fears, and prejudices of the listeners to speak carefully enough to them. I had offended them unnecessarily. As time went on, these meetings had a profound impact on my sermon preparation. As I studied the biblical text with the objections and questions of my new friends still ringing in my ears, I saw implications and applications of the text I hadn't seen before. I would think of a skeptic I had met with that week and say, "That is *exactly* what she was complaining about!" or "This answers his question very well."

Immersion in the pastoral needs of people in our community and continued involvement in evangelistic venues could not be more important. If we are deeply involved in the lives, questions, and concerns of the people, then when we study the Bible in order to preach it to them, we will see God's answers to their questions. If we are living in the culture and developing friendships with people, contextualization should be natural and organic. It will simply bubble up from the relationships in our lives and in our pastoral ministry.

What to Look For as You Enter a Culture

Contextualized communication adapts to the "conceptuality" of the hearers. That is, the illustrations we use in communication are taken from the people's social world; the emotion expressed is within their comfort range; the questions and issues addressed are highly relevant to them; the authorities cited are respected by them.[5] Contextualized gospel communication will adapt to a culture in the way it persuades, appeals, and reasons with people. Missiologist David Hesselgrave speaks of three basic ways to reason. He calls them conceptual (or "Western"), concrete relational (or "Chinese"), and intuitional (or "Indian").[6] I summarize his categories this way:

- **Conceptual.** People make decisions and arrive at convictions through analysis and logic. This involves syllogistic reasoning in which premises are established and then necessary conclusions are drawn.
- **Concrete relational.** People make decisions and arrive at convictions through relationships and practice. These are people likely to believe what their community believes. They also are concerned with practical living. They will believe a principle only if they see "how it works."
- **Intuitional.** People make decisions and arrive at convictions through insight and experience. Intuitional people find stories and narratives more convincing and mind-changing than proving propositions through reasoning.

No one way of persuasion is inherently better than the others. All of them can lead to (or away from) the knowledge of God. The conceptual person may demand that we prove the existence of God; the intuitional person may refuse to make commitments that go against feelings; the practical person may not care much about truth and focus only on results. Yet the biblical authors use all of these appeals. If we have "entered" a culture, we will begin to discern which of these approaches and their many variants will have the most impact with the people we seek to reach. For example, on the whole, less educated people are more concrete and intuitional than educated people. Western people are more rational and conceptual than non-Western people. But keep in mind that culture is far more complex than these simple distinctions imply. Even within these broad categories there are generational and regional differences.

The eighteenth-century pastor and scholar Jonathan Edwards spent most of his career preaching at the Congregational Church of Northampton, the most important town in western Massachusetts, and a church filled with many prominent people. But when he was turned out of the congregation, he went to Stockbridge, Massachusetts, on the American frontier, where he preached often to a congregation that included many Native Americans. Edwards's sermons changed dramatically. Of course, they changed in content—they became simpler. He made fewer points and labored at establishing basic theological concepts. But in addition, he changed his very way of reasoning. He used more stories, parables, and metaphors. He made more use of narrative and insight and less use of syllogistic reasoning. He preached more often on the accounts of Jesus' life instead of on the propositions of the Pauline epistles.[7]

To enter a culture, another main task is to discern its dominant worldviews or belief systems, because contextualized gospel ministry should affirm the beliefs of the culture wherever it can be done with integrity. When we enter a culture, we should be looking for two kinds of beliefs. The first are what I call "A" beliefs, which are beliefs people already hold that, because of God's common grace, roughly correspond to some parts of biblical teaching. Because of their "A" beliefs, people are predisposed to find plausible some of the Bible's teaching (which we may call "A" doctrines). However, we will also find "B" beliefs—what may be called "defeater" beliefs—beliefs of the culture that lead listeners to find some Christian doctrines implausible or overtly offensive. "B" beliefs contradict Christian truth directly at points we may call "B" doctrines.

In this first stage, it is important to identify the "A" beliefs—the wisdom and witness to the truth that God, by his common grace, has granted to the culture. Remember that "A" beliefs differ from culture to culture, so we will need to listen carefully. To use an obvious example, in Manhattan, what the Bible says about turning the other cheek is welcome (an "A" belief), but what it says about sexuality is resisted (a "B" belief). In the Middle East, we see the opposite—turning the other cheek seems unjust and impractical, but biblical prohibitions on sexuality make sense.

In our gospel communication, we enter the culture by pointing people to the overlapping beliefs they can easily affirm: *Do you see this in your culture? Do you see this well-known belief? The Bible says the same thing—even more strongly, even more clearly.* Paul does this in his speech in Athens when he quotes pagan poets in order to establish the creation and providence of God (Acts 17:28). Spend time building in your listeners' minds a respect for biblical wisdom in this way. A culture that puts a high value on family relationships and community should be shown that there is a strong biblical basis for the family. A culture that puts a high value on individual human rights and justice should be shown how the biblical doctrine of the image of God is the historical and logical foundation for human rights. One of the reasons we should take great care to affirm the "A" beliefs and doctrines is that they will become the premises, the jumping-off points, for challenging the culture.

Keep in mind that you never stop entering or identifying with a culture. It is not just a "stage" that you leave behind. Always show respect and empathy, even when you are challenging and critiquing, saying things such as, "I know many of you will find this disturbing." Show that you understand. Be the kind of person about whom people conclude that, even if they disagree with you, you are someone they can approach about such matters.

Challenging and Confronting the Culture

As we saw in the previous chapter, Paul's strategy was not simply to rail against the Greeks' love of intellect and the Jews' love of power, but to show them they were pursuing those things in a self-defeating way. Valuing strength (as the Jews did) was a good thing, but without Christ, the pursuit of power leads to weakness, while Christ's apparent weakness brings true power. Paul does not simply dismiss a culture's aspirations; rather, he both affirms and confronts, revealing the inner contradictions in people's understanding. This is why it is so important to enter a culture before challenging it. Our criticism of the culture will have no power to persuade unless it is based on something that we can affirm in the beliefs and values of that culture. We can challenge some of the wrong things they believe from the foundation of those right things they believe. As we have said, each culture includes some rough areas of overlap between its own beliefs and Christian beliefs. These Christian beliefs (the "A" doctrines) will make a lot of sense to members of the culture. Others will be quite offensive (the "B" doctrines).[8] It is important to learn how to distinguish a culture's "A" doctrines from its "B" doctrines because *knowing which are which provides the key to compelling confrontation.* This happens when we base our argument for "B" doctrines *directly on* the "A" doctrines.

Here is an illustration of what I mean. We all know that logs float and stones sink. But if you lash several logs together and then put the stones on top of the logs, you can get both the logs and stones across the river. If you try lashing the stones together and putting the logs on top, the stones will sink and the logs will scatter, and nothing will get across the river. You always float stones on logs, not the other way around. In the same way, we need to "float" "B" doctrines on top of "A" doctrines. Every culture (including our own) can readily grasp part of the truth but not all of it. And we know that biblical truth, because it is from God, is coherent and *consistent* with itself. What we refer to as "A" and "B" doctrines are equally true and interdependent, and they follow from each other. The confrontation occurs because every culture is profoundly *inconsistent*, conforming to some biblical truths but not to others. If those in a particular culture hold certain "A" beliefs, they are inconsistent not to hold "B" beliefs because the Scriptures, as the revealed truth of God, are always consistent. These inconsistencies reveal the points where a culture is vulnerable to confrontation.

Paul reasons this way in Acts 17 when he speaks on Mars Hill. In verse 28, Paul quotes pagan sources that teach the idea that God is the source of all existence and life. Then in verse 29, he states this: "Therefore since we are God's offspring, we should not think that the divine being is like gold or silver or stone—an image made by human design and skill." Notice that Paul does not call him "the Lord" or talk of creation *ex nihilo*—for these would have highlighted the differences between the Bible and pagan beliefs. Instead, for the sake of argument, Paul stresses the similarity between his hearers' beliefs and the Bible's. But then he turns on them, arguing something like this: "If we have been fashioned by God, how can he be fashioned by us—and worshiped as we wish, through images and temples we devise?" Paul is showing them that their beliefs fail *on the basis of their own premises*. He challenges idolatry by showing that it is *inconsistent* with the pagans' own (and better) impulses about God. He tells them, essentially, "If you believe 'A' about God—and you are right—how can you believe in 'B'?" David Peterson in his Acts commentary concludes, "Paul's critique seems to go out of its way to find common ground with philosophers and poets, but his presuppositions are not drawn from Platonism or Stoicism but unambiguously from the Old Testament."[9]

This, then, is how we confront a culture and persuade faithfully. Our premises must be drawn wholly from the Bible, yet we will always find some things in a culture's beliefs that are roughly true, things on which we can build our critique. We will communicate something like this: "You see this 'A' belief you have? The Bible says the same thing—so we agree. However if 'A' is true, then why do you not believe 'B'? The Bible teaches 'B,' and if 'A' is true, then it is not right, fair, or consistent for you to reject 'B.' If you believe *this*—how can you not believe *that*?" We reveal inconsistencies in the cultural beliefs and assumptions about reality. *With the authority of the Bible we allow one part of the culture—along with the Bible—to critique another part.*[10] The persuasive force comes from basing our critique on something we can affirm within the culture.

God's Love and Judgment

I once spoke to a missionary who worked among prostitutes in Korea some years ago. He found that women in that culture simply could not accept the idea of God extending grace to them. Their self-loathing was too great. No matter how much the missionary showed them narratives of Jesus' forgiveness or passages about God's love and grace, he got nowhere. Finally, the missionary, who was a Presbyterian, came up with a radical idea. He decided to talk to these non-Christian Asian prostitutes about the doctrine of predestination.

No one denies there are biblical texts that talk about God predestining and electing people to believe in him, though there is plenty of controversy about what these passages exactly mean. In our Western, democratic, egalitarian culture, the idea of God's sovereignty and his control of all things is definitely a "B" doctrine. We don't like those parts of the Bible that talk about God being completely in charge of history, or those parts where he opens the hearts of those chosen for eternal life (Acts 13:48; 16:14). So when sharing the gospel, we avoid this doctrine at all costs. For most of us in the West, predestination is not just a "B" doctrine; it's a "C" doctrine!

This missionary, however, realized that this was not necessarily true in mid-twentieth-century Korea. So he told the prostitutes about a God who is a King. Kings, he said, have a sovereign right to act as they see fit. They rule—that's just what kings do. And this great divine King chooses to select people out of the human race to serve him, simply because it is his sovereign will to do so. Therefore, his people are saved because of his royal will, not because of the quality of their lives or anything they have done.

This made sense to the women. They had no problem with the idea of authority figures acting in this way—it seemed natural and right to them. But this also meant that when people were saved, it was not because of pedigree or virtue or effort, but because of the will of God (cf. John 1:13). Their acceptance of this belief opened up the possibility of understanding and accepting the belief in salvation by grace. They asked my missionary friend a question that a non-Christian in the West would never ask: "How can I know if I am chosen?" He answered that if as they heard the gospel they wanted to accept and believe it, this was a sign that the Holy Spirit was working on their hearts and that God was seeking them. And some of them responded. The missionary had discerned the difference between "A" and "B" beliefs and had built one on top of the other: "If you believe in a sovereign God, why won't you believe that you can be saved by grace despite all that you've done?"

A classic example of this type of argument is found in C. S. Lewis's appeal to his British readers to accept the idea of a jealous, holy God:

> If God is Love, he is, by definition, something more than mere kindness ... He has paid us the intolerable compliment of loving us, in the deepest, most tragic, most inexorable sense ...
>
> When we fall in love with a woman, do we cease to care whether she is clean or dirty, fair or foul? Do we not rather, then, first begin to care? ...
>
> In awful and surprising ways, we are the objects of His love. You asked for a loving God: you have one ... not a senile benevolence that drowsily wishes you to be happy in your own way, not the cold philanthropy of a conscientious magistrate ... but the consuming fire Himself, the Love that made the worlds, persistent as the artist's love for his work ... provident and venerable as a father's love for a child, jealous, inexorable, exacting as love between the sexes. How this should be, I do not know: it passes reason to explain why any creatures, not to say creatures such as we, should have a value so prodigious in their Creator's eyes. It is certainly a burden of glory not only beyond our deserts but also, except in rare moments of grace, beyond our desiring.[11]

Note how Lewis confronts his own culture. He builds on an "A" doctrine held by Western people, namely, that if there is a God, he is a

God of love. Lewis reasons that if this God is truly loving, he will also get angry. He must oppose sin and anything that hurts his beloved. A person may say, "I believe in a God of love, not a God of wrath against sin." But Lewis reasons that if we have a truly loving God, we will *have to* believe in a God of wrath against sin.

Sin as Idolatry

When I first began ministry in Manhattan, I encountered a cultural allergy to the Christian concept of sin. I found that I got the most traction with people, however, when I turned to the Bible's extensive teaching on idolatry. Sin, I explained, is building your life's meaning on any thing—even a very good thing—more than on God. Whatever else we build our life on will drive our passions and choices and end up enslaving us. I often referred to Augustine's description of sin in his *Confessions* as a disorder of love. So, for example, if we love our own reputation more than the truth, it's likely that we'll lie. Or if we love making money more than our family, we'll neglect our children for our career. Disordered love always leads to misery and breakdown. The only way to "reorder" our loves is to love God supremely.

This approach was very effective with young, secular professionals for two reasons. First, it neutralized (for the moment) the postmodern person's sensitivity to cultural diversity. The moment you say to them, "Sin is breaking God's law," they will retort, "Well, but different cultures and different times had different moral standards. Everyone has different ones!" Of course, postmodern people must eventually be challenged about their naive view of truth, but the concept of idolatry is a way to move forward and give them a convicting sense of their need for Christ before getting into these philosophical issues. The concept of idolatry helps them understand their own drivenness, fears, addictions, lack of integrity, envy of others, and resentment in properly theological terms. It tells them they have been looking to their careers and romances to save them, to give them something they should have been looking for only in God. Most important, this approach makes a great case that supports a "B" doctrine ("you are a sinner before God") on the basis of an acceptable "A" doctrine ("you were created to be free"). Former generations in Western society believed it was most important for someone to be a *good* person. Today in the West, our values have shifted, and our cultural narrative tells us it is most important to be a *free* person. The biblical theme of idolatry challenges contemporary people precisely at that point. It shows them that, paradoxically, if they don't serve God, they are not, and can never be, as free as they aspire to be.

From the Old Testament prophets to Paul (see his speeches in Acts 17–20) and beyond, Christian theologians and commentators have often used the category of idolatry for cultural critique. For example, Alexis de Tocqueville's famous book on the United States noted how Americans believed that prosperity could bring deep happiness. But such a hope was an illusion, Tocqueville argued, because "the incomplete joys of this world will never satisfy [the human] heart."[12] As a result, he spoke of a "strange melancholy often haunting inhabitants of democracies in the midst of abundance."[13] This melancholy is, of course, the bitter fruit of idolatry that always leads to disappointment. False gods never give us what they promise.

In the first chapter of *Center Church*, I quoted from the novelist David Foster Wallace's 2005 speech to the graduating class at Kenyon College. In that talk, Wallace said, "In the day-to-day trenches of adult life, there is actually no such thing as atheism. There is no such thing as not worshiping. Everybody worships. The only choice we get is what to worship."[14] Wallace was not a Christian, and his testimony is more powerful for it. First he argues that the biblical teaching—that we are *homo religioso*, "man the worshiper"—is true. It is a powerful exposé. Most people think, *I am just working hard to be a good writer. I am just seeking to find someone to love me. I am working out so I can be a good steward of my body. I am working hard to accomplish something in politics or have a good career or just make a little money for security.* But Wallace won't let us off the hook. He calls all that activity "worship," even though we won't admit it. Then he shows that worshiping some created thing rather than God leads to spiritual devastation: "The compelling reason for maybe choosing some sort of god or spiritual-type thing to worship … is that pretty much anything else you worship will eat you alive."[15]

Until we recognize that what we are doing is worship, we will be eaten alive by it. We will feel enslaved and unhappy, and we won't know why.

I have found that when we describe the things that drive our lives in terms of idolatry, postmodern people do not put up much resistance. They quickly and even sheepishly admit that this is exactly what they are doing. The biblical message of heart idolatry adapts the message of sin to their cultural sensibilities, but it's far from telling them what they want to hear. It convicts them and makes sin more personal. Making an idol out of something means giving it the *love* you should be giving to your Creator and Sustainer. Depicting sin as an act of misplaced love, not just a violation of law, is more compelling to many people in our culture today.

Of course, a complete biblical description of sin and grace must recognize our rebellion against the authority of God's law. But I've found that if people become convicted about their sin as idolatry and misdirected love, it is easier to show them that one of the effects of sin is living in denial about our hostility to God. Why is this? In some ways, idolatry is much like addiction (and the vernacular of addiction is very familiar to the present generation). We become ensnared by our spiritual idols in much the same way that people are snared by drink and drugs. Once we understand this, it is possible to hear the message of Romans 1 and accept that we live in a state of denial — that we repress or "hold down" the truth that we live in rebellion and bear hostility toward God. Communicating the concept of sin through the biblical teaching on idolatry is an effective way to convey the idea of spiritual blindness and rebellion to postmodern people.

Does the understanding of sin as idolatry remain true to the Pauline gospel of justification by faith alone? It does; in fact it provides a natural stepping-stone to get there. Luther, in his Large Catechism, shows that idolatry (violating the first commandment) is the very same thing as trusting something besides Jesus for our justification.[16] Idolatry, then, is always a failure to accept salvation by grace alone through faith in Christ alone. Any sermon that calls for repentance from idols and offers freedom through Christ can also call people to move from justification by works to justification by faith alone.

Other Pressure Points

What are other ways we can challenge our contemporary secular, pluralistic Western culture? There are several other pressure points at which our culture in the West is vulnerable to challenge. Western culture longs for community and for justice — these are "A" beliefs — but the culture's own commitments and beliefs end up destroying these very precious things. Here are a few examples:

1. The commodification of sex. Thinkers have long discerned the difference between a consumer relationship, which is characteristic of the marketplace, and a covenantal relationship, which has historically been characteristic of personal relationships, particularly within the family. A consumer relationship is maintained only as long as the consumer gets goods and services at an acceptable price. There is no obligation for the consumer to stay in the relationship if it is not profitable. However, a covenantal relationship is based not on favorable conditions of value but on a loving commitment to the good of the other person and to the relationship itself. Social historians tell us that increasingly the values of the market are being applied to areas of human life traditionally seen as covenantal. People now feel free to sever family and relational ties if they are not emotionally fulfilling for them. *Commodification* is a technical term for a process by which social relationships are reduced to the terms of economic exchange.

And this brings us to the subject of sex. Traditionally, you did not have sex with someone who was not your spouse. Put another way, you didn't give your body to someone unless you committed your whole life to them (and they to you) and you both gave up your individual freedom to bind yourself in the covenant of marriage. Contemporary adults, however, want freedom, including sexual freedom. So they have sex with each other without committing their lives to one another, which typically leads to chronic loneliness and a sense of being used — and well it should. Sex in our culture is no longer something that unites people together in binding community; it is a commodity for exchange. But the Bible tells us that sex is designed by God, not as a means of self-gratification, but as a means of self-donation that creates stable human community. If the Christian sex ethic is propounded in this way, using the culture's "A" belief in the goodness of community, it can be very persuasive.[17]

2. The problem of human rights. Western society also has a powerful concern for justice and human rights. At the same time, a secular worldview is being promoted that tells us there is no God. We are here by accident and evolution, and there is no supernatural world or afterlife. Increasingly, thoughtful non-Christians admit these two ideas run on tracks that can never meet: There is a contradiction between a belief in human rights and a disbelief in God. The philosopher Jacques Derrida states, "Today the cornerstone of international law is the sacred ... the sacredness of man as your neighbor ... made by God ... In that sense, the concept of crime against humanity is a Christian concept and I think there would be no such thing in the law today without the Christian heritage."[18] Jean-Paul Sartre makes the same point in a negative form: "God does not exist, and ... it is necessary to draw the consequences of his absence right to the end ... There can no longer be any good *a priori*, since there is no infinite and perfect consciousness to think it ... Dostoevsky once wrote 'If God did not exist, everything would be permitted' ... Everything is indeed permitted if God does not exist."[19]

You see, if we are merely the product of evolution — the strong eating the weak — on what basis can we object to strong nations oppressing weak ones, or powerful people oppressing marginalized ones? This is completely *natural* to the world if this material world is all there is. And if people are not made in the image of God but are simply the accidental product of blind forces, why would human beings be more valuable than, say, rocks and trees? This is a significant pressure point today. Because young adults are particularly sensitive to injustice, it is possible and necessary to show them that human rights and justice make far more sense in a world made by God than in a world that is not made by God.[20]

3. The loss of cultural hope. In his book *The Real American Dream*, Columbia University scholar Andrew Delbanco gives a history of what American culture has put its hope in over the years, under the headings

"God," "Nation," and "Self." He observes that the original Americans believed that life had meaning and our nation had a purpose because we lived for the glory of God. This later changed to a narrative of scientific and moral progress—and particularly of democratic values—promoted in the world through the growth of the United States. However, today "hope has narrowed to the vanishing point of the self alone," so that America's history of hope is "one of diminution."[21] In the last part of his short book, Delbanco argues that we are now in a cultural crisis. To say that the meaning of life is mere self-fulfillment cannot give a society the resources necessary to create a cohesive, healthy culture. A narrative must give people a reason for sacrifice—for living and dying—and the self-fulfillment narrative cannot do it.

Delbanco quotes the philosopher Theodor Adorno, who "recognized that in modern culture the 'pretense of individualism ... increases in proportion to the liquidation of the individual'—by which he meant that the modern self tries to compensate with posturing and competitive self-display as it feels itself more and more cut off from anything substantial or enduring."[22]

A few pages later, Delbanco writes the following:

[Alexis de] Tocqueville's detection of a "strange melancholy in the midst of abundance" has a special salience today—because while we have gotten very good at deconstructing old stories (the religion that was the subject of my first chapter was one such story; the nationalism that was the subject of my second chapter was another), when it comes to telling new ones, we are blocked ... We live in an age of unprecedented wealth, but ... the ache for meaning goes unrelieved.[23]

In short, if we are allowed the absolute freedom to define and create ourselves, we become untethered from anything bigger or more enduring than ourselves. The result is meaninglessness, loss of moorings, and increasing hopelessness about the future. This is an enormous opening and opportunity for persuasive gospel communication to contemporary secular people.

Appealing to and Consoling the Listeners

As we have seen in 1 Corinthians 1:18–2:16, Paul's approach to his listeners was not simply to denounce their culture. He does not merely critique the Greek passion for intellect and the Jewish desire for practical power. Instead, he shows them that the ways they are pursuing these good things are ultimately self-defeating and then urges them to find ultimate fulfillment of their cultural aspirations in Jesus Christ. And so he ends on a positive note, a note of invitation and consolation, though it always comes with a call to repent and believe.[24]

Having entered a culture and challenged its idols, we should follow the apostle Paul in presenting Christ to our listeners as the ultimate source of what they have been seeking. When we enter a culture with care, we earn the ability to speak to it. Then, after we challenge a culture's belief framework, our listeners will feel destabilized. Now, in this final stage of contextualization, we can reestablish equilibrium. Having confronted, we now console, showing them that what they are looking for can only be found in Christ. Put another way, we show our listeners that the plotlines of their lives can only find a resolution, a "happy ending," in Jesus. *We must retell the culture's story in Jesus.*

This aspect of appeal and invitation should not be seen as a third stage cut off from the other stages of contextualization. All throughout our gospel communication, we are seeking to connect to our listeners' deepest desires. We are trying to heed the advice of Blaise Pascal, who, in one of his pensées, wrote, "Men despise religion; they hate it and fear it is true. To remedy this, we must begin by showing that religion is not contrary to reason; that it is venerable, to inspire respect for it; then we must make it lovable, to make good men hope it is true; finally, we must prove it is true."[25]

How can we make our appeal? In chapter 2 of *Center Church*, I note that the intercanonical themes uniting the Bible are richly diverse. They speak of sin and salvation, using the language of exile and homecoming; of temple, presence, and sacrifice; of covenant and faithfulness; of kingdom and victory. When we seek to communicate the gospel to a particular culture, we will find that some of these themes resonate more deeply than others. Paul was able to speak to a wisdom-obsessed culture by using one of the great themes of the Bible, the wisdom of God as it comes to its climax in Jesus Christ (see 1 Cor 1:18–2:16). The Bible has enough diversity to enable us to connect its message to any baseline cultural narrative on the face of the earth.

Atonement "Grammars"

It is commonly said that the Bible contains several different "models" of atonement. I prefer to call these different "languages" or "grammars" by which the saving work of Christ on the cross is presented.

1. **The language of the battlefield.** Christ fought against the powers of sin and death for us. He defeated the powers of evil for us.
2. **The language of the marketplace.** Christ paid the ransom price, the purchase price, to buy us out of our indebtedness. He frees us from enslavement.
3. **The language of exile.** Christ was exiled and cast out of the community so we who deserve to be banished could be brought in. He brings us home.
4. **The language of the temple.** Christ is the sacrifice that purifies us and makes us acceptable to draw near to the holy God. He makes us clean and beautiful.
5. **The language of the law court.** Christ stands before the judge and takes the punishment we deserve. He removes our guilt and makes us righteous.

It is sometimes implied we can choose which of these models we prefer and ignore the others, but this is misleading. Each way of communicating the atonement reflects a piece of inspired Scripture, and each tells us great things about our salvation that the others do not bring out as clearly. Each will have special resonance with certain temperaments and cultures. People who are fighting oppression or even enslavement and long for freedom will be helped by the first two grammars (the battlefield and the marketplace). People seeking relief for guilt and a sense of shame will be especially moved by the last two—the temple and the law court. People who feel alienated, rootless, and rejected will find the exile grammar intensely engaging.

But perhaps the single most consoling and appealing theme is what theologian Roger Nicole has called the one, irreducible theme that runs through every single one of these models—the idea of *substitution*.[26] Dr. Nicole taught that, regardless of the grammar being used, the essence of the atonement is always Jesus acting as our substitute. Jesus fights the powers, pays the price, bears the exile, makes the sacrifice, and bears the punishment *for* us, in our place, on our behalf. In every grammar, Jesus does for us what we cannot do for ourselves. *He* accomplishes salvation; we do nothing at all. And therefore the substitutionary sacrifice of Jesus is at the heart of everything.

This act—giving one's life to save another—is the most compelling, attractive, and electrifying story line there is. J. K. Rowling, for example, could hardly end her Harry Potter series in any other way because it is the ultimate drama, the most moving ending possible. Lifting up the substitutionary sacrifice of Christ is the ultimate way to appeal to any culture, to attract them to him. The various ways of speaking about the atonement furnish us with wonderfully fitting ways of showing each culture how this atoning work of Jesus specifically solves its greatest problems and fulfills its greatest aspirations.

● ● ●

We live in the first era of history that considers happy endings to be works of inferior art. Modern critics insist that life is *not* like that—rather, it is full of brokenness, paradox, irony, and frustration. Steven Spielberg was denied Oscars until he stopped making movies with happy endings and directed *Schindler's List*. Yet people continue to flock to movies and read books that have fairy-tale endings. There are deep human longings that modern realistic fiction can never satisfy: to escape death and live forever; to hold communion with other personal beings like elves or aliens or angels; to find love that perfectly heals and from which we never part. Most of all, we want to see and, if possible, participate in the final triumph over evil in the world. People turn to fairy tales because they depict these desires coming true.

The gospel is by no means a sentimental view of life. In fact, the Bible has a far darker vision of reality than any secular critic. It tells us that Satan and his legions of demons are at work in the world. It tells us we are so deeply flawed and cruel we can't save ourselves without God's intervention. And yet the gospel has an astonishing message about these longings for love and death and triumph. First, the gospel *explains* them. Human beings have been made in the image of God, which means we were originally designed to know and experience all of these things. We were created to live forever. Second, the gospel tells us that the resurrection of Jesus Christ is hard *proof* that all of these things will come true again. If you believe in Jesus Christ, you will see and know escape from death, love without parting, and triumph over evil. You will talk to angels and supernatural beings. You will live forever. And why will we get eternal life? Because he was killed. We get eternal love because he was forsaken. We triumph over evil because he was tortured, murdered, and defeated. In the salvation of Jesus Christ, we learn that the happy ending we long for is not a fairy tale.

The gospel is the deepest consolation you can offer to the human heart. Once you have taken care to enter and have found the courage to challenge the world of your hearers, be sure to offer this consolation with the passion of one who has experienced it firsthand.

DISCUSSION QUESTIONS

1. Keller writes, "The first task of contextualization is to immerse yourself in the questions, hopes, and beliefs of the culture so you can give a biblical, gospel-centered response to its questions." What are some ways you have found to read and study the culture around you? What questions is the culture asking? How has involvement in the pastoral needs of your community helped you to better understand the culture and people you seek to reach?

2. This chapter highlights three ways of reasoning: conceptual, concrete relational, and intuitional.

- **Conceptual.** People make decisions and arrive at convictions through analysis and logic.
- **Concrete relational.** People make decisions and arrive at convictions through relationships and practice.
- **Intuitional.** People make decisions and arrive at convictions through insight and experience.

Which of these three approaches resonates most with you? With the people you are trying to reach? If they are different, what can you do to bridge the gap?

3. Another task of contextualization is discerning the dominant worldviews and belief systems of a culture. Keller writes, "Contextualized gospel ministry should affirm the beliefs of the culture wherever it can be done with integrity." He identifies "A" beliefs, which "roughly correspond to some parts of biblical teaching," and "B" beliefs, which contradict Christian truth ("B" doctrines) and "lead listeners to find some Christian doctrines implausible or overtly offensive."

Take a moment to identify a key "A" doctrine—a teaching from the Bible that would be generally accepted and affirmed by your target culture—and how it expresses itself in the culture through "A" beliefs. What is an example of a "B" belief in your culture, and what "B" doctrines does it conflict with directly?

4. Keller writes, "It is important to learn how to distinguish a culture's 'A' doctrines from its 'B' doctrines because *knowing which are which provides the key to compelling confrontation*. This happens when we base our argument for 'B' doctrines *directly on* the 'A' doctrines." Using the examples you discussed in the last question, how might you do this?

5. This chapter gives a summary of several cultural pressure points and atonement grammars. Which of these pressure points and grammars are less familiar or natural to you, but worth investigating? How might adding them to your repertoire strengthen your effectiveness in mission?

REFLECTIONS
ON GOSPEL
CONTEXTUALIZATION

*Daniel Strange, lecturer in culture, religion, and public
theology at Oak Hill Theological College, London, UK*

My response to these chapters begins with a spoiler alert: I am largely in agreement with Tim Keller's description of, biblical rationale for, and application of gospel contextualization. Let me say this more effusively: I believe these chapters are an immensely helpful resource for faithful and fruitful gospel ministry. These chapters are a support rather than a substitute for proclaiming Christ and him crucified and in forming Christlike disciples and communities in our dizzyingly diverse world.

I appreciate the model Keller presents not because it is new and innovative *but precisely because it is not*. I've become increasingly satisfied with a similar model, albeit of an older vintage, and see Keller to be in direct continuity. Yes, his trimmings and accessories may look a little newfangled to some; yes, his driving style may be a little racy for others; and yes, he may want to take us to some new destinations hitherto unexplored. But the basic chassis is as solidly orthodox and traditional as it ever was. We can be confident that an upgrade will not involve a betrayal of the brand.

That said, I do think some fine-tuning or tuning up needs to be done, and this will involve opening up the hood and getting our hands dirty. In what follows, I wish to make some opening remarks on Keller's own context before getting down to what really matters for those who affirm *sola scriptura*: the biblical justification for his model.

Contextualizing Timothy Keller

Keller's chapters on gospel contextualization remind us that as humans we are all located, particular beings—we all come from somewhere.[1] I am no different. I am a forty-year-old ethnically half white/half Indo-Guyanese British man who happily lives and moves and has his being in a confessionally conservative evangelical seminary in London with its own peculiar ecosystem and networks. Therefore, for a few moments I need to be openly contextual. From within my world, how is Keller being heard in these chapters?

Having read a number of reviews of the original publication of *Center Church*, while there is a general recognition that Keller is getting at something important, there are also some "worries" and "concerns" about his emphasis on contextualization. Even in the increasingly pagan cultural context out of which I operate in the UK, my gang doesn't intuitively embrace words like *plausibility*, *persuasion*, or *effectiveness*. At best, Keller is overcomplicating things to the point of confusion. Do we really need to think about this stuff? Might it even inhibit ministry, causing us to second-guess and dither on things that previously had always been natural? At worst, even if Keller himself is not in danger of syncretizing, accommodating, culturally relativizing, and being too worldly (and some think he is), then less mature and more gung ho practitioners will be: *Obviously we can make adjustments for what he is saying and won't fall into the traps, but others ...*

Putting it candidly, I think some worry that contextualization de-powers the gospel. We don't think there's enough power in the message itself, so we try to make up for it with clever contextualization. Our attempts to make it more plausible or "stronger" ironically de-power it and make it weaker, which takes us back to 1 Corinthians material. The underlying fears are that people will be either tricked into "easy believism" and will not be genuinely converted, or that they will not be converted at all because it's not the power of God at work. contextualization is seen as another case of turning to another power to make evangelism work. Liberal theology from Schleiermacher onward did this by removing the supernatural; others have done it with signs and wonders — and now Keller is doing this with contextualization.

If Keller is right, though, and I think he is, then in reacting against a perceived syncretism, my constituency is in danger of falling off the horse on the other side into a cultural fundamentalism, which, irony of ironies, *is precisely the same ground* — syncretistic, accommodating, culturally relativizing, and worldly. At this point, his regular refrain of maintaining "balance" is a little misleading and counterproductive. In terms of contextualization, the right approach is not halfway between under- and overadapting. Underadapting *is* overadapting. This is an important point for us conservative evangelicals who claim to resist con- textualization but who actually have been blown about by philosophical winds, usually those of modernity.

Where Keller is correct is that we cannot just put our fingers in our ears, hum loudly, and pretend this discussion is not happening. Nor can we have the mentality of "if in doubt, go for caution, play it safe, and underadapt." Rather, we must reflect intentionally and transparently, given our belief and confidence in the truth, stability, and magiste- rial power of God's revealed Word (ministered to us in the "pattern of sound teaching" and the "rule of faith"), and its ability to expose and demolish cultural idols, including our own, with its foolish scandalous message.[2] I hope that Keller's bold linking of faithful contextualization as an implication of the gospel of salvation by grace alone through faith alone might act as the wake-up call or, to put it more strongly, a cattle prod where we might have become somewhat sedentary and risk averse. Yes, there might be some initial pain, discomfort, and stiffness as we get active again, but our hearts will be better for it.

So in the name of transparency, what is causing us to have these hearing problems and how can they be addressed?

First, Tim Keller is a located, particular "body and soul" human being made in God's image. I've only met him personally on a few occa- sions, so my perception of him comes from watching him and reading his works. He can be described in terms of physical appearance (tall, white, balding, wearing glasses, etc.), general manner and demeanor (generally measured in his speech, academic and "bookish" in tone, warm and relational, etc.), and interests (media, arts, sociology, psychology, etc.). Here's my point: Keller speaks and writes on the need for plausibility, persuasion, and winsomeness, and he seems to be plausible, persuasive, and winsome. His human characteristics (including the physical ones) seem to complement his teaching. One might think this a happy providence, thank God, and go about our lawful business. However, for those who are nervous about being persuasive and winsome (because of a perception that this negates the scandal, foolishness, and offensiveness of the cross), I'm sure his manner adds to the worry, especially because the primary culture into which he ministers seems to be drawn to him as a person.

That said, Keller seems sufficiently self-aware, theologically aware (in recognizing that it is the sovereign work of the Holy Spirit who is ultimately responsible for making dead hearts beat again), historically aware (in terms of church history), and globally aware (in terms of world Christianity) not to succumb readily to the temptation of overly cultivating his image. Recognizing the role of personality does not mean subscribing to the cult of personality.

Second, Keller is writing here in a particular context. He is writing for practitioners and not for specialists. He is attempting to have transtribal appeal in wanting to reach a broad spectrum of evangelical belief. This is a laudable aim. Moreover, one of his great gifts is as a communicator. He has that knack of being able to communicate complex concepts in a clear and concise manner. In the hardcover, single-volume publication of *Center Church*, this material is presented in a textbook style to be referred to and returned to. Keller will know, therefore, what communication theorists call the "curse of knowledge": "the difficulty of remembering what it is like not to know something."[3] For these reasons, he doesn't answer the nitty-gritty, tradition-specific questions we might have, but we shouldn't blame him for not dealing with every question we might have. Although these chapters do show some of his workings (and intentionally so), there are other levels of theological depth he doesn't attempt to plumb.

Third, in a world of specialization and compartmentalization where theological disciplines are often hermetically sealed, Tim Keller is one of those rare breeds who seeks to bridge disciplines in order to bring greater depth and clarity to the Christian mission. How would you describe him? Pastor? Preacher? Theologian? Apologist? Missiologist? In the best sense of the term, he is a generalist and an integrator. To my mind, one of his lasting contributions, like Lesslie Newbigin before him, will be to have brought a cross-cultural, missiological mentality and missiological tools into a conservative church context that has viewed missiology suspiciously as a somewhat exotic and peripheral discipline.

Here's the rub, and here I reveal myself as primarily a theologian, not a missiologist (and, yes, I have been asking myself why Tim Keller would ask a theologian to respond to these chapters rather than a missiologist), there is a lot of baggage weighing down the very term *contextualization*, which for an average pastor and Christian leader can be intimidating and confusing. Keller bravely attempts to define what he means by the term and why we need to think about it. I wonder whether we might cut through some of the complexities here by simply thinking about contextualization as nothing more than gospel communication, gospel application, and gospel living. Under these more widely accepted terms, I wonder whether he would get an even wider hearing, especially in those parts where contextualization is shorthand for "selling out." Surely his plea for us to be more consciously self-aware, self-reflective, and self-critical so we are more God-glorifying and gospel-shaped in our lives and ministries is not an unreasonable request. It's certainly not meant as a rejection of faithful, fruitful gospel ministry, both historically or presently.

Fourth, and most importantly, Keller's exposition of contextualization *is not balanced*, and its imbalance is why I agree with it! The Zondervan marketing team may not like me for saying this, but his exposition is very tradition-specific and confessional. Keller is Reformed theologically, apologetically presuppositional, and, in terms of missiology, in a definite genealogical heritage of Dutch Reformed thinking, a lineage going back hundreds of years. He notes his indebtedness to his teacher at Westminster Theological Seminary, Harvie Conn. What I want to bring out more in my response is how J. H. Bavinck (my hero!), who had a major influence on Conn, might offer a slightly different nuance to Keller's model. But any such nuance is all part of an intra-familial discussion. It's wonderful that Keller is able to communicate and persuade those outside this confessional family, but let's not forget that his theological presuppositions are rooted here, and that he is not confessionally neutral when it comes to some of the big tectonic plates that make up a Reformed worldview. While the rhetoric "balance" and "center" may give the impression of fence-sitting or, to use an English idiom, "having your cake and eating it,"[4] it seems clear to me that there is a distinctiveness to Keller's model of contextualization that is under-pinned by a distinct theology and anthropology.

Showing these connections is important. Using a little presupposi-tional twist of my own, Keller's model of contextualization can only float on a raft of Reformed logs. These logs should stop anyone from taking his model and floating off into streams of syncretism and cur-rents of cultural accommodation. One immediate implication here is that teaching on contextualization in churches, courses, and seminaries cannot replace the rigor of knowing Scripture and being well drilled in those mutually complementary (and I hope integrated) disciplines of exegesis, biblical theology, systematic theology, and church history.[5] I will return to this theme of education later on.

Back to Athens

Given our similar theological foundations, Keller's grammar and parsing of contextualization are very similar to my own "subversive fulfillment" model, which I have developed,[6] in terms of the gospel's relationship to other religions, but which can be applied to culture in general.[7] It's been encouraging to see former students taking models like Keller's, my own,[8] and those of other friends who have similar sympa-thies[9] and test-driving them in their own different ministry contexts. Just the other day, a former student shared this with me:

> I was recently asked to talk about faith to a group of professional
> sportsmen. I began by exploring the issue of identity and tried to
> highlight how their impression of themselves has been determined
> by the opinion of others from a very early age. Parents identify their

talent and push them. When they play well, home is fun; when they don't, it isn't. Teachers, coaches, age group coaches, professional coaches, international coaches, media, fans ...

In the eyes of these people, their value is determined by their performance, and I tried to get them to see that tying their joy or satisfaction, ultimately their identity, to these things is a volatile thing that leaves them very vulnerable. I drew on the statistics of cricket suicides (there is a weird phenomenon of cricketers who commit suicide when they retire — more than in any other sport!) to show that this can and does have serious consequences. The talk was discursive, and one of the players said he agreed with this and that was why he didn't put "all his eggs in the sport basket." His "faith" was his family. I then explored how that too will ultimately leave you vulnerable. There were other lines of thought explored that all ended up in the same place, leaving one's identity hanging on a fragile edge.

From there, I held out Christ as the only certain and sure place to stand, and the only place where identity is secure. I said that as long as our family, coaches, fans, media make their demands, we will have to measure up, and as such, we will lie and put on a front when things are bad. Christ knows the worst about us and accepts us anyway. The opinions and love of others are fickle, changing according to our performance. Christ accepts us unconditionally, liberating us to be honest and humble toward others. Culture accepts us for what we can do, but even when we can't perform, Christ accepts us because of who we are as a redeemed image bearer of the God who made us for himself.

Of course, I had to show them how living with the focus on themselves as the end of all things might be offensive to God. Having your identity caught up in the opinions of others is a toxic combination of worshiping them and yourself. Finding security in Christ can only happen if you repent of those things. One guy asked me what he needs to do to become a Christian, and now another wants to read a gospel. I'm 100 percent certain this wouldn't have happened if my presentation had been a standard, "God's in charge, you have sinned, it's going to go badly, so you better repent" approach.

Other examples in very different settings can be illustrated as well—e.g., Islam[10] and within more working-class and socially deprived areas.[11]

To reiterate, all these models have a great deal of similarity. However, in what remains, I would like to bring out a few subtle differences I may have with Keller at the level of theological anthropology. *Who cares?* you might say. *Do we have to nitpick? Can't we just get on with the task?* Well, remember, I'm a theologian! Little nuances at these foundational levels can have important implications at a more practical level.

Keller, recognizes, as do I, that the gospel both confronts and connects with every culture. But what is the dynamic between these two elements? He writes, "Every human culture is an extremely complex mixture of brilliant truth, marred half-truths, and overt resistance to the truth" (p. 51). The doctrines of the "antithesis" (see his discussion on the fall, pp. 252–54), image of God, and common grace support this view of culture. The concept of idolatry brings all these doctrines together. Idolatry allows us to talk about a superficial structural similarity between Christianity and all other worldviews because idols are counterfeit and parasitic.

In other words, it is not surprising that throughout history, human beings have asked similar questions about life, the universe, and everything.[12] However, I wonder whether the nature of suppressed truth (Rom 1:18) and the totalizing, all-infecting, assimilating nature of idolatry lead to a slightly more confrontational and challenging stance to non-Christian culture than Keller takes. Here I'm not talking so much about our tone, manner, or even the percentage or order of confronting or connecting. Rather, I mean the full implications of the stark discontinuity between the gospel and idolatrous culture. In other words, all connection is in the context of confrontation. Bavinck writes, "There is no direct uninterrupted path from the darkness of paganism to the light of the gospel ... The transition from paganism to Christianity is not continuous and smooth, and it would be dishonest and unfaithful to Christ if it were to try to camouflage the gulf separating the two."[13]

Let me illustrate by returning to Acts 17. Now I'm aware that some think that far too much weight is put on this passage. While I don't want to be guilty of having a "canon within a canon," I do think that

Luke (under God's superintendence) intended this incident and the other apostolic encounters recorded in Acts to be exemplars in terms of the communication of the gospel in different cultural settings.[14] I also think Acts 17 is a particularly relevant example with which to lead, given my particular cultural context in Britain at the moment.

Shadows and Sunbeams

The framing for Paul's address is his violent revulsion and righteous anger at the idolatry he sees in Athens, a whole city submerged in idolatry. Just as God himself is provoked by idols in Deuteronomy 32:16–19, so Paul is provoked as he surveys the scene in front of him (Acts 17:16). This introduction must never be left out. It is this deeply negative reaction that gives us the mood for the whole encounter. However respectful, intellectual, and contextual Paul may be in what follows, we must not forget this backdrop. If anyone were to doubt this anti-idolatry mood throughout, then the climactic call to repentance (v. 30) nails it all down securely.

Do we have the biblical eyes and, frankly, the biblical nerve to see and feel all our evangelistic and apologetic encounters in the context of idolatry and its provoking nature? I'm not talking about an application that issues in facile ranting and raving, but about a background theological commitment that understands, however it might look to the contrary on the surface, the real theological nature of all that which is not of Christ. Should we be more "distressed" than we often are? Would there be a renewed urgency to our mission if we were?

Keller is right that idolatry is such a helpful tool for understanding sin and the damage it causes to ourselves and relationships. But it's the damage it causes in our relationship with God that is always primary. Yes, idolatry can, as Keller notes, reveal to unbelievers that we suppress the truth and bear hostility toward God (p. 80), but we also need to show that because of God's holiness and our rebellion, *he bears hostility to unbelievers*, seen in what I call shadows and sunbeams.

The "wrath of God ... being revealed from heaven" (Rom 1:18) is a *shadow* of what the Bible calls "the coming wrath" (1 Thess 1:10), brought forward into the present (what Ted Turnau calls "hell writ small").[15] Part of contextualized communication is to start with the "felt wrath" that unbelievers experience in myriad ways every day, and to show how these are warning signs (indeed, providentially gracious ones) of hell writ large. Similarly God's common grace, his goodness shown to all creation, are *sunbeams* (what can be called "heaven writ small"), pointing toward the source of all goodness, God himself. They are to be interpreted as such and to be received with thanksgiving. However, when the gift is mistaken for the giver (idolatry), when we do not give thanks (Rom 1:21), then this has consequences—eternal consequences that at some point must be pointed out.[16]

Whether it's shadows or sunbeams, the only appropriate responses are repentance and faith. I would suggest, in Kelleresque fashion, that our gospel communication cannot stop at the shadows and sunbeams but must use them to point to that which they signify. However, neither should we simply bypass the shadows and sunbeams, for these presenting issues are revelatory points that helpfully link the concrete specifics of people's lives and contexts with eternal realities that people often don't "feel." Superficial relationships with our non-Christian friends and acquaintances just won't do; we need to have relationships with people that enable us to engage in terms of their whole life—intellect, will, emotion, as well as in terms of past, present, and future.

The "Point of Attack"

It would help for us to be a little more precise in our thinking of what Keller calls "A" doctrines. He describes them as beliefs that "roughly correspond" to biblical teaching (p. 72). Although such beliefs through God's common grace certainly serve as a way in and point of contact, Paul's opening statement to the "religious" Athenians with their "unknown God" is not a straightforward commendation, affirmation, or prescription of their undoubted religiosity, but rather a description of their idolatrous and ignorant speculation and searching. It's not so much the contact of a warm handshake but rather more the contact of a wrestle. Bavinck writes:

From a strictly theological point of view there is no point of contact within pagan thought which offers an unripe truth that can simply be taken over and utilized as a basis for our Christian witness. If this is what is meant by point of contact, then there just is none. But, practically speaking, in actual missionary experience, we cannot avoid making frequent "contact"; no other way is open. But, we must never lose sight of the dangers involved, and we must endeavor to purify terms we have borrowed of their pagan connotations. This is what the apostles did with concepts such as salvation, redemption, *logos*, and many others, which undoubtedly could easily have led to a world of misunderstanding. We would like to distinguish, therefore, a "point of attack" from a "point of contact." The point of attack signifies for us the awareness of need, poverty, and inability, which we frequently encounter in non-Christian nations, as well as in our own surroundings.[17]

I believe that Paul's quotation of the pagan poets in Acts 17:28 is still within the context of "ignorance" and "groping in the dark."[18] As Greg Bahnsen notes, "Paul did not utilize pagan ideas in his Areopagus address. He used pagan expressions to demonstrate that ungodly thinkers have not eradicated all ideas, albeit suppressed and distorted, of the living and true God."[19] So while we must recognize the existence of "A" doctrines, we must never atomize or separate them from the overall idolatrous structure in which they are inextricably associated. Moreover, do we recognize the perils associated with our need to communicate cross-culturally? Bavinck notes that we "inadvertently swallow a number of pagan conceptions every moment ... Infected terms are used simply because it is impossible not to use them ... The missionary exhales many pagan ideas with every word that he speaks. He cannot do otherwise, since he has no other vocabulary at his disposal, but he will shudder at times when he is conscious of what he is doing."[20]

A "Run-Up" and "Run-Through"

As Paul stands up and explains himself on the Areopagus, he invites a comparison and head-on collision of worldviews. As Luke records in Acts, the whole buildup to the speech has been talking about the good news of Jesus, his death, and his resurrection. At the beginning of chapter 17, we learn that Paul "reasoned with them from the Scriptures, explaining and proving that the Messiah had to suffer and rise from the dead" (17:2–3). In Athens itself, he has been proclaiming "the good news about Jesus and the resurrection" (17:18), before being brought before the Areopagus. Christ and him crucified is very much present and correct. But the reception of this message is one of confusion. Therefore, when Paul stands up and starts to speak, his purpose is not to reduce the scandal of the message but to give a defense of this good news, to put it in the context of life, the universe and everything, to show its implications and applications for humanity. Both ignorance and biblical illiteracy have to be dealt with. As D. A. Carson notes, "What Paul provides is the biblical metanarrative. This is the big story in the Bible that explains all the little stories. Without this big story, the accounts of Jesus will not make any sense."[21] What Paul is doing here is giving a *run-up* and then a *run-through*. For the good news of Jesus to make sense in Athens, Paul needs the longer run-up, which gets some basic concepts in place—concepts the Athenians just don't have. That's why his speech is a run-through of a Christian worldview. Paul is saying, "OK, let's get back to basics. You Athenians may have all kinds of views about the nature of ultimate reality, creation, time, the end of it all, but I'm going to lay out how I see it." A God both absolute and personal, both far and near; a creation distinguished from its Creator; a view of providence that has a purpose; a fall (the "groping after"), a time of long-suffering; and an end to history, with a judgment coming. Without these basic building blocks in place, Jesus and his resurrection do not make sense. Paul recognizes the need to point out these differences pretty early on; indeed, the quotations from the pagan philosophers occur *after* this setting out of the Christian worldview has been laid down.

Do we need to be starting further back in our conversations with unbelievers? Do we need to spend more time running through these worldview basics, putting together a picture into which Jesus and his resurrection make sense? Please don't mishear me at this point: Our goal is always to get to the good news about Jesus. This running-up and running-through is not a *substitute* for gospel proclamation but rather a *support* for such proclamation. And it will take more time and patience and prayer than maybe we've needed in the past.

Concluding Reflections

The above section has concentrated solely on the issue of contextualization as gospel communication. It needs to be remembered that contextualization is not simply about communication but also about living, worshiping, culture building, and theologizing.

In whatever area of contextualization we are talking about, the more "active" and even "forceful" stance we've spoken about in terms of the collision between the gospel and idolatrous culture remains. For example, the discourse of gospel accommodation or adaptation must be questioned. Bavinck's notion of *possessio* is more appropriate:

> The Christian life does not accommodate or adapt itself to heathen forms of life, but it takes the latter in possession and thereby makes them new. Whoever is in Christ is a new creature. Within the framework of the non-Christian life, customs and practices serve idolatrous tendencies and drive a person away from God. The Christian life takes them in hand and turns them in an entirely different direction; they acquire an entirely different content. Even though in external form there is much that resembles past practices, in reality everything has become new, the old has in essence passed away and new has come.[22]

While not denying the practical complexity and dangers of what and how we might "possess," I wonder whether we would be less anxious and more open to contextualization because it is positively "possessing" for Christ rather than passively "accommodating" to culture.

Second, and following on, we need to ask whose responsibility it is to do the possessing. Here, we need to be alive to the relational dynamic, well-known in missiological circles, between the culture of the Bible, the culture of the cross-cultural communicator, and the "new" indigenous culture into which this communication comes. I am sympathetic to the view that our overall aim is for the new indigenous culture to be engaging directly with the Bible and not having to go back through the cross-cultural communicator's culture to get to the Bible. We should be encouraging indigenous leadership and self-theologizing, the goal of which is mutual edification:[23]

> Instead of appealing to principles of contextualization to justify the assumption that every interpretation is as good as every other interpretation, we will recognize that not all of God's truth is vouchsafed to one particular interpretive community—and the result will be that we will be eager to learn from one another, to correct and to be corrected by one another, provided only that there is a principled submission to God's gracious self-disclosure in Christ and in the Scriptures. The truth may be one, but it sounds less like a single wavering note than like a symphony.[24]

What needs to be noted is that for *any* culture, the sandpit within which we creatively contextualize and "possess" has definite boundaries. The categories of "orthodoxy" and "orthopraxis" do exist; there is an apostolic "pattern of sound teaching" (contrasted with gangrenous teaching); and of the ministerial "rule of faith."[25] We return to the need for theological education and formation in our churches.

In conclusion, one of the worries about all this contextualization talk is that it will *translate out* the richness of the Bible, its categories, and its plotline rather than capturing our imagination and *drawing us into* a new vision of the world, with its own language, practices, and plausibility. As Richard Lints notes:

> It is a fundamental challenge facing contemporary theology to educate a church that is largely ignorant of the Scriptures and therefore largely ignorant of the controlling biblical images and metaphors

that have informed theology in ages past. The translation of the redemptive-historical message of the Scriptures into the vernacular of modern culture will be meaningless unless and until the church is educated in the vernacular of the Scriptures. We have to go back before we go forward.[26]

John Piper has made the point that preaching is as much about "concept creation" by a work of the Spirit in us as it is about the contextualization of existing conceptual categories.[27] However, if we recognize the counterfeiting nature of idolatry, if we acknowledge the radical subversion but real fulfillment that the gospel of Christ brings, and if we talk about possessing rather than accommodating, then maybe we can affirm a view of contextualization that recognizes cultural continuity in discontinuity, that recognizes newness and strangeness, but the nature of which is actually the re-creation of the old and familiar cultures in which God has providentially located us and in which we can worship and glorify him in our unity and in our diversity. Maybe we *can* have our cake and eat it.

RESPONSE TO DANIEL STRANGE

Timothy Keller

Grateful

Dan Strange's fine essay starts by saying that my work on contextualization may be "a little racy" for some but still "orthodox"—a bit provocative but sound. It's amusing for an aging, balding (yes, he mentions that too) white man to hear himself called racy in any context at all. So I accept the compliment! And I greatly appreciate his recommendation of the material on gospel contextualization as "immensely helpful" (p. 89).

I also appreciate that Strange is, a little ironically, doing his own version of contextualization by recommending my work to his own context of British evangelicalism. He confirms the message that those who are too afraid of a "perceived syncretism" are themselves in danger of "falling off the horse on the other side into a cultural fundamentalism, which, irony of ironies, *is precisely the same ground*—syncretistic, accommodating, culturally relativizing, and worldly" (p. 91). His own flourish adds that my counsel to maintain a "balance" between overadapting and underadapting can mask the fact that "underadapting is overadapting."

Strange also does a great job of arguing that my basic approach to contextualization is not something either newfangled or syncretistic, but is rather a practical outworking of an approach to missions and apologetics that is in the "definite genealogical heritage of Dutch Reformed thinking, a lineage going back hundreds of years" (p. 93). As Strange points out, I developed the more theoretical aspects of my approach during my years of teaching at Westminster Seminary in the 1980s, where Harvie Conn, who had taught apologetics there in the tradition of Abraham Kuyper, Cornelius Van Til and the Bavincks (Herman and J. H.), was applying this to the project of defining an evangelical approach to contextualization. Because he and I have these same intellectual ancestors, his thinking about apologetics as a theologian and mine as a practitioner have developed along fundamentally similar lines.

Indeed, when I saw Strange call his model "subversive fulfillment" (p. 94), the name immediately resonated as an excellent short descriptive of exactly what I am trying to accomplish as well. We identify the particular desires and aspirations in the culture that have become idolatrous. We show how destructive, illusory, and self-defeating the idols are. But then we point to the gospel as both subverting and challenging the idol, yet fulfilling the very desire that the idol cannot fulfill. He outlines this model in his essay endnotes, and it essentially describes the method of the Gospel Contextualization chapters.

Because of this central agreement, Dan Strange's critiques definitely feel more like improvements to the model rather than efforts to change it.

Helpful

Strange's first critique is a proposal that I just drop using the word *contextualization* at all. He points out that what I am talking about in these chapters is only the communicative aspect, that contextualization comprehensively considered includes also "living, worshiping, culture building, and theologizing" (p. 101). Therefore, why call these chapters "Gospel Contextualization" when what I am really discussing is gospel communication and application? He says I try "bravely" (p. 93) to define contextualization in the defiance of its original pedigree within the circles of the World Council of Churches. But why try to hold on to a word with all that baggage, a word that immediately raises red flags in more orthodox circles. I think Strange here is giving me some hints on how to better contextualize contextualization for certain contexts. (Did I write that?)

I feel the force of this argument because I have indeed met resistance for this material in some quarters, even where the resistors admitted their problem was with hardly any of the actual content of these chapters — it was mainly with the name. Their complaint was that the word *contextualization* (much like, unfortunately, in their own ways, the terms *gospel-centered* and *grace renewal*) had become a kind of banner to fly over a host of unhelpful attitudes and practices. Many younger leaders who are achingly concerned to appear culturally sophisticated use the term as they move away from traditional, pointed expository preaching and evangelism that calls for repentance. (For more of this discussion, see Michael Horton's essay on Gospel Theology and my response in the first book in this series, *Shaped by the Gospel*.)

My response to all this is to grant that in many situations I should indeed call this teaching gospel communication or even apologetics. But I still share the original concern of Harvie Conn, John Stott, J. I. Packer, and others at the 1978 Consultation on Gospel and Culture that evangelicals had fallen into the deadly illusion that the gospel message could be communicated without deep reflection on the human culture from which the message comes and to which it is proclaimed.[1]

Strange's next critique is a significant one, despite his kind use of the word *slightly*. He writes that what is warranted is "a slightly more confrontational and challenging stance to non-Christian culture than Keller takes" (p. 96). He hastens to add that he is not talking about "tone, manner, or even the percentage or order of confronting or connecting." Rather, he means that "all connection is in the context of confrontation." He cites J. H. Bavinck: "It would be dishonest and unfaithful to Christ if it were to try to camouflage the gulf separating the two [the gospel and paganism]."

As a practitioner rather than a theologian, I might ask how this more confrontational stance actually shows itself if it does not change one's tone, manner, or even the actual amount of time challenging the listener? Strange does give two answers. One comes as he examines Paul's distress and revulsion at the idols of Athens. While not wanting "facile ranting and raving," Strange asks whether we should not be more "distressed" by the idolatries of our culture. I think he is saying we should be more grieved and less reconciled to the lies and delusions around us, so as to have more "urgency to our mission" (p. 97). I see that this distress and urgency is not part of the gospel contextualization material. If anything, I as a writer want my evangelical readers to be more willing to engage nonbelieving culture in a less condescending and insensitive way than they usually do. Strange warns us not to lose our distress over what is warped and dark. He is right.

The other practical way to maintain a more challenging stance is that in our engagement we must convey to nonbelievers not simply that their sin creates unfulfilled longings but also that it brings God's hostility. Strange, quoting other writers, talks about "shadows" of God's wrath, "hell writ small" experiences and intuitions found within "the concrete specifics of people's lives" that are actually evidences of their alienation from God but also of his alienation from us.

I completely agree with the importance of this caution as well. It is true, that in a "subversive fulfillment" model, it is too easy to put all the emphasis on the way the gospel fulfills one's deepest longings, thereby giving listeners the impression that sin only hurts them and doesn't also grieve, dishonor, and anger God. Strange gives no concrete examples of how to do this. But there are many ways to do this, which I've referred to in my preaching over the years.

One of the ways I've done this is to mention a figure from history or fiction—like Lady Macbeth, who is wounded by guilt. Then I admit that the very idea of guilt seems old-fashioned to modern people. And yet if the preacher speaks as follows, there is always a silence:

> But. But. You may not believe in sin; you may not believe in hell; you may not believe in a divine law—and yet, you've got a sense of condemnation that you can't shake. There is a voice (is there not?) that calls you a fraud, an imposter, says you are not living up. You try to explain it by saying it's some kind of psychological complex, by saying maybe your parents didn't affirm you, but I want you to know those of us with affirming parents hear it anyway. You feel stained. And it goes deeper than just "not living up to your own standards."
>
> One of the reasons our guilt has an indelibility, immediacy, and freshness to it, according to the Bible, is that it is not only the memory of

something we did in the past. Our consciences are in contact with some-
thing that keeps refreshing them. There is a divine bar of judgment, and
our consciences are like radio monitors that pick up transmissions from
it. Deep down, we know we aren't what we should be because Somebody
keeps telling us. There's a court before which we all stand. There's a justice
with which we all must deal. There's a standard we've all violated, and
we all know it, and we all stand before it underdressed, without defense.

So Strange is right that we must show not only how sin harms us
but also how it warrants God's displeasure and wrath, and we must
find ways to show nonbelievers evidences of God's judgment in their
lives. These aspects are not emphasized in the gospel contextualization
chapters and rightly belong here, together with more support on how to
convey to contemporary people the biblical doctrine of sin in general.

Intriguing

The "meatiest" theological discussion is at the end of Strange's essay,
in which he discusses whether there are really "'A' doctrines"—namely,
beliefs that the non-Christian shares with believers, common ground
on which to build (pp. 98–99). The practical heart of my model is to (1)
agree with the listener at some point, (2) then show them something I
think is wrong and inconsistent with the agreed-on belief, and (3) then
press them to be consistent. "If you believe this, why believe that?" Dan
Strange takes the position of J. H. Bavinck and Greg Bahnsen that there
are not, ultimately, any common beliefs, that even these similar-looking
beliefs are at bottom idolatrous, that therefore there is no "point of contact" but only a "point of attack." I theoretically agree. Yet it is intriguing
to see Bavinck, who was a working missionary in Indonesia, admitting
there is no alternative but to deploy "infected terms . . . used because it is
simply impossible not to use them." And I have listened to recordings of
Greg Bahnsen's debates, in which he also uses these commonly accepted
terms and concepts and presses his opponent on their inconsistency in
exactly the same way I would. So, I wonder, what's the difference on the
ground? Perhaps it goes back to Strange's exhortation that we maintain

our inner distress and also never forget the idolatrous matrix in which the agreed-on term and concept is embedded.

This helps me see something that will make me a much better teacher. I have done far more actual evangelizing and apologetics than writing and reflecting on it. (That is true of the *Center Church* topics across the board. I reflect on that in my note in the front of this book.) Everything Dan Strange says he would like to see added or refined in my model of contextualization is something I already do in my practice, but it is not well represented in the reflection and training on how to do it. That means I need to keep listening to subject matter experts in each field so that theory and practice can be better integrated as we train the next generation of church leaders.

Part 2

CITY VISION

Chapter 5

THE TENSION
OF THE CITY

M any Christians today, especially in the United States, are indifferent or even hostile toward cities. Some think of them as a
negative force that undermines belief and morality, while others see
them as inconsequential to Christian mission and living. It may also be
true that some young Christians are adopting a romanticized view of
the city.[1] But the attitude of the biblical authors is quite different. The
biblical view of cities is neither hostile nor romantic. Because the city is
humanity intensified — a magnifying glass that brings out the very best
and worst of human nature — it has a dual nature.[2]

This is why the Bible depicts cities as places of perversion and violence and also as places of refuge and peace. Genesis 4 and 11 depict
city builders as those in the line of Cain (the first murderer). Genesis
also depicts the evil of the cities of Sodom and Gomorrah. Yet Psalm
107 speaks of a group of wandering people "finding no way to a city
where they could settle ... and their lives ebbed away. Then they cried
out to the LORD ... He led them by a straight way to a city where they
could settle. Let them give thanks to the LORD" (vv. 4–8). The psalmist
depicts life for people without a city as a bad thing. The assumption
behind this psalm is that the city is a place where human life thrives — it
is a positive social form. The depiction of the city in the Bible is therefore finely nuanced. It highlights how the capacities of this positive
social form can be realized for God's glory yet also demonstrates how
it can be a vehicle for enhancing human rebellion against God. And
as we will see in chapter 6, the city plays a pivotal role in the arc of
redemptive history.

In this chapter, I want to look at this tension between the city's God-exalting promise and its man-exalting shadow. We will find this dual nature played out in the pages of Scripture and mirrored in our contemporary world, for in most ways our cities are still today as they have always been.

The City Defined

But first we must ask, What do we mean by a city? Today, a city is usually defined in terms of population size. Large population centers are called "cities," smaller ones "towns," and the smallest ones "villages." We must be careful, however, not to impose our current cultural understanding of city onto the biblical term. The most common Hebrew word for city, *'îr*, meant any human settlement surrounded by some fortification or wall.[3] Most ancient cities numbered only about one thousand to three thousand in population but the residents were tightly packed within the city wall.[4] Therefore, according to the Bible, the essence of a city was not the population's size but its density. A city is a social form in which people physically live in *close proximity* to one another.

Psalm 122:3 refers to this density: "Jerusalem, built as a city should be, closely compact."[5] In a fortified city, the people lived close to one another in small residences on narrow streets. City life was street life — physical human presence at all times and in all places. In fact, most ancient cities were estimated to be five to ten acres in size, containing an average of 240 residents per acre.[6] By comparison, the island of Manhattan in present-day New York City houses only 105 residents per acre — with high-rises! After Nehemiah rebuilt Jerusalem's city wall, there were far too many vacant homes for Jerusalem to flourish as a city (Neh 7:4). In other words, the city wasn't densely populated enough to function as a city should. So 10 percent of the nation was commanded to move into the city to fill it (Neh 11:1). When cities first arose, they created a distinct kind of human life within their walled, protected space. Out of this dense proximity flowed three signal features that mark urban human life.

Safety and Stability

First, because early cities had walls, a city meant greater *safety* and therefore *stability*. Cities' primary importance lay in their resistance to hostile forces, whether opposing armies, marauders, blood feud avengers, or wild animals. The walled safety of a city allowed for a far more stable life than was possible outside the city, and this led to the growth of human civilization. *Civilized* literally means "citified." When the Israelites were conquering Canaan, they were amazed at the strength of its fortified cities (Deut 1:28; 9:1; Josh 14:12), and as they settled the land, they built cities for themselves (Num 32:16 – 42). It should not surprise us that in the Bible the city is used as a metaphor for confidence (Prov 21:22; cf. Deut 28:52). Proverbs 25:28 tells us that a man without self-control is like a city without a wall. Cities were places where life was not dangerously out of control.

Because of this stability, systems of law and order were able to develop first in urban settings. Early cities had gates where the elders sat and decided cases according to the rule of law. Outside the gates, disputes were settled by the sword, which led to blood feuds, destruction, and social disorder. The wall and the gate made it both necessary and possible to develop systems of jurisprudence so matters could be settled fairly, without violence. God commanded the Israelites to build "cities of refuge" to which individuals who killed someone accidentally could flee and plead their case (Num 35:6).

The idea of the city as a place of safety and stability does not immediately strike modern readers as intuitive. We may accept that cities were safe places in earlier times, but today we think of cities as places of high crime. The latest studies indicate that this concept—that higher crime is inevitable in cities—is a mistake.[7] And we must broaden our definition of "the city as safe space." This concept continues to drive the growth and success of many cities in chaotic parts of the world. Even modern-day cities such as Hong Kong, Singapore, and Gaborone (in Botswana) have thrived because they have established themselves as bastions of the rule of law in disorderly parts of the world, thereby attracting a disproportionate amount of economic investment and human talent.

But another way in which most cities thrive is that they have become places of refuge to which minority groups and individuals can flee from powerful interests. In Bible times, accused criminals could flee blood avengers, seek refuge in the city, and have their case heard by the city elders (Num 35; Deut 19; Josh 20). Even today, economically pressed or politically oppressed people who need to move out of their homeland to achieve a better life usually emigrate to cities. It is in these places of density and proximity that immigrant groups can create "mini-cities" with their own institutions that enable newcomers to enter and learn the ways of the new country. And it's not just immigrants who feel cities are safe places to live. All demographic minorities (e.g., older single people, racial minorities) feel less conspicuous and odd in cities where more of the people in their group live. Cities, then, continue to thrive today because significant numbers of people perceive them to be safe places to live — in the broadest sense of the term.

Diversity

Second, the biblical understanding of a city also implies greater *diversity*, which is a natural result of density and safety. In the church in Antioch, we see leaders from different ethnic groups (Acts 13:1) — a natural occurrence when the gospel goes forth in cities, in which many different people groups reside. Because minorities find them to be safe places to live, cities tend to become racially and culturally diverse. And this is not the full extent of their diversity. Cities are marked by diversity not just of population but of land use as well.

Human society requires several elements:

- an economic order, where people work and business transactions take place
- a cultural order, where people pursue scholarship, art, and theater
- a political-legal order, where cases are decided and governing officials meet

If you think of these elements as components of a pizza (tomato sauce, cheese, pepperoni, dough), the city is a place where every neighborhood is a slice of pizza. Along with residences, it has places to work, shop, read, learn, enjoy art and music, worship, and play, as well as public government buildings such as town halls and courts. All are mixed and compacted together within walking distance. In ancient times, rural areas and even villages could not provide all these elements; only cities could sustain them all. This is why some define a city as a "walkable, mixed-use settlement."[8] And in modern times, the dominant arrangement—the suburb—deliberately avoids this urban pattern. Suburbs are normally dedicated to large, single-use zones—so places to live, work, play, and learn are separated from one another and are reachable only by car, usually through pedestrian-hostile zones. Suburbs and rural areas have the pizza ingredients, but not in pizza form. It is tomatoes here, dough there, and pepperoni over there.[9]

Productivity and Creativity

Third, in the Bible, cities were places of greater *productivity* and *creativity*. As we will see below, human culture—technology, architecture, the arts—began to develop as cities were built (see Gen 4; 11). The city features street life and marketplaces, bringing about more person-to-person interactions and exchanges in a day than are possible anywhere else. The more often people of the same profession come together, the more they stimulate new ideas and the faster these new ideas spread. The greater the supply of talent, the greater the productivity of that talent, and the demand for it follows. As a testimony to this fact, the purpose of modern conventions is *connection*—a place where people connect with expertise, peers, money, and other resources—and the best way to facilitate these connections is to create a temporary city! All the connections lead in the end to creativity—new alliances, ideas, art, and movements.

So ever since the beginning of recorded history, cities have been the centers of cultural intensity—for better or for worse. And what makes a city a city is not so much population size but proximity. Edward Glaeser writes, "Cities are the absence of physical space between people."[10] This is what gives the city its distinctiveness and potency among all other human living arrangements.

The City throughout the Old Testament

We have said the Bible has a balanced understanding of how both good and evil operate in a city. We will call this the "tension" of the biblical view of the city. The tension takes time to come into focus, as the city plays a definite role at every stage in the history of salvation. As redemptive history progresses, the Bible moves from a largely negative view of the city (emphasizing the city's rebellion) to a more positive one (emphasizing the city's strengths, power, and strategic importance). To illustrate, we turn to a detailed study of the city in early biblical history.

The Primeval City

The first occurrence of the word *city* (*'îr*) in the Bible is in Genesis 4:17, where Cain, after committing fratricide and being sent away from the presence of the Lord, settles east of Eden in the land of Nod (Gen 4:16). Cain, the rebel, then *builds a city*.[11] This has led some to see "a possible reflection of the antiurban bias in Genesis."[12] But this association misses the subtleties of the narrative. First, the founding of the city comes as the result of Cain's search for security in the world and of God's granting his request (Gen 4:14–15). In other words, the city is seen as a refuge, even from the very beginning. In addition, Genesis 4:17–22 links the founding of the city with the beginnings of the creation of culture. Immediately after Cain establishes city life, we see the first development of the arts in the musicianship of Jubal (v. 21) and of technology in the tool making of Tubal-Cain (v. 22). Architecture, agriculture, the arts, and technology all begin when cities begin. Cities are places of human productivity.

This list of cultural expressions would have been shocking to Israel's ancient Near Eastern neighbors who believed that cultural advances like the sciences, writing, and the arts were the product of divine or mythological characters. The historical, human nature of their origins runs counter to the prevailing cultural view of the ancient Near East. In the Genesis narrative, we see man becoming a contributor under God in the ongoing work of creation, through the development of culture. We learn that city life is not to be seen as simply a punishment for humanity after the banishment from the garden. Rather the city has inherent capacities for bringing human beings together in such a way that enhances both security and culture making.

However, as can be seen in the line of Cain, these capacities, under the influence of sin and rebellion against God, can be generators of great evil. The song of Lamech, Cain's descendant, shows the Cainite city dwellers using all their advances to form a culture of death (Gen 4:23 – 24). Here is the first clear indicator of the dual nature of the city. Its capability for enormous good — for the culture-making creation of art, science, and technology — can be used to produce tremendous evil. Henri Blocher does not consider it a coincidence that the first mention of anti-God culture making is tied to the first instance of city building, but he warns against drawing the wrong conclusion:

> It is no doubt significant that [in Genesis 4] progress in arts and in engineering comes from the "city" of the Cainites. Nevertheless, we are not to conclude from this that civilization as such is ... the fruit of sin. Such a conclusion would lead us to Manichaeism or to the views of Jean-Jacques Rousseau ... The Bible condemns neither the city (for it concludes with the vision of the City of God) nor art and engineering.[13]

Blocher may be responding to writers such as Geerhardus Vos, who in his *Biblical Theology* points to "the problem of the city" and asserts that "the city, while an accumulator of the energies of culture, is also an accumulator of potencies of evil (Amos 3:9; Micah 1:5)."[14] Sometimes these seats of culture making can be established to bring glory to God's name (1 Cor 10:31) and therefore be a means of serving God and neighbor (e.g., Bezalel in Exod 31:3 – 5), or they can be erected to "make a name for ourselves" (Gen 11:4), resulting in a culture of human pride, self-salvation, violence, and oppression (Gen 4:17 – 24).

Vos adds that what makes the human city fallen is not its density of population (indeed, this is what makes it an "accumulator of the energies of culture"), but its "spirit of rebellious self-dependence over against God."[15] A horse is a more valuable animal than a mouse, yet a crazed horse is capable of far more damage than a crazed mouse; so too a city's strengths under sin can unleash more destructive evil. As the Genesis narrative unfolds, we see that warring with the city's great potential is a profound bent toward corruption and idolatry.

For most of the rest of Genesis, the city is seen in a negative light. The city is mentioned in connection with the accursed Ham (Gen 10:12). The next substantive appearance is in Genesis 11:4 when the people dwelling in the plain of Shinar (11:2) gather together *to build a city*. The naming of Shinar is significant because of its associations with Babylon (see Gen 10:10; Isa 11:11; Dan 1:2). It is in this city that the people gather as one and say to each other, "Come, let's make bricks and bake them thoroughly." The writer of Genesis states:

> They used brick instead of stone, and tar for mortar [again, the city is depicted as the place of technological achievement]. Then they said, "Come, *let us build ourselves a city*, with a tower that reaches to the heavens, so that we may make a name for ourselves; otherwise we will be scattered over the face of the whole earth."
>
> But the LORD came down to see *the city* and the tower the people were building.
>
> Genesis 11:3–5, emphasis mine

The spirit of the line of Cain reaches its climax in this effort to build the city of Babel. The new city and its tower are designed to help residents gain an identity apart from service to God. Here we see the essence of how cities can magnify our sinful drive for self-glorification and self-salvation. The efforts of the people working together for their own glory attract the notice of God, who reacts by confusing their language and scattering them "from there over all the earth," lest they succeed in their plans. The result of God's judgment was that they "stopped building the city" (v. 8).

The Patriarchs and the City

The rest of Genesis continues to highlight the dark side of the city—particularly the infamous Sodom and Gomorrah. Again, God "goes down" to judge Sodom (Gen 18:21), just as he did with Babel. Babel, later called Babylon in the Bible, comes to serve as the archetype for urban culture arrayed against God (see Isa 13:19). The Sodom narrative stands in the midst of a long period in which we see city dwellers opposed to God, while God's people remain rural nomads. God called Abram to leave Ur, one of the great cities of the day, and remain a shepherd all his life. Genesis shows us that Abram's nephew Lot made a grave mistake in choosing urban life. While he remained a righteous man within Sodom and was distressed by the sinful lifestyle there, the behavior of his wife and daughters showed that Lot's decision to live in a city without a believing community led to spiritual disaster for his family.[16]

Nevertheless, we later learn that Abraham's refusal to enter the cities of his time and place lay in his longing for God's city: "By faith Abraham ... lived in tents ... For he was looking forward to the city with foundations, whose architect and builder is God" (Heb 11:8–10). If the city as a social form is intrinsically bad for human beings or for our faith, it wouldn't make sense for it to be idealized as the source of Abraham's sustaining hope. Cities in the service of human self-aggrandizement may work to unravel and destroy the world God made and to contest his lordship over it. But as we will see, the city form, in service to God, actually fulfills the will of God for human life.

Israel and the City

With the establishment of Israel in the Promised Land, the biblical depiction of cities becomes more positive. When God settled the Israelites in Canaan, he commanded them to build cities of refuge: "Select ... your cities of refuge, to which a person who has killed someone accidentally may flee. They will be places of refuge from the avenger, so that anyone accused of murder may not die before they stand trial before the assembly" (Num 35:11–12). Why did God command the building of cities? Cities with walls and a gathered population could protect an accused person and conduct a trial in a way that villages and rural areas could not. Without cities, a crime or accident could lead to an endless cycle of violence and reprisals. The safety and density of cities enabled a system of jurisprudence to develop around the rule of law. There the elders could hear and settle cases in peace (Deut 19:11–12). God commands the establishment of cities in Israel to establish justice.

But the biggest change in the city's role within redemptive history comes with the establishment of Jerusalem. Unlike Babel, established to "make a name for ourselves" (Gen 11:4), Jerusalem becomes the city that is the dwelling place for God's Name (1 Kgs 14:21). This begins when Jerusalem is captured by David (2 Sam 5), the ark of the covenant is brought to the city (2 Sam 6), and finally the temple is built by Solomon. Jerusalem is appointed to be an urban culture that is a witness to the nations and a symbol of the future City of God (2 Sam 7:8–16). God directs that the temple be built on Zion, an elevated location within the city, so it rises above the city as its "skyscraper." God's city is different from human cities (like Babel) where skyscrapers are designed for their builders' own prosperity and prominence. By contrast, God's city is "the joy of the whole earth" (Ps 48:2). The city's cultural riches are produced, not for the glory of the producers, but for the joy of the entire earth and the honor of God. The urban society in God's plan is based on service, not on selfishness.

The Prophets and the City

From the time of David onward, the prophets speak of God's future world as an urban society. Bible scholar J. Alec Motyer writes, "The Isaianic literature could be accurately described as 'the book of the city.'"[17] He notes that in Isaiah, *Jerusalem*, *Zion*, *mount/mountain*, and *city* are interchangeable terms showing the city's centrality in the divine thought and plan.[18] At this point the spiritual battle lines of history become clear. The great spiritual conflict of history is not between city dwellers and country dwellers but is truly "a tale of two cities." It is a struggle between Babylon, representing the city of man, and Jerusalem, representing the city of God.[19] The earthly city is a metaphor for human life structured without God, created for self-salvation, self-service, and self-glorification. It portrays a scene of exploitation and injustice. But God's city is a society based on his glory and on sacrificial service to God and neighbor. This city offers a scene of peace and righteousness. As Saint Augustine put it, "The humble City is the society of holy men and good angels; the proud city is the society of wicked men and evil angels. The one City began with the love of God; the other had its beginnings in the love of self."[20]

John concludes his Apocalypse (Rev 22:19) by warning those who take words away (*aphelē*) from "this scroll of prophecy" that God will take away (*aphelei*) from them their "share in the tree of life and *in the Holy City*" (*kai ek tēs poleôs tēs hagias*, emphasis mine). Throughout Revelation, John draws a consistent contrast between "the great city," Babylon,[21] and the city of God, Jerusalem.[22] The former receives the eschatological judgment of God, while the latter receives (and mediates) eschatological blessing and salvation.[23]

The City of Exile

When we get to the book of Jonah, we come to a new phase in the unfolding biblical theology of the city. Throughout Israel's history, prophets are raised up and sent to preach to God's people, to call them to repentance and renewal. But Jonah is given a unique mission. For the first time, a prophet is sent to preach to a pagan, foreign city—Nineveh. Jonah's response is first (in Jonah 1–2) to run away from the city. In chapter 3, after his famous encounter with the great fish, Jonah does preach to Nineveh—and the people respond in repentance. God does not destroy the city as he had warned he would. This response displeases Jonah greatly, and in Jonah 4:10–11 (NASB), God scolds Jonah for his lack of compassion for the lost people of Nineveh. Listen to God's argument:

> Then the LORD said, "You had compassion on the plant for which you did not work and which you did not cause to grow, which came up overnight and perished overnight. Should I not have compassion on Nineveh, the great city in which there are more than 120,000

persons who do not know the difference between their right and left hand, as well as many animals?"

Here God makes a case for the importance of the city from the sheer number of the human beings in residence. He is saying, "How can you look at *so many* lost people and not find compassion in your heart?" This is a critical reason that the city is so important today. We might call it the *visceral* argument for the city. God "has compassion on all he has made" (Ps 145:9). But of all the things he has made, human beings have pride of place in his heart, because they were made in his image (Gen 9:6; James 3:9). Cities, quite literally, have more of the image of God per square inch than any other place on earth. How can we not be drawn to such masses of humanity if we care about the same things that God cares about?

Why did God send an Israelite prophet to a pagan city? Some have argued that this is intended to prepare the Jews for the next stage of their own history — the period of exile — in which they will be residing not in Jerusalem but literally in Babel — in Babylon. The importance of Jerusalem had been obvious; it was to be "the joy of the whole earth" (Ps 48:2), a model urban society demonstrating to the world what human life under God's lordship could be. But what happens when Israel goes to live in a wicked, pagan, bloodthirsty city in Jeremiah 28–29? How will the people of God relate to the great human cities of the earth now?

A major part of the Babylonian Empire's strategy was to eradicate the spiritual identity of its conquered peoples. A defeated nation's professional and elite classes were often taken to Babylon to live before being allowed to return home.[24] Judah had been deported, partially in the hope that the children and grandchildren of the Israelites would assimilate and lose their identity as a distinct people. The false prophet Hananiah, who could not imagine Israel's life in Babylon long-term, dishonestly prophesied that God would bring Israel back to Jerusalem within two years (Jer 28:3–4). Had the exiles followed Hananiah's advice, they would have remained disengaged in Babylon, waiting indefinitely for God's imminent deliverance.

Instead God, through the prophet Jeremiah, contradicts both the Babylonians' strategy and the false prophet's counsel. On the one hand,

God tells his people to "increase in number there; do not decrease" (Jer 29:6) to retain their distinct community identity and to grow, but he also tells them to settle down and engage in the life of the great city.[25] They are to build homes and plant gardens (v. 5). Most striking of all, God calls them to serve the city—to "seek the peace and prosperity of the city" and to "pray to the LORD for it" (v. 7). While living in Babylon, they are not simply to increase their tribe in a ghetto within the city; they are to use their resources to benefit the common good.

This is quite a balance! From Genesis 11 all the way through Revelation, Babylon is represented as the epitome of a civilization built on selfishness, pride, and violence—the ultimate city of man. The values of this city contrast absolutely with those of the city of God; yet here the citizens of the city of God are called to be the *very best* residents of this particular city of man. God commands the Jewish exiles not to attack, despise, or flee the city—but to seek its peace, to love the city as they grow in numbers.

God is still primarily concerned with his plan of salvation. He must establish his people; the gospel must be proclaimed; human beings must be reconciled to him. Yet he assures his people that serving the good of this pagan city is part of this very plan: "If it prospers, you too will prosper" (Jer 29:7). Loving and serving the city not only shows love and compassion; doing so also strengthens the hands of the people of God, who bear the message of the gospel to the world. Because the Jews in exile obeyed this command, they accrued the influence and leverage needed to eventually return to and restore their homeland. God ties, as it were, the fortunes of the people of God to the effectiveness of their urban ministry.

● ● ●

Sadly, there has never been a city on earth that is not saturated with human sin and corruption. Indeed, to paraphrase a Woody Allen joke, cities are just like everywhere else, only much more so. They are both better and worse, both easier and harder to live in, both more inspiring and oppressive, than other places.

As redemptive history unfolds, we begin to see how the tension of the city will be resolved. The turn in the relationship between the people of God and the pagan city becomes a key aspect of God's plan to bless the nations and redeem the world. In the New Testament, we find cities playing an important role in the rapid growth of the early church and in spreading the gospel message of God's salvation.

DISCUSSION QUESTIONS

1. How would you describe your own attitude toward cities? Indifferent? Hostile? Romanticized? Positive? In what way has this chapter challenged your attitude toward cities?

2. Cities are places of safety, diversity, and productivity. How does each of these characteristics uniquely define urban culture?

3. Keller writes, "Cities, quite literally, have more of the image of God per square inch than any other place on earth. How can we not be drawn to such masses of humanity if we care about the same things that God cares about?" What are some of the reasons that people avoid ministry in the city? What are some of the reasons that they are attracted to urban ministry?

4. How can you and the community of believers to which you belong work to "seek the peace and prosperity of the city"? What does this look like in your context?

Chapter 6

REDEMPTION AND THE CITY

A s we saw in the last chapter, God unexpectedly calls Israel to serve the pagan city of Babylon—to seek its prosperity—while living in exile there. And in a sense, the people of God have yet to return from that state of exile. In this chapter, we will see how this exilic model helps us understand the relationship of the church to the city in New Testament times—and even today—and how God plans to resolve the great tension of the city at the end of time.[1]

During the exile, Israel no longer existed in the form of a nation-state with a government and laws. Instead, it existed as a counter-cultural fellowship contained within other nation-states. In many ways, this is also the form of the New Testament church, as Peter and James suggest when they address believers as "the Dispersion" (Jas 1:1 ESV) and "exiles" (1 Pet 1:1 ESV). Twice Peter uses *parepidēmoi* as a word for "exiles"—a word we sometimes translate as "resident aliens." *Parepidēmoi* were citizens of one country and yet full-time residents of another. Their primary allegiance was to another country, and that country's culture was formative for their beliefs and practices. Yet they lived in their country of residence as full participants in its life. In other words, "resident aliens" lived neither as natives nor as tourists. Though they were not permanently rooted, neither were they merely travelers who were just passing through.

Christians are now considered citizens of "the Jerusalem that is above" (Gal 4:26; see Phil 3:20). Indeed, in a significant statement, Jesus tells his followers that they are a "town built on a hill" (Matt 5:14). Communities of Christ followers are God's "city" within every earthly city. They are the renewed people of God (see Isa 32:14; Dan 9:16). Their ultimate allegiance belongs to God and his kingdom, yet, in keeping with the phrase used by Peter and James, believers are not just "passing through" their earthly cities. This reflects the same balanced attitude that Jewish exiles were called to have toward Babylon. The Jewish exiles were not to hate the pagan city as they bided their time, waiting for the day of their departure. They were to be fully involved in its life, working in it and praying for it. At the same time, they were not to adopt its culture or lose their distinctive identity as God's holy people. God called the Jewish exiles to accept and embrace the tension of the city for the sake of God's glory—and this is exactly what today's Christians are called to do as well.

Resident aliens will always live with both praise and misunderstanding. Jesus taught that Christians' "good deeds" are to be visible to the pagans (Matt 5:16), but he also warns his followers to expect misunderstanding and persecution (v. 10). In a similar way, Peter calls Christians to live in the midst of pagan society in such a way that others will see their "good deeds and glorify God" (1 Pet 2:12), but he warns them to expect persecution nonetheless. Both Peter and Jesus indicate that these "good deeds" (which in the Greek meant not merely personal morality but also acts of service to others) will lead at least some pagans to glorify God.

Despite these similarities, the Christian church differs from the Jewish exiles in two significant ways. First, the Jews "increase in number" in Babylon almost exclusively by having children and growing families (Jer 29:6). The church must also multiply and increase in the pagan city as God's new humanity, but this happens especially through evangelism and discipling (Acts 6:1, 7; 9:31; 12:24). We also see a significant shift in God's call to mission between the Old and New Testaments. In the Old Testament, mission was *centripetal*; the flow was in toward the center. Israel was called to be an obedient people, becoming a society that displayed God's glory for the nations to see (Deut 4:6–8). The nations were called to look and to "come in" and worship God. But in the New Testament, mission becomes *centrifugal*—moving outward from the center. The people of God are sent out to the world to proclaim the gospel (Matt 28:16–20; Acts 1–2). The Babylonian exile and Jonah's mission are foreshadowings of this future change.

Second, despite their engagement with Babylonian society, the Jews still kept the Mosaic code, so that their dress, food, and other practices continued to set them culturally apart from the Babylonians (see, e.g., Dan 1:8). Their dietary laws alone virtually dictated that Jews eat separately from pagans. In the book of Acts, God has to send Peter a vivid and forceful vision to get him to even consider accepting an invitation to enter a Gentile soldier's home (10:28–29). In Christ, these ceremonial and cultural regulations and distinctions become obsolete (Mark 7; Acts 15:1–35). Jesus eats with tax collectors and sinners as a strategy for ministry. Adopting these New Testament teachings frees Christians to participate in a city's culture more fully than the Jews in Babylon could. However, this freedom also makes the danger of assimilation and compromise more acute for Christians. As future citizens of heaven, Christians must see and avoid the idolatries and injustices of their culture, even as they continue to enjoy its common-grace blessings.

So why should we apply the exhortations of Jeremiah 29 to the church today? In the Bible, we see the people of God living in three configurations. From Abraham's day onward, God's people existed as an *extended biological family*. From the days of Moses, they existed as a *nation-state*, with laws and a king and an army to enforce those laws by civil sanctions. During the exile, however, God's people existed as a *dispersed fellowship of congregations* (synagogues) living in many different nation-states. God's laws did not take a civil form during that period—the disobedient were expelled from the congregation, but they were not executed.

After the exile, the Jews went back to being a nation-state. Yet the New Testament does not envision the Christian church in this way. Instead, it shows that *the church continues to exist as a dispersion of people from every nation under heaven* (Acts 2), just as Israel did in the exile (see Jas 1:1; 1 Pet 1:1). Therefore, it seems reasonable to conclude that the church should continue to relate to the human cities of our time, not as the people of God did under Abraham, Moses, or David, but as they did during the time of the exile.

City Ministry in the Early Church

In the early church, God's redemptive mission no longer centered on a particular city such as Jerusalem or Babylon. All of the cities of the world become primary targets of God's mission. The *Dictionary of Biblical Imagery* in its article on "City" states the following:

> The world that we enter in the book of Acts is the most modern in all the Bible by virtue of its urban identity. Most of the action occurs in the famous cities of the Greco-Roman world, not in the local villages or the countryside. This prevailingly metropolitan world is, moreover, international and cosmopolitan. There is a sense in which the city is vindicated in the history of the early church — not in the sense that the city is mainly good or cordial to the gospel but in the sense that the city is where most people now live and where the influential power structures exist ... It is easy to see that *the mission strategy of the early church was to evangelize the city*. It is no exaggeration to say that in Acts the church is almost exclusively associated with the city.[2]

In Acts 17, Paul travels to Athens, the *intellectual* center of the Greco-Roman world. In Acts 18, he goes to Corinth, one of the *commercial* centers of the empire. In Acts 19, he arrives in Ephesus, perhaps the Roman world's *religious* center, the hub of many pagan cults and particularly of the imperial cult, with three temples for emperor worship. By the end of Acts, Paul has made it to Rome itself, the empire's capital of *military and political power*. John Stott concludes, "It seems to have been Paul's deliberate policy to move purposefully from one strategic city-centre to the next."[3]

Paul's ministry in Ephesus reveals several of the strengths of urban ministry. In Acts 19:1 we read, "While Apollos was at Corinth, Paul took the road through the interior and arrived at Ephesus." Stott remarks that virtually all the roads in that part of the world went through Ephesus.[4] Similarly, all major cities are the unavoidable crossroads for their regions and societies. Paul entered Ephesus and rented the "lecture hall of Tyrannus" (v. 9). Stott notes that the lecture hall would have been a school that stood vacant for two to three hours at midday when people took a break from work for a meal and rest.[5] There Paul did gospel *dia-legomenos*, arguing and persuading his hearers dialogically — not simply by preaching but by making his case that the Messiah was Jesus and engaging with people's questions and objections. "This went on for two years, so that all the Jews and Greeks who lived in the province of Asia heard the word of the Lord" (v. 10). Because Paul's ministry took place in the region's major city, virtually everyone in the Lycus River valley would have been exposed to the preaching of the gospel.

Stott observes that "all the inhabitants of Asia visited Ephesus from time to time, to buy or sell, visit a relative, frequent the baths, attend the games in the stadium, watch a drama in the theatre, or worship the goddess [Artemis]."[6] By reaching the city, Paul reached all segments of society, as evidenced in the letter to the Colossians. In this epistle, Paul follows up with disciples in cities along the Lycus Valley — Laodicea, Hierapolis, and Colossae (Col 4:13 – 16) — who were likely converted through his Ephesian ministry, even though he had never visited those places personally. This suggests that if the gospel is unfolded at the urban center, you can effectively reach the region and the surrounding society. Stott cites J. A. Alexander's insight that Acts shows the spread of the gospel "by the gradual establishment of radiating centres or sources of influence at certain salient points throughout a large part of the Empire."[7] Stott concludes:

> This process of urbanization ... constitutes a great challenge to the Christian church. On the one hand, there is an urgent need for Christian planners and architects, local government politicians, urban specialists, developers and community social workers, who will work for justice, peace, freedom and beauty in the city. On the other, Christians need to move into the cities, and experience the pains and pressures of living there, in order to win city-dwellers for Christ. Commuter Christianity (living in salubrious suburbia and commuting to an urban church) is no substitute for incarnational involvement.[8]

The early church was largely an *urban* movement that won the people of the Roman cities to Christ, while most of the rural countryside remained pagan. Because the Christian faith captured the cities, however, it eventually captured the ancient Greco-Roman world. As the city went, so went the culture.[9] Why? The urban elites were, of course, important, but the Christian church did not focus on them alone. Then, as now, the cities were filled with the poor, and urban Christians' commitment to the poor was visible and striking. Through the cities, Christians changed history and culture by winning the elites as well as by identifying deeply with the poor. Richard Fletcher, in *The Barbarian Conversion*, shows that this same thing occurred during the Christian mission to Europe from AD 500 to 1500.[10]

Consummation: Cultivating the City

Beginning with the Old Testament prophets, God's future redeemed world is depicted as a city. And in Revelation 21–22, when God's creational and redemptive intentions are fully realized, we see that the result is indeed a city, with walls and gates and streets. In some ways, this city is unlike our current cities, more of a "garden-city" that perfectly balances the glorious benefits of human density and diversity with the beauty and peace of nature. The city of God's old enemy, Babylon, is finally overthrown, and God's people thrive in peace and productivity (Rev 18).

What is most striking about this holy city is that it has not been built from scratch. In its midst flows a crystal river, and on each side of the river is "the tree of life" that bears fruit and leaves to heal the nations of all the effects of the divine covenant curse (Rev 22:1–3). This city is, in fact, the same garden we see in the Genesis account, which was also marked by a central river and the presence of the tree of life (Gen 2:8–10), but it has been expanded and remade into the garden-city of God. *It is the garden of Eden*, yet faithfully cultivated—the fulfillment of the purposes of the Eden of God.[11] Indeed, the very word used for "garden" in Genesis 2 denotes not a wilderness but a "park,"[12] a well-tended plot of land one would find in a city or near a royal palace.

Why is this important? God's directive that Adam and Eve "rule over" the earth (Gen 1:28) is often called "the cultural mandate." This is a call for them to "image God's work for the world by taking up our work in the world."[13] It is a call to develop a culture and build a civilization that honors God. Gardening (the original human vocation) is a paradigm for cultural development. A gardener neither leaves the ground as is, nor does he destroy it. Instead, he rearranges it to produce food and plants for human life. He *cultivates* it. (The words *culture* and *cultivate* come from the same root.) Every vocation is in some way a response to, and an extension of, the primal, Edenic act of cultivation. Artists, for example, take the raw material of the five senses and human experience to produce music and visual media; literature and painting; dance and architecture and theater. In a similar way, technologists and builders take the raw material of the physical world and creatively rearrange it to enhance human productivity and flourishing. Because we are called to create culture in this way, and because cities are the places of greatest cultural production, I believe that city building is a crucial part of fulfilling the mandate.

As we have already pointed out, the first evidence for this connection between the city, the culture, and the flourishing of human beings is found in Genesis 4, where Cain is "building a city" (v. 17). Immediately after the city is built, we see the first development of the arts, agriculture, and technology—the beginnings of the human cultural creativity that God had called for. Even though Cain's purpose in building the city was rebellious, its power was good. The tension of the city was present from its very start.

The cultural mandate, our failure to fulfill it in accord with God's design, its connection to city building, and the progressive importance of the city of man to the city of God—all these plotlines resolve at the end of the book of Revelation. Though the first Adam failed to faithfully heed God's call, the second Adam—Jesus Christ—*will* fulfill the mandate of the first Adam. He will save a people, subdue the earth, and bring in a civilization that honors the Father (1 Cor 15:22–25). Since the Bible reveals to us that a city is the final result of the work of the second Adam on our behalf, it seems fair to assume this was what God had intended when he gave the cultural mandate to the first Adam. In other words, God called Adam and Eve to expand the borders of the garden, and when God's will is finally done and Jesus fulfills the cultural mandate on our behalf, the garden of Eden becomes a garden *city*.

Many Christians assume that the final goal of Christ's redemption is to return us to a rural, Edenic world. Based on this assumption, the work of Christians is exclusively to evangelize and disciple. But Revelation shows us this is not the case. God's intention for human endeavor is that it raise up civilizations — cities — that glorify him and steward the endless wonders and riches that God put into the created world. This insight has led Harvie Conn to write that the cultural mandate "could just as easily be called an urban mandate."[14]

● ● ●

The city is an intrinsically positive social form with a checkered past and a beautiful future. As redemptive history progresses, we see that God's people begin as wanderers and nomads outside of cities, and as city rebels (Babel). Then God directs them to be city builders and rebuilders (Jerusalem) and city-loving exiles (Babylon). In New Testament times, the people of God become city missionaries (indeed, New Testament writings contain few glimpses of nonurban Christianity). Finally, when God's future arrives in the form of a city, his people can finally be fully at home. The fallen nature of the city — the warping of its potential due to the power of sin — is finally overcome and resolved; the cultural mandate is complete; and the capacities of city life are freed in the end to serve God. All of God's people serve him in his Holy City.

DISCUSSION QUESTIONS

1. Keller writes, "The church should continue to relate to the human cities of our time, not as the people of God did under Abraham, Moses, or David, but as they did during the time of the exile." In what ways is the situation of the Christian church different from that of the exiles in Babylon? In what ways is it similar? How does this affect the mission of the church today?

2. From Acts 17 through the end of the book of Acts, Paul has strategically traveled to the intellectual (Athens), commercial (Corinth), religious (Ephesus), and political (Rome) centers of the Roman world. What are the centers of power and influence in your own local context? How is your church seeking to strategically reach these different centers of cultural influence?

3. Keller writes, "Then, as now, the cities were filled with the poor, and urban Christians' commitment to the poor was visible and striking." Do you believe this is still true of the Christian church? If so, give an example. If not, how can this legacy be recaptured?

4. Keller writes, "Gardening (the original human vocation) is a paradigm for cultural development. A gardener neither leaves the ground as is, nor does he destroy it. Instead, he rearranges it to produce food and plants for human life. He *cultivates* it. (The words *culture* and *cultivate* come from the same root.) Every vocation is in some way a response to, and an extension of, the primal, Edenic act of cultivation." Discuss how different vocations are a response to our call to cultivate culture. How does the creation mandate transform our understanding of work and vocation?

Chapter 7

THE CALL TO THE CITY

Paul and other Christian missionaries went to great cities because when Christianity was planted there, it spread regionally (cities were the centers of transportation routes); it also spread globally (cities were multiethnic, international centers, and converts took the gospel back to their homeland); and finally it more readily affected the culture (the centers of learning, law, and government were in the cities). As we will see in this chapter, the importance of cities for Christian mission today is, if anything, even greater.

Today, cities are more important than ever before. In 1950, New York and London were the only world cities with metro-area populations of over ten million people. Today, however, there are more than twenty such cities—twelve of which achieved that ranking in the last two decades—with many more to come.[1] All of these new megacities are developing in what was once called the Third World. But why?

In the eighteenth century, a combination of population growth and technology brought rural Europe to its "carrying capacity," creating a surplus population. Virtually all of the land was owned and developed, and so every family had some members who left the family farm, the countryside, and the small towns to make a living elsewhere. As a result, the great cities of Europe (and, in the nineteenth century, America) swelled in size. Many experts now believe that this type of shift has begun to occur in Africa, in Asia, and to a lesser extent in Latin America, where cities are exploding with people from the rural areas. If the urban-to-rural ratio of these populations stabilizes near 75 percent to 25 percent, as it did in Europe and North America, the next three decades will see over half a billion people move into the cities of Africa and Asia alone—in other words, one new Rio de Janeiro (ten million people) *every two months*.[2] Currently, Western cities such as New York City grow at approximately 125,000 people per year, but cities such as Dhaka and Lagos are growing at a rate of more than half a million per year. By most estimates, we have reached the point where over 50 percent of the world population now lives in cities, compared to around 5 percent two centuries ago.[3]

Globalization and Renaissance

The significance of cities today lies not only in their growing size but also in their growing influence, and this influence is due to the rise of globalization. The technological revolution has led to an unprecedented mobility of people, ideas, and capital. Because of the Internet and other forms of electronic communication, people around the world are more connected than ever before, and Western urban values in particular are spreading everywhere.

What is the effect of this "flattening" of the world due to globalization?[4] First, globalization *connects cities to the world*. Some people predicted that the rise of technology would end up weakening cities, that it would make agglomeration (a cluster of usually disparate elements) obsolete.[5] Social networking and communication online, it was argued, would make it unnecessary to pay the high costs of living in the city. But as Edwin Heathcote has written, "Digital networking has not, as was forecast, led to a decline in the city. Rather, it has led to an urbanization of the rest of the planet."[6] People, especially young people, want to live in cities. The rise of new forms of technology and mobility has not weakened this desire. Instead, it has dramatically expanded the reach and influence of urban culture. This urbanizing influence now extends far beyond the city limits, affecting even the most rural areas of remote countries. Children in Mexico and Romania are becoming more like young adults in Los Angeles and New York City than the adults in their own locales.

Second, globalization *connects cities to cities*. Not only does globalization connect the rest of the world to urban ideas and culture; it also connects cities to one another, enhancing their power and influence.[7] World cities are more connected to others around the world than they are to their own nations. The elites of New York, London, and Tokyo not only work for the same multinational companies, but they also graduate from common educational institutions, take vacations and buy homes in the same places, and share common social and cultural values. They are better able to identify with the urban elites of other nations than with the nonurban citizens of their own countries.

The strong connections among major cities exist not only through the elites, however. Huge, diverse immigrant populations in global cities tie each urban area tightly to scores of other countries. They travel frequently and communicate daily with their homelands. This means, for example, that thousands of residents of New York City are in much closer communication with people in Athens, Manila, Port-au-Prince, Bogota, Hong Kong, and Lagos than they are with the residents of New Jersey and Connecticut. Each global city is a portal to others.

These networked world cities are quickly becoming more economically and culturally powerful than their own national governments. Governments are increasingly losing control of the flow of capital and information and have far less influence than the multinational corporations and international financial, social, and technological networks based in global cities. According to the American journalist Neal Peirce, "Great metropolitan regions—not cities, not states, not even the nation states—are starting to emerge as the world's most influential players."[8]

Cities not only grow and mature, but they can also be reborn. Despite the pessimism about Western cities during the late twentieth century, many have regenerated during the 1990s and the first decade of the twenty-first century. During the twenty years from 1970 to 1990, many American cities went into sharp decline. Immigration of blacks from the South to northern cities resulted in white flight, and many poor people were trapped in inner-city ghettos. In the late 1970s and early 1980s protracted recessions diminished tax revenues and drove some cities near or into actual bankruptcy. Meanwhile, urban planning in the mid-twentieth century privileged the suburbs. Whole urban neighborhoods were bulldozed to create expressways that gave suburban residents easy access to center-city jobs. Planners also favored big stores and stadiums with lots of parking, as well as massive housing projects for the poor. All of this led to downtown urban centers that were like ghost towns after dark. The middle class flight to the suburbs took many jobs, leaving the poor poorer and most neighborhoods riddled with crime. Cities hollowed out into "doughnuts," with poor nonwhite centers and affluent white suburbs.

However, since 1990, American cities have experienced an amazing renaissance.[9] During this time, many cities' population declines have begun to reverse. People began to move back into cities, and center cities began to regenerate at their cores. Why? One of the primary reasons is that during this time the U.S. economy experienced a sustained period of growth, which created a great deal of new wealth and new jobs in knowledge sectors. Second, crime went down in cities for the reasons liberals cite (more jobs) and for the reasons conservatives cite (tougher enforcement). Third, a cultural mood developed (which some call postmodern) embracing eclecticism, the mixture of the old and new, asymmetry, messiness and unmanageability, cultural diversity, and the artistic and organic. All of these are features of city life rather than of suburban culture. Younger adults began to prefer city life and started moving to urban areas in greater numbers. Fourth, changes in immigration law opened the door to an influx of immigrants from non-European nations. Between 1965 and 1970, U.S. immigration doubled. Then, from 1970 to 1990 it doubled again. Most of this immigration wave emptied into America's cities, renewing and diversifying many neighborhoods. It also completely changed the older, gridlocked, binary black-white dynamic of urban politics into a far more complex, multi-polar situation, with many ethnicities and nationalities.

As a result, many American cities began to surge. Professionals streamed into center-city neighborhoods, while new ethnic communities developed within older working-class and poor neighborhoods. Sometimes the gentrification process was more destructive and disruptive to the social fabric; in other cases it had a more wholesome effect. The major actors in this renewed upsurge included empty-nester boomers returning to cities, young professionals seeking cities to live and work in, and a wave of immigrants in inner-city neighborhoods and inner suburbs that eventually produced second-generation college graduates who moved into the center city to live and work. These groups joined the gays and artists who have always chosen to live in urban communities.[10]

Edward Glaeser points out that not all cities have succeeded in the past generation—and he points to Detroit, Michigan, and Leipzig, Germany, as examples. But most cities have found the power to reinvent themselves, argues Glaeser, because the essence of what makes a city a city is the bringing of people together to innovate. At one level, this means bringing together the most highly trained and talented people, the "elites." Yet at another level, it means bringing together the most energetic, ambitious, and risk-taking people from among the poor and middle classes of the world. Cities are cauldrons of reengineering and reinvention, and so it should not surprise us to find that they are always reinventing themselves.

Perhaps the most interesting example of contemporary urban reinvention is what has been called the "consumer city." The post–World War II years brought about the rise of suburbanization and the creation of the commuter city. People chose suburban life for its amenities and comforts and commuted into the city only for work and the occasional show. But Vancouver and Los Angeles are two urban areas that reversed the trend. They became *consumer* cities marked by a new phenomenon—the reverse commuter. Increasingly, these and other cities offer residents a quality of life they could not find elsewhere in the region—a dizzying variety of artistic, educational, cultural, and entertainment events and venues, but also (now) safe streets, good schools, and excellent public transportation. Many people now move to London, New York, and Paris and are willing to pay a premium to live in the center of the city, even if their jobs take them out of the core of the city each day.[11]

The Future of Cities

Few people now believe we will see a significant decline in the population growth and importance of global cities, at least in the foreseeable future. The growth trends and culture shifts are on too strong a trajectory. However, the Great Recession and hard economic times in the United States and Europe mean that city governments in these countries are being forced to make deep, painful cuts to their budgets, while the private sector faces the prospect of years of high unemployment. The gaps in social service offerings are likely to widen in many cities. These changes will certainly have an impact on the quality of life in cities.[12]

So will Western cities return to the economic and population decline they experienced in the 1970s and 1980s? Several trends are likely to help many cities in the West continue flourishing, at least for the foreseeable future. First, the world will continue to globalize—and globalization is a boon to cities that connect to it. More cities will imitate the biggest and most established cities in the West—New York, Los Angeles, and London—whose strong international connections and influences will help to keep real estate values up and provide a constant source of jobs (regardless of how national economies are faring). As a result, most globalizing cities should be able to remain economically stable.

Second, current urban planning in Western cities has returned to the classic urban form—compact, public transit–oriented, and walkable, mixed-use development (with residences, businesses, retail outlets, educational and cultural institutions, and entertainment venues situated together). The emphasis will be on developing neighborhood schools, "complete" streets with sidewalks for pedestrians, and lanes for bicyclists. This renewed emphasis on older forms is sometimes called "New Urbanism" or "Smart Growth," and there are many factors driving this trend. One relates to environmental concerns. Suburban and rural dwellers consume far more energy—electricity, fossil fuels, and other forms—than urban residents.[13] The increasingly urgent search for energy sustainability will continue to press societies to urbanize. Cities, therefore, will remain a very attractive alternative to the suburbs as a social arrangement.

Third, immigration laws have not significantly changed (as of this writing), and so it is likely that the United States will continue to receive immigrants from around the world. Though some trends have seen immigrants moving straight into the suburbs, the structure of city life continues to provide most new immigrants with the essential support resources they need to successfully transition into a new society. Cities today will compete for immigrants, knowing that the urban areas that receive the most immigration will be best positioned for future success.

Fourth, one of the greatest fears about cities—that high, life-threatening crime is inevitable in very large urban areas—is fast eroding. Led by New York City, many cities in North America have seen startling drops in crime over the past two decades; and this is one of the main drivers of economic and population growth in cities. The decline in crime is often attributed entirely to better police practices, as Mayor Michael Bloomberg of New York recently claimed.[14] But criminologists have shown that policing can only account for part of the decline, and that crime only falls off drastically when a variety of factors converge, many of which are impossible to measure directly.[15] These may include the strengthening of "civil society"—in the flourishing of voluntary associations such as stronger parent-teacher alliances, growth in religious institutions, growth in various nonprofit agencies, and greater public-private cooperatives.[16]

Fifth, as far as I can tell, the postmodern mood that leads many young adults to prefer city life to suburban life will continue. This trend is difficult to quantify or fully explain, but the appeal of city life for young people remains quite strong, and the presence of youthful energy and creativity will continue to sustain the growth and strength of cities. According to the *Wall Street Journal* and *The Atlantic*, approximately 32 percent of Americans in the Millennial generation live in cities—and 88 percent of them want to.[17]

Some of the most troubled cities, such as Detroit, will need to make drastic changes, shrinking their urban footprint and redesigning into smaller municipalities. But this is unlikely to become the norm in the United States. I believe globalization and the current cultural mood will continue to make cities highly desirable destinations for ambitious and innovative people, and this will be a decisive factor in continuing the growth and dominance of urban culture.

Now, more than ever, cities set the course of society and life as a whole, even in areas of the world, such as Europe and North America, where cities are not growing as rapidly.[18] All current signs lead us to believe that the world order of the twenty-first century will be global, multicultural, and urban.

The Challenge of Ministry in Cities

The massive growth and influence of cities in our time confront Christian mission with an enormous challenge. The first problem is one of sheer scale and economics. It is critical that we have Christians and churches wherever there are people, but the people of the world are now moving into the great cities of the world many times faster than the church is. Christian communication and ministry must always be translated into every new language and context, but the Christian church is not responding fast enough to keep up with the rapid population growth in cities.

There are five million new people moving into the cities of the developing world every month—roughly the size of the metropolitan areas of Philadelphia or San Francisco. Think of that—how many churches ought there to be in a city the size of Philadelphia? Even if there were one church for every five thousand people—which is five times fewer than the United States average[19]—this means we should be planting a thousand urban churches in the world every month.

But the challenge is not just numerical; it is also conceptual and methodological. Our very models for ministry must become increasingly urbanized. U.S. missions agencies are finding that more and more they must send their workers to live and minister in the growing cities. But seldom are these Americans experienced at life or ministry in the city. A couple of years ago, I met with American missionaries who had been sent to one of the fast-growing megacities of China. They told me their mission agency had assumed that the training they needed had to do with learning the language and understanding Chinese culture.

But after a while they realized they knew nothing about living in cities. Each member of their team had grown up in small towns in southern and midwestern areas of the United States. They struggled more with urban life than with life in China per se. And they also came to see that the people they were trying to reach were more like people living in Los Angeles and Manhattan than like those in the Chinese countryside. The leader of the team told me, "Only the language training we received was helpful. We were given no training in how to live in cities and how to reach urban people, and as a result we've been ineffective."

Urbanization is not only transforming how we in the West do mission overseas; it is also transforming the mission landscape in the West itself. Waves of immigration from the Southern and Eastern Hemispheres are coming to the cities of North America and Europe. Many of these immigrants come from parts of the world where belief in orthodox, supernatural Christianity is on the rise. As a result, thousands of new churches are being planted by non-Westerners in the formerly secular cities of London, Paris, and New York.[20] In fact, most of the largest, well-attended churches in London and Paris are led by Africans, and in New York City we have seen hundreds of new churches started by Christians from Asia, Latin America, the Caribbean, and Africa. At first, these new Christian churches remain somewhat isolated from the broader society, evangelizing and growing within ethnic enclaves. But as the children of these Christians become educated in national universities and move into the center city, they will begin to wield greater power and influence in areas of finance, media, and culture. Anglo elites have begun inviting many of these young nonwhites into the upper echelons of business and government, not realizing that a large percentage of them are Christians.[21]

Globalization and urbanization are removing the very distinction between "home" and "foreign" missions (to use, for a moment, the old terminology).[22] Consider the example of a church I know in the borough of Queens in New York City. This church has planted three daughter churches—one in New York's neighboring College Point, one in New York's neighboring Bronx, and one in the "neighboring" Philippines. They had reached so many Filipino immigrants in their own neighborhood that these new Christians wanted to plant a daughter church among their friends and relatives in their country of origin. So they sent a large group of people out from New York City to plant a new church. This is not an isolated case. Every major city is now a portal for reaching the nations of the world. In other words, one of the very best ways to reach the far parts of the world is to reach your own city![23]

Now consider another example. We planted Redeemer Presbyterian Church in the middle of New York City—in central Manhattan. Within a few years, we had planted daughter churches in Westchester County, New York, and New Jersey (the two principal "bedroom communities" of the city). If we had originally located in any particular suburb, however, we would never have been able in so short a time to plant churches in Manhattan or in the other suburbs. Why not? You can't reach the city from the suburbs, but you can reach the suburbs from the city. Cities are like a giant heart—drawing people in and then sending them out. Students come to cities to attend school, and then they graduate and move out. Singles meet in the city, get married, and move out to the suburbs when children are born. Immigrants come to the city and live in ethnic enclaves, but as they amass assets and become more established in their new country, they move outward to gain additional space for their growing families. In each case, the movement is from the center outward. As a result, a church that thrives in the city will create a community whose members will spread naturally throughout the adjoining region and into other great cities. In other words, one of the best ways to reach a region and country is to reach your own city!

The Opportunity of Ministry in Cities

The growth in size and influence of cities today presents the greatest possible challenge for the church. Never before has it been so important to learn how to do effective ministry in cities, and yet, by and large, evangelical Christianity in the United States is still nonurban.

Along with these challenges comes a range of unique opportunities. I see four important groups of people who must be reached to fulfill the mission of the church, and each of them can best be reached in the cities.

1. The younger generation. The prospects for advancement, the climate of constant innovation and change, the coming together of diverse influences and people—all of these appeal to young adults. In the United States and Europe, the young disproportionately want to live in cities, and for the highly ambitious, the numbers are even higher. In a *New York Times* op-ed column, "I Dream of Denver," David Brooks looks at Pew Research Center data that shows the sharp difference between younger Americans and older Americans as to their preference for cities:

> Cities remain attractive to the young. Forty-five percent of Americans between the ages of eighteen and thirty-four would like to live in New York City. But cities are profoundly unattractive to people with families and to the elderly. Only 14 percent of Americans thirty-five and older are interested in living in New York City. Only 8 percent of people over sixty-five are drawn to Los Angeles.[24]

This means, of course, that if the church in the West remains, for the most part, in the suburbs of Middle America and neglects the great cities, it risks losing an entire generation of American society's leaders.

One of the reasons cities are filled with young adults is that they are also usually filled with students. In university towns it is obvious to the casual observer that students are an important part of the demographic. In large cities, however, there are often enormous numbers of undergraduate and graduate students, but the size and diversity of the urban population make college students less visible. Yet students constitute an extremely important mission field, and urban students have far more local job opportunities available to them after graduation than do those who go to school in "college towns." As a result, college students in cities who are won to the faith are a significant source of future leaders for urban churches.

2. The "cultural elites." The second group is made up of those who have a disproportionate influence on how human life is lived in a society because they exert power in business, publishing, the media, the academy, and the arts. These people live or spend much of their time in city centers. Since cities now influence the culture and values of the world more than ever, the single most effective way for Christians to influence the culture of a nation is to have large numbers of them stay in cities and simply "be the church" there. Also, for all the reasons noted above, ministry that is effective in a world city travels well. Ministry in rural areas of a country may have little transferability to rural areas in other countries. But ministry forms that are effective in one center city are likely to have wide appeal to other center cities, especially with the younger generation.

Some Christians may complain, "We are losing the culture wars." This comment comes from the fact that relatively small groups living disproportionately in cities exert far more cultural influence than evangelical Christians, who live disproportionately outside of cities. Every time I exit the 42nd Street subway station in Manhattan, I pass Viacom, the parent company of MTV. Few institutions have had a greater cultural impact on an entire generation than MTV. I once read that years of Communist rule had not been able to erode the distinct ethnic identity of the Hungarian minority in Romania. Now, however, a global youth culture is turning Hungarian youth away from their cultural roots. Global consumer youth culture is pumped from Manhattan and Hollywood into the digital devices of kids all around the world. Fifteen-year-olds in rural Mexico are now more "urban" in their sensibilities than their parents are. If churches are to have any influence on the people who create institutions like MTV, they will have to live and minister in the same places where these people live—in the city.

3. Accessible "unreached" people groups. Many people speak about the importance of engaging in mission to the hard-to-reach religious and cultural groups, people who live in remote places or in nations that forbid Christian mission work. But the currents of history are now sweeping many of these formerly unreachable people into cities as rural economies fail to sustain old ways of life.

Millions of these newcomers in the burgeoning cities of the world are more open to the Christian faith than they were in their original context. Most have been uprooted from their familiar, traditional setting and have left behind the thicker kinship and tribal networks they once relied on, and most cities in the developing world often have, in the words of Philip Jenkins, "next to nothing in working government services."[25] These newcomers need help and support to face the moral, economic, emotional, and spiritual pressures of city life, and this is an opportunity for the church to serve them with supportive community, a new spiritual family, and a liberating gospel message. Immigrants to urban areas have many reasons to begin attending churches, reasons that they did not have in their former, rural settings. "Rich pickings await any groups who can meet these needs of these new urbanites, anyone who can at once feed the body and nourish the soul."[26]

But there is yet another way in which cities make formerly hard-to-reach peoples accessible. As I noted earlier, the urban mentality is spreading around the world as technology connects young generations to urbanized, global hyperculture. Many young people, even those living in remote places, are becoming globalized semi-Westerners, while their parents remain rooted in traditional ways of thinking. And so ministry and gospel communications that connect well with urban residents are also increasingly relevant and effective with young nonurban dwellers.

4. The poor. A fourth group of people who can and must be reached in cities is the poor. Some have estimated that one-third of the people representing the new growth in cities in the developing world will live in shantytowns. A great majority of the world's poor live in cities, and there is an important connection between reaching the urban elites and serving the poor of your city. First, an urban church's work among the poor will be a significant mark of its validity. It is one of the "good deeds" that Scripture says will lead pagans to glorify God (Matt 5:16; 1 Pet 2:12). Similarly, once cultural elites are won to Christ, discipling them includes reorienting them to spend their wealth and power on the needs of the poor and the city instead of on themselves. In other words, an urban church does not choose between ministry to the poor and ministry to the professional class. We need the economic and cultural resources of the elites to help the poor, and our commitment to the poor is a testimony to the cultural elites, supporting the validity of our message.

● ● ●

We can be confident that the cities of the world will continue to grow in significance and power. Because of this, they remain just as strategic—if not more so—than they were in the days of Paul and the early church when Christian mission was predominantly urban. I would argue that there is nothing more critical for the evangelical church today than to emphasize and support urban ministry.

The need is great, as is the cost—ministry in city centers is considerably more expensive on a per capita basis than it is away from the urban core. But the church can no longer ignore the profound and irreversible changes occurring in the world today. If Christians want to reach the unreached, we must go to the cities. To reach the rising generations, we must go to the cities. To have any impact for Christ on the creation of culture, we must go to the cities. To serve the poor, we must go to the cities.

Many people who are not naturally comfortable in the city will have to follow the example of Abraham. Abraham was called to leave his familiar culture and become a pilgrim, seeking the city of God (Gen 12:1–4; Heb 11:8–10). And while Christians should not deliberately seek difficulty for its own sake, can we not follow the example of the incarnate Christ, who did not live in places where he was comfortable but went where he was useful (Matt 8:20; John 4:34; Rom 15:3)? Can we not face difficulty for *his* sake (cf. Heb 11:26), embracing both the difficulties and the riches of city living?

DISCUSSION QUESTIONS

1. Where have you witnessed some of the things discussed in this chapter (globalization, gentrification, city renaissance, reverse commuting, postmodernism, etc.) in the life of your nearest city? How do they affect life in that city? How do they affect ministry in that city?

2. If our future will be largely an urban culture, what changes should the church be making today to prepare and adapt?

3. One significant trend discussed in this chapter is the influx of Christian immigrant populations and their increasing access to elite levels of business and society. How do you believe their contributions will shape the future of your ministry?

4. Which of the following city-prone groups do you feel most passionate to reach: the younger generation, the "cultural elites," accessible "unreached" people groups, or the poor? Is that group present in your setting right now? How is urbanization affecting them? Take a moment to reflect on what it would be like to minister meaningfully to the group you have identified.

Chapter 8

THE GOSPEL
FOR THE CITY

I have made as strenuous a case as I can that the city is one of the highest priorities for Christian life and mission in the twenty-first century. Now I want to press even further. These chapters on City Vision may have given you the idea that I think all Christians should move into cities and serve there. To be clear, this is *not* what I am saying. I believe there must be Christians and churches everywhere there are people. In one sense, there are no "little" places or people.[1] God loves to use unimportant people (1 Cor 1:26–31) and unlikely places (John 1:46) to do his work. Jesus wasn't from Rome or even Jerusalem but was born in Bethlehem and raised in Nazareth—perhaps to make this very point. We have been told that now something like 50 percent of the world's population live in cities—but this means that half the population does *not* live in urban areas, and therefore we must not discourage or devalue gospel ministry in the hundreds of thousands of towns and villages on earth. And ministry in small towns may not change a country, but it surely can have a major impact in its region.[2]

And yet a thought experiment may be illuminating here. Imagine you are in charge of establishing new churches in two different towns—one has a hundred residents, while the other has ten thousand residents. Imagine also that you have only four church planters. Where would you send them? Regardless of philosophy, I doubt anyone would send two church planters to each town on the premise that all places are equally important in ministry. It simply would not be good stewardship of God's human resources to send two pastors to a town with only a hundred residents. It is good stewardship, though, to insist that we should increase our attention and emphasis on urban ministry in a day when nonurban areas typically have more churches than cities and when cities are increasingly exerting more influence on how human life is lived in the world.

So I am not saying that all Christians should pack up and go to live and minister in urban areas. What I *am* saying is that the cities of the world are grievously underserved by the church because, in general, the people of the world are moving into cities faster than churches are. And I am seeking to use all the biblical, sociological, missiological, ecclesial, and rhetorical resources at my disposal to help the church (particularly in the United States) reorient itself to address this deficit.

But the call to the city doesn't end there. Everywhere in the world is more urban than it was ten or twenty years ago. Wherever you live, work, and serve, the city is coming to you. In a sense, every church can and must become a church for its particular city—whether that city is a great metropolis, a university town, or a village. As a result, I believe you can benefit by allowing yourself and your ministry to be intentionally shaped by the realities and patterns of urban life and culture. In order to accomplish this, we must look first at how the dynamics of the city affect our lives and then consider how churches with City Vision will minister in response to these dynamics.

How the City Works On Us

By many people's reckoning, the "death of distance" should have led to a decline in cities, but it has not. If you can learn things over the Internet, the thinking went, why pay big-city prices for housing? But real learning, communication, and community are far more complex than we may care to acknowledge. A great deal of research has shown that face-to-face contact and learning can never be fully replaced by any other kind.

It is no surprise, then, that research shows us that productivity is significantly higher for companies that locate near the geographic center of "inventive activity" in their industry. Why? Proximity to others working in your field enables the infinite number of interactions, many of them informal, that turns neophytes into experts more quickly and helps experts stimulate each other to new insights. Edward Glaeser observes, "Much of the value of a dense work environment comes from unplanned meetings and observing the random doings of the people around you. Video conferencing will never give a promising young worker the ability to learn by observing the day-to-day operations of a successful mentor."[3] Other studies reveal that a high percentage of patent applications cited older patents in the same metropolitan region, so "even in our age of information technology, ideas are often geographically localized."[4]

Urban theorists call this "agglomeration." Agglomeration refers to the economic and social benefits of physically locating near one another.[5] It is not surprising, then, that more movies are produced in Los Angeles and Toronto than in Atlanta, because those cities have far larger pools of skilled laborers—writers, directors, actors, technicians—who can make movies happen. It is not surprising that new innovations in financial services come out of Manhattan or new technologies out of Silicon Valley. Why? Agglomeration. The physical clustering of thousands of people who work in the same field naturally generates new ideas and enterprises. But the benefits of agglomeration are not limited to locating near people who, *like* you, work in the same field. There are benefits to be reaped of living near large groups of people who are *unlike* you but who have skills that supplement yours.

A good case study is the world of the arts. "Artistic movements are often highly localized," even more so than in other fields.[6] Urban scholar Elizabeth Currid interviewed New York City cultural producers (fashion designers, musicians, and fine artists) and gatekeepers (gallery owners, curators, and editors), as well as owners of clubs and venues frequented by these groups, people in the media and sometimes the academy, the directors of foundations that supported the arts, and prosperous businessmen and women who often acted as patrons.[7] Art "happened" when complex interactions occurred among people in these diverse sectors of the arts ecosystem—not typically through business meetings in workplaces but through interactions at social gatherings and spontaneous meetings in informal situations. Currid found that the cultural economy depends on having "artistic and cultural producers densely agglomerated," part of a "clustered production system."[8] When these various classes of persons live in geographical proximity, thousands of enterprise-producing, culture-making, face-to-face interactions take place that could not take place otherwise.[9] As Ryan Avent puts it, "Cities are a lot like a good group of friends: what you're doing isn't nearly as important as the fact that you're doing it together."[10]

How do the dynamics of agglomeration bear on the real life of the average city Christian? First, *the city uniquely links you with many people* **like** *you*. The city's challenges and opportunities attract the most talented, ambitious, and restless. So whoever you are, in the city you will encounter people who are far more talented and advanced than you are. Because you are placed among so many like-but-extremely-skilled people in your field, you will be consistently challenged to reach down and do your very best. You feel driven and pressed by the intensity of the place to realize every ounce of your potential. Cities draw and gather together human resources, tapping their potential for cultural development as no other human-life structure can. But sin takes this strength feature of the city—its culture-forming intensity—and turns it into a place tainted by deadly hubris, envy, and burnout. This is what sin does. It is a parasitic perversion of the good. The gospel is needed to resist the dark side of this gift.

Second, *the city uniquely links you with many people* **unlike** *you*. The city attracts society's subcultures and minorities, who can band together for mutual support. It is inherently merciful to those with less power, creating safe enclaves for singles, the poor, immigrants, and racial minorities. Because you are placed among such inescapable diversity, you will be consistently challenged in your views and beliefs. You will be confronted with creative, new approaches to thought and practice and must either abandon your traditional ways and beliefs or become far more knowledgeable about and committed to them than you were before. Again, sin takes a strength feature of the city—its culture-forming diversity—and turns it into a place that undermines our prior commitments and worldviews. And again, the gospel is needed to resist the dark side of this gift.

How should Christians respond to these ways in which the city challenges us? We must respond with the gospel. And how, exactly, does the gospel help us face these challenges with joy rather than fear? Obviously, it is true that we must bring the gospel to the city and hear the gospel while in the city. But we must also recognize how much *the city itself brings the gospel to us.* The city will challenge us to discover the power of the gospel in new ways. We will find people who seem spiritually and morally hopeless to us. We will think, "*Those* people will never believe in Christ." But a comment such as this is revealing in itself. If salvation is truly by grace, not by virtue and merit, why should we think that *anyone* is less likely than ourselves to be a Christian? Why would anyone's conversion be any greater miracle than our own? The city may force us to discover that we don't really believe in sheer grace, that we really believe God mainly saves nice people—people like us.

In cities we will also meet a lot of people who hold to other religions or to no religion who are wiser, kinder, and more thoughtful than we are, because even after growth in grace, many Christians are weaker people than many non-Christians. When this surprises you, reflect on it. If the gospel of grace is true, why would we think that Christians are a better kind of person than non-Christians? These living examples of common grace may begin to show us that even though we intellectually understand the doctrine of justification by faith alone, functionally we continue to assume that salvation is by moral goodness and works.

Early in Redeemer's ministry, we discovered it was misguided for Christians to feel pity for the city, and it was harmful to think of ourselves as its "savior." We had to humbly learn from and respect our city and its people. Our relationship with them had to be a consciously reciprocal one. We had to be willing to see God's common grace in their lives. We had to learn that we needed them to fill out our own understanding of God and his grace, just as they needed us.

I believe many Christians in the West avoid the city because it is filled with "the other." Because cities are filled with people who are completely unlike us, many Christians find this disorienting. Deep down, we know we don't *like* these people or don't feel safe around them. But see how easily we forget the gospel! After all, in the gospel we learn of a God who came and lived among us, became one of us, and loved us to the death, even though we were wholly other from him. The city humbles us, showing us how little we are actually shaped by the story and pattern of the gospel.

The gospel alone can give us the humility ("I have much to learn from the city"), the confidence ("I have much to give to the city"), and the courage ("I have nothing to fear from the city") to do effective ministry that honors God and blesses others. And in time we will see that, for our own continuing spiritual growth and well-being, we need the city perhaps more than the city needs us.

What Should Christians Do about Cities?

If this is how the city can change us for the better, what can we do to return the favor?

1. Christians should develop appreciative attitudes toward the city. In obedience to God, Jonah went to the city of Nineveh, but he didn't love it. In the same way, Christians may come to the city out of a sense of duty to God while being filled with great disdain for the density and diversity of the city. But for ministry in cities to be effective, it is critical that Christians appreciate cities. They should love city life and find it energizing.[11] Why is this so important?

First, because so many who live in and have influence in the city do actually *enjoy* living there. If you try to draw them into your church, they will quickly pick up on your negative attitude, which can erect a barrier in their willingness to listen to the gospel. Second, if a church consists primarily of people who dislike urban living, those people won't be staying very long. Your church will be plagued with huge turnover (as if turnover and transience aren't enough of a problem already in the city!).

Preaching and teaching that produce a city-positive church must constantly address the common objections to city living, which include beliefs that city life is "less healthy," too expensive, and an inferior place to raise families. Two additional objections are especially prevalent. One objection I commonly hear is this: "The country is wholesome; the city is corrupting." Christians should be able to recognize the bad theology (as well as bad history) behind this idea. Liberal humanism of the nineteenth and early twentieth centuries viewed human nature as intrinsically good and virtuous, so they concluded that human problems came from wrong socialization. In other words, we become violent and antisocial because of our environment. They taught that human society—especially urban society—teaches us to be selfish and violent. As we have seen, however, the Bible teaches that the city is simply a magnifying glass for the human heart. It brings out whatever is already inside. In the previous chapter, we examined the city's strengths for culture making, as well as its spiritual dangers. But we must remember that the city itself is not to blame for the evil that humans have sinfully brought into it.

Here is another common objection: "The country inspires; faith dies in the city." While the countryside can indeed inspire, it is quite wrong to say that the urban environment is a harder environment to find and grow in faith. As we noted earlier, many people coming from regions where Christianity is suppressed by the culture hear the gospel for the first time in the great cities where there is more of a "free market" of ideas. Millions of people who are virtually cut off from gospel witness are reachable if they emigrate to cities. Also, many who were raised as nominal Christians come to the cities where they are challenged in new ways and brought to vital, solid faith in the process. I have seen this occur thousands of times during my ministry at Redeemer. The city is, in fact, a spiritual hotbed where people both lose faith and find it in ways that do not happen in more monolithic, less pluralistic settings. This is, yet again, part of the tension of the city we see addressed in the Bible (see ch. 5).

Sometimes the contrast of the countryside and the city is drawn even more starkly. My colleague at Westminster, Harvie Conn, told me about a man who said to him, "God made the country, and man built the suburbs, but the devil made the city." The theology behind this statement is dubious to say the least. And theologically, it is not a good idea to think of the countryside as intrinsically more pleasing to God. An urban missionary, Bill Krispin, explains why. Bill once said to me, "The country is where there are more plants than people; the city is where there are more people than plants. And since God loves people much more than plants, he loves the city more than the country." I think this is solid theological logic. The apex of creation is, after all, the making of male and female in the image of God (Gen 1:26–27). Therefore, cities, which are filled with people, are absolutely crammed full of what God considers the most beautiful sight in his creation. As we have noted before, cities have more "image of God" per square inch than anywhere else, and so we must not idealize the country as somehow a more spiritual place than the city. Even those (like Wendell Berry) who lift up the virtues of rural living outline a form of human community just as achievable in cities as in small towns.

How can you as a church or an individual live out this value if you are not located near a metropolitan area? I believe the best strategy is to include urban ministry in your global missions portfolio. This may mean supporting individual missionaries who serve in cities; an even more effective strategy is to support church-planting ministries in global cities.[12] Another promising trend is the creation of metro-wide partnerships of churches and other agencies to support the holistic work of spreading the gospel throughout the city.

2. Christians should become a dynamic counterculture where they live. It will not be enough for Christians to simply live as individuals in the city, however. They must live as a particular kind of community. In the Bible's tale of two cities, man's city is built on the principle of personal aggrandizement (Gen 11:1–4), while "the city of our God ... is beautiful in its loftiness, the joy of the whole earth" (Ps 48:1–2). In other words, the urban society God wants is based on *service*, not selfishness. Its purpose is to spread joy from its cultural riches to the whole world. Christians are called to be an *alternate city* within every earthly city, an *alternate human culture* within every human culture—to show how sex, money, and power can be used in nondestructive ways; to show how classes and races that cannot get along outside of Christ can get along in him; and to show how it is possible to cultivate by using the tools of art, education, government, and business to bring hope to people rather than despair or cynicism.

Someone may ask, "Can't Christians be an alternate city out in the suburbs?" Absolutely! This is one of our universal callings as Christians. Yet again, though, the earthly city magnifies the effect of this alternate city and its unique forms of ministry. In racially homogeneous places, it is harder to show in pragmatic ways how the gospel uniquely undermines racial barriers (see Eph 2:11–22). In places where few artists live, it is pragmatically harder to show the gospel's unique effect on art. In economically homogeneous places, physically removed from the human poverty that is so pervasive in the world, it is pragmatically harder for Christians to realize how much money they are spending on themselves. What is possible in the suburbs and rural towns comes into sharper focus in the city. The city illustrates in vivid detail the unique community life that is produced as the fruit of the gospel.

3. Christians should be a community radically committed to the good of their city as a whole. It is not enough for Christians to form a culture that merely "counters" the values of the city. We must also commit, with all the resources of our faith and life, to serve sacrificially the good of the whole city, and especially the poor.

It is especially important that Christians not be seduced by the mind-set of the "consumer city"—the city as adult playground. Cities attract young adults with a dizzying variety of amenities and diversions that no suburb or small town can reproduce. Even when holding constant factors such as income, education, marital status, and age, city residents are far more likely to go to a concert, visit a museum, go to the movies, or stop into a local pub than people outside of urban areas.[13] On top of this, urban residents, more than their country cousins, tend to take an unmistakable pride in sophistication and hipness. Christians must not be tempted to come to the city (or at least not to remain in the city) for these motivations. Christians indeed can be enriched by the particular joys of urban life, but ultimately they live in cities to serve.

Christians must work for the peace, security, justice, and prosperity of their neighbors, loving them in word and deed, whether or not they believe the same things we believe. In Jeremiah 29:7, God calls the Jews not just to live in the city but to love it and work for its shalom—its economic, social, and spiritual flourishing. Christians are, indeed, citizens of God's heavenly city, but *these citizens are always the best possible citizens of their earthly city.* They walk in the steps of the One who laid down his life for his opponents.

Christians in cities must become a counterculture for the common good. They must be radically different from the surrounding city, yet radically committed to its benefit. They must minister to the city out of their distinctive Christian beliefs and identity. We see this balance demonstrated when we examine the early Christian understanding of citizenship. Paul used his Roman citizenship as leverage and defense in the service of his wider missional aims (Acts 16:37–38; 22:25–29; cf. 21:39; 23:27). He tells the Ephesians that because of the work of the gospel, "You are no longer foreigners and strangers, but *fellow citizens with God's people* and also *members of his household*, built on the foundation of the apostles and prophets, with Christ Jesus himself as the chief cornerstone" (Eph 2:19–20, emphasis mine).

And to the church in Philippi, Paul writes, "Our citizenship is in heaven. And we eagerly await a Savior from there, the Lord Jesus Christ, who, by the power that enables him to bring everything under his control, will transform our lowly bodies so that they will be like his glorious body" (Phil 3:20–21). Though Roman citizenship was a beneficial badge and indeed carried valuable social status, Paul is clear that Christians are, first and foremost, citizens of heaven.

Joseph presents an interesting Old Testament demonstration of this tension. When he is made prince of the land (Gen 41:39–40), he pursues the wealth and good of *Egypt*, just as he had previously done in prison and in Potiphar's house. Through his pursuit of the good of the city, salvation comes to the people of God. This story is especially striking because God puts Joseph in the position to save *the city* from hunger, not just the people of God.

In the end, Christians live not to increase the prosperity of our own tribe and group through power plays and coercion but to serve the good of all the people of the city (regardless of what beliefs others hold). While secularism tends to make people individualistic, and traditional religiosity tends to make people tribal, the gospel should destroy the natural selfishness of the human heart and lead Christians to sacrificial service that benefits the whole city. If Christians seek power and influence, they will arouse fear and hostility. If instead they pursue love and seek to serve, they will be granted a great deal of influence by their neighbors, a free gift given to trusted and trustworthy people.

Christians should seek to live in the city, not to *use* the city to build great churches, but to use the resources of the church to seek a great, flourishing city. We refer to this as a "city growth" model of ministry rather than a strictly "church growth" model. It is the ministry posture that arises out of a Center Church theological vision.

Seven Features of a Church for the City

It is infinitely easier to *talk* about living out this posture "on the ground" in our cities than to actually do it. The challenge is to establish churches and other ministries that effectively engage the realities of the cities of the world. The majority of evangelical Protestants who presently control the United States mission apparatus are typically white and nonurban in background. They neither understand nor in most cases enjoy urban life. As I have been arguing, many of the prevailing ministry methods are forged outside of urban areas and then simply imported, with little thought given to the unnecessary barriers this practice erects between urban dwellers and the gospel. Consequently, when ministers go into a city, they often find it especially hard to evangelize and win urban people—and equally difficult to disciple converts and prepare Christians for life in a pluralistic, secular, culturally engaged setting. Just as the Bible needs to be translated into its readers' vernacular, so the gospel needs to be embodied and communicated in ways that are understandable to the residents of a city.

I believe churches that minister in ways that are indigenous and honoring to a city—whatever its size—exhibit seven vital features:

1. Respect for urban sensibility
2. Unusual sensitivity to cultural differences
3. Commitment to neighborhood and justice
4. Integration of faith and work
5. Bias for complex evangelism

6. Preaching that both attracts and challenges urban people

7. Commitment to artistry and creativity

We'll unpack each of these characteristics in more detail here.

1. Respect for urban sensibility. Our culture is largely invisible to us, which is why it is revelatory to leave one's society and live in a very different culture for a while. This experience enables us to see how much of our thought and behavior is not based on universal common sense but on a particular cultural practice. And it is often easier to see the big cultural differences than the small ones. Christians who move to cities within their own country (or even region) often underestimate the importance of the small cultural differences they have with urbanites. They speak and act in ways that are out of step with urban sensibilities, and if this is pointed out to them, they despise the criticism as snobbishness.

Most American evangelical churches are middle class in their corporate culture. That is, they value privacy, safety, homogeneity, sentimentality, space, order, and control. In contrast, the city is filled with ironic, edgy, diversity-loving people who have a high tolerance for ambiguity and disorder. On the whole, they value intensity and access more than comfort and control. Center-city people appreciate sophistication in communication content and mode, and yet they eschew what they consider slickness, hype, and excessive polish. Being able to strike these nuanced balances cannot be a matter of performance. Christian leaders and ministers must genuinely belong to the culture so they begin to intuitively understand it.

Center-city culture in particular is filled with well-informed, verbal, creative, and assertive people who do not respond well to authoritative pronouncements. They appreciate thoughtful presentations that are well argued and provide opportunities for communication and feedback. If a church's ministers are unable to function in an urban culture, choosing instead to create a "missionary compound" within the city, they will soon discover they cannot reach out, convert, or incorporate the people who live in their neighborhoods.

2. Unusual sensitivity to cultural differences. Effective leaders in urban ministry are acutely aware of the different people groups within their area. Because cities are dense and diverse, they are always culturally complex. This means not only that different races and socioeconomic classes are in closer physical proximity than in other settings, but that other factors, such as ethnicity, age, vocation, and religion, create a matrix of subcultures. In New York City, for example, older downtown artists (over the age of fifty) are significantly different from younger artists. The Jewish community in New York City is vast and variegated. The cultural differences among African Americans, Africans, and Afro-Caribbeans are marked, even as they share a broad sense of identity over against white culture. Some groups clash more with particular groups than others (e.g., African Americans and Koreans in some cities). The gay community is divided between those who want to be more integrated into mainstream culture and those who do not. Asians talk about being "1.0, 1.5, or second generation."

Fruitful urban ministers must first notice these differences and avoid thinking they are inconsequential. Then they must seek to understand these different people respectfully and navigate accordingly in communication and ministry without unnecessarily offending others. In fact, urban ministers should constantly surprise others with how well they understand other cultures. If you are an Anglo man, for example, you should occasionally hear something like, "I didn't think a white man would know about that."

Those raised in culturally homogeneous areas who move to a city soon come to realize how many of their attitudes and habits—which they thought of as simply universal common sense—were deeply tied to their race and class. For instance, Anglo-Americans don't see themselves as making decisions, expressing emotions, handling conflict, scheduling time and events, and communicating in a "white" way—they just think they are doing things the way everybody knows things ought to be done. In an urban setting, people typically become more sensitive to these blind spots. Why? Because they are acquainted with the aspirations, fears, passions, and patterns of several different groups of people through involvement with friends, neighbors, and colleagues who come from these groups. They have personally experienced how members of different ethnic or even vocational groups use an identical word or phrase to mean different things.

No church can be all things to all people. There is no culturally neutral way of doing ministry. The urban church will have to choose practices that reflect the values of *some* cultural group, and in so doing it will communicate in ways that different cultural groups will see and hear differently. As soon as it chooses a language to preach in, or the music it will sing, it is making it easier for some people to participate and more difficult for others.

Nevertheless, the ever-present challenge is to work to make urban ministry as broadly appealing as possible and as inclusive of different cultures as possible. One of the ways to do this is to have a racially diverse set of leaders "up front." When we see someone like ourselves speaking or leading a meeting, we feel welcomed in a hard-to-define way. Another way is to listen long and hard to people in our congregation who feel underrepresented by the way our church does ministry. In the end, we must accept the fact that urban churches will experience recurring complaints of racial insensitivity. Urban ministers live with the constant sense that they are failing to embrace as many kinds of people as they should. But they willingly and gladly embrace the challenge of building racial and cultural diversity in their churches and see these inevitable criticisms as simply one of the necessary costs of urban ministry.

3. Commitment to neighborhood and justice. Urban neighborhoods are highly complex. Even gentrified neighborhoods, full of professionals, may actually be "bipolar." That is, alongside the well-off residents in their expensive apartments, private schools, and various community associations and clubs is often a "shadow neighborhood" filled with many who live in poverty, attend struggling schools, and reside in government housing.

Urban ministers learn how to exegete their neighborhoods to grasp their sociological complexity. They are obsessed with studying and learning about their local communities. (Academic training in urban ethnography, urban demographics, and urban planning can be a great help to a church's lay leaders and staff members.) But faithful churches do not exegete their neighborhoods simply to target people groups, although evangelistic outreach is one of the goals. They are looking for ways to strengthen the health of their neighborhoods, making them safer and more humane places for people to live. This is a way to seek the welfare of the city, in the spirit of Jeremiah 29.

Urban churches train their members to be neighbors in the city, not just consumers. As we have seen, cities attract young professionals by providing something of a "theme park" with thousands of entertainment and cultural options, and many new urban residents tend to view the city as simply a place where they can have fun, develop a résumé, and make friends who will be of help to them in the future. They plan to do this for a few years and then leave. In other words, they are *using* the city rather than living in it as neighbors (as Jesus defines the term in the parable of the good Samaritan in Luke 10:25–37).

In the middle years of the twentieth century, Jane Jacobs wrote the classic *The Death and Life of Great American Cities*. Jacobs's great contribution came in demonstrating the importance of street life for civil society. She observed how foot traffic and street life and a mixture of residences and businesses (viewed negatively by suburban zoners and even many urban planners at the time) were critical for economic vitality, for safety, for healthy human relationships, and for a strong social fabric. Jacobs was a major opponent of large-scale urban projects in the mid-twentieth century, the very projects that eventually ruined neighborhoods and the street life she had promoted. Jacobs writes the following:

> Looking at city neighborhoods as organs of self-government, I can see evidence that only three kinds of neighborhoods are useful: (1) the city as a whole; (2) street neighborhoods; and (3) districts of large, subcity size (composed of 100,000 people or more in the case of the largest cities).
>
> Each of these kinds of neighborhoods has different functions, but the three supplement each other in complex fashion.[14]

Jacobs explains how each of these is indeed a neighborhood and how each requires the participation of all urban residents to keep the city healthy. In other words, you must know your literal neighbors (your street neighborhood) and have some familiarity with the blocks around your residence (your district). And yet this in itself is not enough. "Ward politics" — in which one neighborhood pits its own good against the good of the other parts of the city — is unwholesome and unhealthy. So it is important for Christians and Christian ministries to find ways to be neighbors to the whole city, not just to their immediate street neighborhood. Failing to engage in the interests of the entire city often results in a lack of involvement in helping the poorest residents of the city. It is equally important that a church not minister just to the whole city while ignoring its local neighborhood. If this happens, a church can become a commuter church that no longer knows how to reach the kind of people who live in their immediate vicinity.

Urban churches, then, should be known in their community as a group of people who are committed to the good of all their neighbors, near and far. It takes this type of holistic commitment from all residents and institutions to maintain a good quality of life in the city, and a church that is not engaged in this manner will (rightly) be perceived by the city as tribal.

4. Integration of faith and work. Traditional evangelical churches tend to emphasize personal piety and rarely help believers understand how to maintain and apply their Christian beliefs and practice in the worlds of the arts, business, scholarship, and government. Many churches do not know how to disciple members without essentially pulling them out of their vocations and inviting them to become heavily involved in church activities. In other words, Christian discipleship is interpreted as consisting largely of activities done in the evening or on the weekend.

Many vocations of city dwellers — fashion and the media, the arts and technology, business and finance, politics and public policy — demand great amounts of time and energy. These are typically not forty-hour-a-week jobs. They are jobs that dominate a person's life and thinking, and urban Christians are confronted with ethical and theological issues every day in the workplace. Preaching and ministry in urban churches must therefore help congregants form networks of believers within their vocational field and assist them in working through the theological, ethical, and practical issues they face in their work.

In addition to the practical issues of how to do their individual work, urban Christians need a broader vision of how Christianity engages and influences culture. As we have discussed, cities are culture-forming incubators, and believers in such places have a significant need for guidance on how Christian faith should express itself in public life. For more on this subject, see part 3 ("Cultural Engagement").[15]

5. Bias for complex evangelism. Two kinds of urban churches can grow without evangelism. The first is the ethnic/immigrant church. While many ethnic churches are evangelistic, it is possible for them to grow without conversions, as new immigrants are always looking for connections to their own people in the city. Ethnic churches therefore become informal "community centers" for people of the same race and subculture—and they can grow simply by gathering new immigrants who want to be part of the fellowship. Second, churches in Western center cities can grow without evangelism by meeting the needs of one particular "immigrant subculture"—evangelical Christians—through preaching, music, children's programs, and so forth. In the past, in cities outside of the southern and midwestern United States, there simply was no constituency of "church shoppers" to attract. However, during the urban renaissance of the last fifteen years, this situation has changed, and cities have become desirable destinations for young adults from all over the country. Redeemer Presbyterian Church's experience is a good way to understand this phenomenon.

Redeemer was begun in Manhattan at the end of the 1980s, during the end of an era of urban decline. Crime was high and the city was losing population, and there were few or no Christians moving into New York City from the rest of the country. During the first several years of Redeemer's existence, it grew through aggressive but winsome evangelism. An evangelistic consciousness permeated the young congregation, and several hundred people came to faith out of nonbelief and nonchurched backgrounds over the first five years.

By the mid-1990s, the urban regeneration had begun, and we noticed that young adults from Christian backgrounds were moving to the cities. By the end of the decade, we found that we could (and did) grow substantially by drawing these folks in and helping them live out their Christian lives in service to the city. This is, of course, a very good and important thing, but it can also mask a lack of evangelism, and in the end, nonevangelistic church growth can't help reach the city in the most profound way. Recognizing this danger, our church has recommitted itself to reigniting our ethos of evangelism.

Not only must an urban church be committed to evangelism; it must be committed to the *complexity* of urban evangelism. There is no "one size fits all" method or message that can be used with all urban residents. For example, it is impossible for a Christian minister in London to share the gospel in exactly the same way with an atheist native Scot or a Muslim from Pakistan—yet they may both be the minister's literal neighbors. Urban evangelism requires immersion in the various cultures' greatest hopes, fears, views, and objections to Christianity. It requires a creative host of different means and venues, and it takes great courage.

6. Preaching that both attracts and challenges urban people. Perhaps the greatest challenge for preachers in urban contexts is the fact that many secular and nonbelieving people may be in the audience. Of course, urban congregations can be as ingrown as any others, but certain dynamics of urban life can more readily make city church gatherings "spiritually mixed" and filled with nonbelievers. Urban centers have higher percentages of single people, and it is far easier for a single Christian to get a single, non-Christian friend to come to a church gathering than it is for a Christian family to get an entire non-Christian family to come. Singles make unilateral decisions (without having to consult others), tend to spend more time out of their homes, and are more open to new experiences. Also, cities are not "car cultures"; they are pedestrian cultures, and it is not unusual for people to simply walk off the street into a church out of curiosity. Finally, people who come to cities come to "make it," are often separated from extended families, and are under a great deal of stress. As a result, urban people are often in a spiritual search mode and can be hungry for human connection and a sense of belonging.

The challenge for the urban preacher is to preach in a way that edifies believers and engages and evangelized nonbelievers at the same time. Here are some pointers:

First, be sure to preach sermons that ground moral exhortation in Christ and his work. Show how we live as we should only if we believe in and apply Christ's work of salvation as we should. In this way nonbelievers hear the gospel each week, yet believers have their issues and problems addressed as well.

Second, be very careful to think about your audience's premises. Don't assume, for example, that everyone listening trusts the Bible. So when you make a point from the Bible, it will help to show that some other trusted authority (such as empirical science) agrees with the Bible. Use it to promote trust of the Bible, saying something like, "See, the Bible was telling us centuries ago what science now confirms." That will help convince your hearers of that point so you can move on. By the end of the sermon, of course, you will be appealing only to God's Word, but in the early stages of the sermon you invite nonbelievers along by showing respect for their doubts about the Bible's reliability.

Third, do "apologetic sidebars." Try to devote one of the three or four sermon points mainly to the doubts and concerns of nonbelievers. Keep in your head a list of the ten or so biggest objections people have to Christianity. More often than not, the particular Scripture text has some way to address them. Always treat people's typical doubts about Christianity with respect. Jude reminds us to "be merciful to those who doubt" (Jude 22). Never give the impression that "all intelligent people think like I do." Don't hesitate to say, "I know this Christian doctrine may sound outrageous, but would you consider this ...?"

Fourth, address different groups directly, showing that you know they are there, as though you are dialoguing with them: "If you are committed to Christ, you may be thinking this—but the text answers that fear," or "If you are not a Christian or not sure what you believe, then you surely must think this is narrow-minded—but the text says this, which speaks to this very issue."

Fifth, consider demeanor. The young secularists of New York City are extremely sensitive to anything that smacks of artifice to them. Anything that is too polished, too controlled, too canned will seem like salesmanship. They will be turned off if they hear a preacher use noninclusive gender language, make cynical remarks about other religions, adopt a tone of voice they consider forced or inauthentic, or use insider evangelical tribal jargon. In particular, they will feel "beaten up" if a pastor yells at them. The kind of preaching that sounds passionate in the heartland may sound like a dangerous rant in certain subcultures in the city.

Sixth, show a deep acquaintance with the same books, magazines, blogs, movies, and plays — as well as the daily life experiences — that your audience knows. Mention them and interpret them in light of Scripture. But be sure to read and experience urban life across a spectrum of opinion. There is nothing more truly urban than showing you know, appreciate, and digest a great diversity of human opinion. During my first years in New York, I regularly read *The New Yorker* (sophisticated secular), *The Atlantic* (eclectic), *The Nation* (older, left-wing secular), *The Weekly Standard* (conservative but erudite), *The New Republic* (eclectic and erudite), *Utne Reader* (New Age alternative), *Wired* (Silicon Valley libertarian), *First Things* (conservative Catholic). As I read, I imagine dialogues about Christianity with the writers. I almost never read a magazine without getting a scrap of a preaching idea.

7. Commitment to artistry and creativity. According to the United States census, between 1970 and 1990 the number of people describing themselves as "artist" more than doubled, from 737,000 to 1.7 million. Since 1990, the number of artists continued to grow another 16 percent to nearly two million. Professional artists live disproportionately in major urban areas, and so the arts are held in high regard in the city, while in nonurban areas little direct attention is typically given to them. Urban churches must be aware of this. First, they should have high standards for artistic skill in their worship and ministries. If you do not have such standards, your church will feel culturally remote to the average urban dweller who is surrounded by artistic excellence even on the streets where talented artists sing and perform.

Second, city churches should think of artists not simply as persons with skills to use. They must connect to them as worshipers and hearers, communicating that they are valued for both their work and their presence in the community. This can be done in a variety of ways. One way includes being sensitive to your own region's or city's particular art history (e.g., Nashville is a music center; New England and the Midwest have many writers; New Mexico is a center for visual artists). Take time to listen to the artists and musicians in your church to understand something about the nature of the local artistic community and how the creative process works. Do your best to work with local artists and musicians rather than flying in your favorite artists long-distance for concerts or shows. When you make use of artists' gifts, take their advice on how the music and the art should be done; don't simply give orders to them.

●　●　○

God has given us the city for his purposes, and even though sin has harmed it, we should use the resources of the gospel to repair broken cities. Jesus himself went to the city and was crucified "outside the city gate" (Heb 13:12), a biblical metaphor for forsakenness. By his grace, Jesus lost the city-that-was, so we could become citizens of the city-to-come (Heb 11:10; 12:22), making us salt and light in the city-that-is (Matt 5:13–16).

So we urge *all* the people of God to recognize and embrace the strategic intensity of cities—and therefore to respond to the urgent call to be *in the city* and *for the city* from every coordinate on the globe. City Vision recognizes God's creational intentions for cities and calls the people of God to be the city of God within the city of man.

DISCUSSION QUESTIONS

1. If you are not located in a city, how might City Vision shape and improve the fruitfulness of your current ministry?

2. How is agglomeration evident around you? Which types of trades, skills, inventors, or culture makers are concentrated most highly in your area? In what ways can your ministry seek face-to-face opportunities to minister to and through this population—that is, to become an "agglomerizing" church?

3. Keller writes, "The city itself brings the gospel to us. The city will challenge us to discover the power of the gospel in new ways." How does this chapter suggest this happens? How have you experienced this?

4. Which of the seven features of a church for the city does your church currently exhibit? How might those outside your community answer this question?

REFLECTIONS ON CITY VISION

Gabriel Salguero, president of the National Latino Evangelical Coalition

Tim Keller and I are very different and yet very much the same. We both serve as pastors in Manhattan. I serve a Nazarene congregation, and he pastors a Presbyterian church. He is Anglo, and I'm Latino. I'm in my forties, and he's in his sixties. I grew up in the Pentecostal Latino Church, deeply informed by Wesleyanism and Arminian traditions, and he is in the Reformed tradition, drawing deeply from John Calvin.

So on several levels, Keller and I have different optics by which we see and are seen. Nevertheless, we are brothers. Our love for the gospel and the city, and our common commitment to the task of clearly communicating the gospel to contemporary urbanites, unites us.

My entry point into this conversation reflects a tension that is at the very core of the Christian faith. It's a hybridity that is important for understanding both the gospel and cities. As Christians, we serve a "hybrid" Christ who is both God *and* human. We are a church that is made up of both Jews and Gentiles. We are on a mission that is both in this world but not of it. My sense is that precisely this dialectic is at the heart of Keller's articulation of a Christian theological vision for gospel-centered urban ministry. As I read these chapters, his search for balance found me saying yes to this call for gospel-centered urban ministry. Our shared commitment to the gospel allows us to eschew blind idolatries to specific models of urban ministry engagement. Resisting idolatries means drawing from *and* contextualizing our methodologies for the sake of gospel-centeredness and fruitfulness.

In these chapters, I hear the echoes of another famous Christian New Yorker, Reinhold Niebuhr. Keller probes in creatively different ways the same queries of sin and grace, transcendence and history, culture and gospel that Niebuhr grappled with in his works *Faith and History*, *Pious and Secular America*, and *Children of Light and Children of Darkness*. Contemporary urban ministers know that understanding the gospel *and* urban sociology is critical for gospel fruit in cities.

The aesthetic depiction of the new Jerusalem as a city with life-giving trees and fruit (Rev 22:2) is what many urban Christians look to as the goal of gospel-centered ministry. It's a paradoxical metaphor. The idea of bearing fruit in a city invites us to critically analyze our Christian witness and presence. We must clearly articulate what we mean by the gospel and what the gospel means for the "peace and prosperity" of our cities (Jer 29:7). Keller wrestles with what those of us called to live out the gospel in urban centers have long wrestled with: How can we be faithful to the Christian gospel in ways that yield gospel fruit in the city?

Keller's words remind me of the question Dietrich Bonhoeffer asked in the 1940s: "What is bothering me incessantly is the question what Christianity really is, or indeed who Christ really is, for us today?"[1]

Keller is asking us this as well: "Who is Jesus Christ in and for our cities today?"

Who Do You Say That I Am?

The people of the tribe of Issachar "understood the times and knew what Israel should do" (1 Chr 12:32)—and so it is with us today. We need a contextualized theological vision that firmly understands *both* the gospel and the city. Keller reminds us that sound contextualization must not compromise the gospel. A nuanced call for practical contextualization is certainly not new, but it is always good to hear it repeated. Some of the first calls of active actualization by C. René Padilla, Samuel Escobar, and Francis Schaeffer are worth rehearsing for a new generation of urban Christians.[2] Faithful urban witness requires that we answer the existential and social question made famous by the soul singer Marvin Gaye: "What's going on?" What is "going on" in our neighborhoods, on our streets, and in the life of our cities?

We need this reminder that contextual and cultural intelligence in the urban milieu is not *all* that is required for gospel impact in cities. First and foremost, we must intimately know the gospel. As Keller says, in truly knowing the gospel we avoid the perilous temptations of overcontextualization or undercontextualization. Many times, when I was teaching classes on urban ministry, the city became *everything*, and students became so focused on understanding the culture and the context that they lost sight of the gospel and its priority. But the city is *not* everything. In all of our contextualization, we must resist making an idol of the city. We need to return to the gist of Bonhoeffer's question, "Who is Jesus Christ for the city today?" and remember that we preach Jesus Christ *for* the city. This dual knowledge of the gospel and the city is at the heart of the *missio ecclesia*, the mission of the church.

One of the greatest challenges I have seen with a new generation of urban church planters is the dangerous idolatry of methodology. In these chapters, Keller seeks to free us from a one-size-fits-all methodology. His *cantus firmus* to gospel faithfulness and missional fruitfulness challenges our modern love affair with methodologies. This is not to say that methods or taxonomies serve no purpose. They are *ministerium*— servants of the gospel mission—not *magisterium*—lords over it. In this a Latino Nazarene raised in New Jersey is in full agreement with an Anglo Presbyterian from Pennsylvania: The gospel can engage culture while destroying its idols.

Seeing the City as It Really Is

Keller makes it clear that context matters. I like to illustrate this by pointing to the sitcom depictions we see of New York and, in particular, Manhattan on network television (think *Sex in the City*, *Seinfeld*, and *Friends*). The younger generation's understanding of New York City has largely been framed by these sitcom depictions, and for the most part they showed a Manhattan that was predominantly white, upper middle class, and young. It's as if Harlem, Washington Heights, Chinatown, and Loisaida were just not there—not a part of Manhattan.

But these television depictions are a far cry from the diversity of that area. Other shows from the past were more stereotypical in their approach—shows like *Welcome Back Kotter* and *The Jeffersons* in the 1970s and 80s. This homogenization of Manhattan in visual media was not merely descriptive; it somehow became prescriptive for what the city "ought to be." Much of the writing on urban mission has regrettably followed this pattern. Here is where Keller's call for balanced and gospel-centered ministry needs to be heard. The gospel brings a freshness and vibrancy to our thinking and engagement that is far more than a reflection of the spirit of our age.

In short, we need to avoid confusing the "descriptive" of the urban context with the "prescriptive" of the gospel imperative. We need a balance here. Far too often, depictions of urban ministry are simplified so that the city is either a sinful place with gangs, violence, corruption, and godlessness or a place of cultural elites, fashion, power, and finance (à la *West Side Story* and *The Wolf of Wall Street*). Yet neither of these depictions is adequate. The city is a complex topography of both, and far more as well. Gospel-centered ministry requires *both* the descriptive and the prescriptive.

Several months ago, I was invited to speak at Church of Grace to Fujianese in the Lower East Side of Manhattan at an 11:00 a.m. Wednesday morning Bible study. My assumption was that it would be a handful of elderly people gathered around a table. I was very wrong. That morning, I spoke to approximately five hundred Fujianese young people, mostly in their twenties and thirties. I learned that Church of Grace to Fujianese held an early midweek gathering for young immigrants who worked in the restaurant and hotel industries of Chinatown. This is New York City as it is today, and the influence of the global South is not lost on Keller. He rightly draws from Philip Jenkins's understanding of migration patterns for gospel growth in the city: "Waves of immigration from the Southern and Eastern Hemispheres are coming to the cities of North America and Europe. Many of these immigrants come from parts of the world where belief in orthodox, supernatural Christianity is on the rise. As a result, thousands of new churches are being planted by non-Westerners in the formerly secular cities of London, Paris, and New York" (p. 144).

My visit to this Fujianese church was a reminder that there are rich and diverse mission opportunities in every urban center. To put it another way, this is not the New York you see in a sitcom; it's the city as it really is.

Beyond a Flat Picture of the City

The capacity for cities to converge diasporas of generations and cultures has direct and immediate implications for gospel mission. I remember when the testimonies of David Wilkerson and Nicky Cruz in *The Cross and the Switchblade* were published all over the press. Their ministry was captured in a film and a book that were popular in Christian circles. When I read the book, I remember thinking, *Now I have discovered how to reach the city!* This flat portrait of a single, faithful ministry drove many of us to replicate their model as the *only* model for urban ministry. And this is the modern seduction of making the method the message. Today, with the success of models like Redeemer Church, Christian Cultural Center, and Trinity Grace Church, others are equally tempted to think these leaders have found the magic pill for fruitful gospel impact in cities. Keller rightly issues a clear warning here, one I am glad to echo. The complexity of cities cannot be reduced to any one model, no matter how successful or renowned.

Here is where we can benefit from robust dialogue with partners in the global church and Christian leaders in other global cities. Though Keller sounds this note, I found his description of the "historic moment" we face in the urban West to be too flat a view, one that grants only a cursory nod to the reality of global culture. Keller's descriptive of city culture is deeply informed by the thoughts of Lesslie Newbigin, James Davison Hunter, Harvey Cox, and other Western thought leaders in their estimation of late modernity, culture, and secularization. Newbigin, Hunter, and Cox are not wrong in their analysis that cultural shifts of late modernity in the West are moving toward a more secular or post-Christian society. James E. White's *The Rise of the Nones* has shown that the rise of religiously unaffiliated millennials is something we need to pay attention to.[3] Even among Hispanics, Pew Forum has noted that in 2013, the number of unaffiliated Hispanics has risen to close to 10 percent of the U.S. Hispanic population.[4] These numbers highlight the fact that immigrants are becoming more integrated into cities in the global North, yet they tend to assume the move is toward secularism. This misses some of the nuance we find on the ground when we talk with people. While there is much truth and insight to the notion of secularized cultural shifts, we also need the added texture that takes into account globalization and immigration and the diversification of our cities.

So I find myself both nodding in agreement and shaking my head in disagreement when I read Keller saying that *The Bonfire of the Vanities* "captured the spirit of the age of Manhattan in the 1980s" (p. 70). Certainly this is true to some degree. Yet Manhattan, like every other city, is not a monolith. *Down These Mean Streets* and *Savior, Savior, Hold My Hand* by Piri Thomas also captured the spirit of the age in 1980s Manhattan. Manhattan was much more than what *The Bonfire of the Vanities* portended.

Cultural anthropologist Homi Bhabha urges this query of world-view assumptions in his book *The Location of Culture*.[5] Bhabha challenges some of the assumptions of James Davison Hunter's *To Change the World*, namely, that culture is formed primarily in the places of cultural elites and institutions. His contrasting view—that power from below also has the capacity to form and inform culture—is particularly helpful for millennials, who have seen firsthand the power of social media to democratize information and cultural creation. Granted, it is still unclear to what degree social media will be an Internet Pentecost or a Tower of Babel—or possibly both. French postmodernist Michel Foucault argues that power and agency are ubiquitous.[6] Urban ministers should not succumb to flat views of power and agency that can lead to segregated urban missional movements.

Of course, Hunter is correct in saying that institutions and networks have the capacity to channel and commodify these movements. But none of this is fixed. Centers and margins are always moving. The movement of the gospel begins not with Paul in the cities but with Jesus in Galilee. Gospel movements do not follow linear models of transformation, and because of this they have violated modernity's enamorment with hierarchal, elite-only transformation.

Don't Idolize the Center

My hope is that we can somehow avoid falling captive to the temptation to idolize the center. Anyone who knows the power of New York communities to influence larger culture (e.g., the Harlem Renaissance, El Barrio's aesthetics movements, and the Dominican creativity of Washington Heights) can attest to the power of common grace operating *outside* the center. And these movements operating outside the center will continue to change and impact the work of institutions as well, including the church. A truly urban ecclesiology and mission require an integrated holistic model.

Keller emphasizes that multiple cultural streams always coexist in one city at one time. How, then, do we engage these multiple cultural and urban streams in mission and discipleship? Urban centers are attractive to young people and immigrants, and while there are some shared needs, each group also has particular needs. In my visits to Madrid, Amsterdam, Maracaibo, and Mexico City, I have seen how these multiple demographics of Christians serve, worship, and generally "do life" in separate silos throughout the city. The reality in much of the world is that we still have a tale of two cities, where different demographic groups of Christians living in urban areas have only minimal interaction with each other as worshiping communities.

Keller is aware of this, of course. He categorizes opportunities for ministry in cities into four important groups: the younger generation, the cultural elites, accessible "unreached" people groups, and the poor (pp. 145–48). Yet the challenge of integration is even more apparent when we focus on these four groups. We begin to see that the credibility and validity of the gospel message are at stake here. Is the gospel we preach truly universal? Is it able to reach the cultural elites, the poor, and everyone in between? Admittedly, center cities are becoming more and more economically stratified, with stark divides between the elites and the poor. This is true in Manhattan, but it is also seen in the juxtaposition of the *favelas* and towering businesses in Sao Paolo, Brazil and the *caserio* of La Perla and the business and tourist community of El Condado in San Juan, Puerto Rico. Here is where Keller's reminder of the universality of the gospel is needed: "An urban church does not choose between ministry to the poor and ministry to the professional class" (p. 148). Yes, cities offer unique opportunities for ministry we do not find elsewhere; yet there is always the danger of focusing on a specific group and ignoring others.

Avoiding One-Directional Ministry

It is here that some of the nuance of the gospel can be lost in our missional focus. Keller puts it this way to emphasize the need to bridge between the various groups: "We need the economic and cultural resources of the elites to help the poor, and our commitment to the poor is a testimony to the cultural elites, supporting the validity of our message" (p. 148). But this presentation of missional focus seems entirely too unidirectional to me. Though it rightly emphasizes the need for diversity in our mission, it is a ministry *to* the poor rather than *with* and *by* the poor.

Historically, this is manifested in well-intentioned ministries of compassion that rarely translate to shared worship or community. Some in urban centers have called these "drive-by ministries"—providing services of some kind but never asking people to join our community or making an attempt to join theirs. I don't see this as a minor point, for regrettably much of classical urban ministry has emulated bad models of global missions that foster paternalism rather than partnership. These models neglect the work of God through those among the urban poor who are orthodox Christians. In early Christianity, many of these urban poor were men and women who testified to their employers and benefactors the truth of the gospel.

Today we tend to see the poor, as with other groups, as *objects* of ministry rather than as ministry *agents* who are a key part of urban evangelism and transformation. This optic is one of the major hurdles to having truly integrated congregations. In New York, for example, many of the nannies and domestics who serve the cultural elites worship in congregations around the city. During the week, they provide spiritual and biblical instruction to the children of these elites. In my mind, this phenomenon has much in common with the way the early church expanded from the rural regions of ancient Galilee to the center of the Roman Empire. It suggests that Christian discipleship is not just a matter of reaching younger people, cultural elites, and the poor with the gospel. We must also ask if the gospel has penetrated our thinking and our practice in such a way that we see ourselves as one community that is "doing life together." Are we so bound by cultural practices, temperament, and class that we must remain in our silos?

This is more than, as Keller posits, simply doing ministries of compassion and justice *for* the poor or evangelizing cultural elites, unreached groups, and young people. It's what Bonhoeffer called "life together,"[7] living in community with one another despite our very real and noticeable differences. It is not just asking someone if we can share the gospel with them; it is asking, Can I sit with you in worship, even when it causes both of us discomfort?

Beyond Our Personal Preferences

In this sense, our personal capacity for cultural and class sensitivity becomes an essential tool for fruitful and credible ministry and helps break down any lingering walls of hostility (Eph 2:11–14). As urban congregations experience global immigration and the migration of young professionals and artists, we must take a closer look at how we communicate the gospel and engage in Christian discipleship and fellowship.

Speaking to this, Keller gives several pragmatic cautions: "No church can be all things to all people" (p. 164). He expounds on the limits of our flexibility by saying, "We need to stretch as much as we can to be as inclusive as possible. But we must also be aware of our limits. We should not live in the illusion that we can share the gospel so as to make it all things to all people at once" (p. 35).

Yet here is another place where I would push where Keller cautions. If I were to identify one of the lingering challenges to urban ministry today, it is in our capacity to "stretch" beyond the homogenous unit principle affirmations of Donald McGavran's *The Bridges of God*. This remains one of the greatest missional and discipleship challenges that we must confront in global cities. This is more than just having Christians intellectually affirm the gospel; it is asking, What does the gospel do to our idols of comfort and personal preferences?

In my own ministerial journey, one of the most difficult tasks I've engaged has been cultivating broader fellowship with those who are different from me. As part of our ministry to the city, my wife, Jeanette, and I, are involved in discipling some people who would be considered "cultural elites." I host Bible studies with folks from Wall Street, local government, film, and professional sports. This is a part of how we are called to love the city and its people. We also serve a congregation with Chinese and Hispanic immigrants and their children. Even when we all speak English, it is difficult for us to worship together. I am acutely aware of how cultural barriers create obstacles to an integrated church. We all struggle with the idolatry of our cultural preferences. We all have personal preferences as well, and in this, anthropology and sociology are closely linked. We are not just individuals in a vacuum, but individuals formed by cultures.

Nevertheless, the cross calls us to self-emptying and sacrifice for the sake of the *communio sanctorum*—the community of the saints. Homogenized communities in a heterogeneous urban context are an obstacle to the visible witness of the gospel. The sermons I preach and the small groups we lead intentionally call people to "cross borders" by asking the question asked of Jesus: "Who is my neighbor?" (Luke 10:29). So even as we recognize our limitations, we must intentionally and repeatedly lift up the gospel ideal of an inclusive community. This requires intentional gospel-centered preaching and teaching on this subject.

Martin Luther was correct when he said, *"Crux probat omnia"* — the cross tests everything. There is *no* universal presentation of the gospel sans culture, and yet it is also true that we use culture as an excuse to isolate and separate ourselves from those God has called us to love and serve, namely, our neighbors. The cruciform challenge is how to cross cultural and economic boundaries. This is far too easily dismissed with appeals to temperament, styles, and personal preferences. And here is where the call for a *cruciform* gospel-centered ministry challenges me. Too often my ecclesiology is overadapted to the rampant individualism of our age and not to the gospel.

Discipleship and mission in urban centers require cultural sensibilities, but it takes more than this as well. It also requires cultural sacrifice and boundary crossing akin to the incarnational and kenotic model of Philippians 2 and the early church in Acts. Our sociological, cultural, physical, and linguistic limits must be taken seriously, but they must also be challenged by the gospel. We acknowledge our limits, yet the gospel calls us to transcendence.

The Gospel Is Not Always Pragmatic

Another pressing challenge is the triumph of pragmatism, one of the spirits of our age. Pragmatism is doing things simply because they work, not because they're right. Fruitfulness ought never to be seen as synonymous with pragmatism. There is a healthy tension between engaging the city effectively and challenging cultural assumptions of homogenization and stratification that can lead to the evils of tribalism, racism, and parochialism.

For much of my work in urban ministry, I placed mission and discipleship at cross-purposes. But it need not be this way. As Keller writes, biblical contextualization rightly posits that "our stance toward every human culture should be one of critical enjoyment and an appropriate wariness" (p. 51). As urban ministers we must balance the pragmatism of Sancho Panza with a quixotic and prophetic gospel denouncement of the windmills of isolation, tribalism, and classism that alienate us from God and each other.

Fruitful mission and faithful discipleship *can* and *should* walk together. The idea of center churches and center cities that pursue mission at the expense of discipleship or focus on discipleship while never reaching out distorts the balance of gospel-centeredness. I am acutely aware that no single congregation can truly represent the church in a given city. This is where we need to respond to this segregated ecclesiology with what Keller calls gospel movements that are profoundly collaborative. Nevertheless, if all of the congregations in our center cities are homogenized (as is the case in Manhattan and many other urban centers, particularly class homogenization), it indicates that the gospel has not sufficiently challenged our idolatry of class identification.

The late Jorge Lara-Braud, professor at San Francisco Theological Seminary and former director of the Council on Theology and Culture for the Presbyterian Church (U.S.A.) wrote, "A homogenous church in a heterogeneous society is an ecclesiastical heresy."[8] If we cannot worship together and transcend these differences, how has the gospel manifested itself as a new community and a new reality in our cities? Lara-Braud's complaint is akin to the one loudly sounded by Dr. Martin Luther King Jr.: "As a minister of the gospel, I am ashamed to have to affirm that eleven o'clock on Sunday morning, when we sing 'In Christ There Is No East or West,' is the most segregated hour in America."[9]

King's lament has legitimate grounding in the gospel narrative. Fortunately, we have some biblical models to navigate a culturally and economically diverse urban topography.

My Context at The Lamb's

The context in which my wife, Jeanette, and I pastor is a church called The Lamb's on the Lower East Side of Manhattan in Chinatown. The Lower East Side is one of those complex neighborhoods that some urbanologists have labeled "turning neighborhoods." This section, renamed by some of its newer neighbors as LoHo, nexuses Chinatown and Little Italy. Its boundaries stretch from Houston Street to Delancey Street, between the Bowery and the East River. This area once housed African Americans freed from slavery, immigrants from Ireland during the potato famines, Jews, Germans, southern Italians, and many more seeking better lives for their families. The motto of the LES can be read on the welcome signs scattered throughout the community: "Welcome to the Lower East Side ... where cultures mingle."

The Lamb's ministry has called us to examine not just the realities and contours of cultural difference in New York but also how the gospel calls us to respond to these sociological realities. As one of our West Indian parishioners once told me, "This is work that takes a certain level of maturity on behalf of the congregation as well as its leadership." Manuel Ortiz writes, "The experiences, training, and spiritual maturity [of these leaders] will decide the outcome and effectiveness of a multiethnic ministry that is biblically founded and sociologically aware of the community in which it has decided to serve."[10]

The leadership of a church in this context must be deeply aware of how preferences of communications, worship styles, and modes of expressions can lead to cultural syncretism and class captivities not consonant with the gospel. Leaders of the church, while engaging the city in culturally sensitive ways, ought to resist the temptation to replicate models that lead to homogeneity. In the words of Bruce Nicholls, "A contemporary example of cultural syncretism is the unconscious identification of biblical Christianity with 'the American way of life.' This form of syncretism is often found in both Western and Third World, middle-class, suburban, conservative, evangelical congregations who seem unaware that their lifestyle has more affinity to the consumer principles of capitalistic society than to the realities of the New Testament."[11]

This type of gospel-challenging, boundary-crossing ministry is what Jeanette and I have experienced on two trips to other major cities — in Madrid, Spain, and in Amsterdam, Netherlands. About a decade ago, in our church leadership development work in Madrid, we noticed that much of the church growth in evangelical communities was happening among immigrants from Latin America. Churches were sprouting up among Columbian and Venezuelan immigrants. Initially, much of that church growth and planting did not impact the larger Spanish culture. Yet in the years since this migration (which some have called "reverse mission"[12]), there has been significant growth in the progress of the gospel to nonimmigrant Spaniards as well. The ongoing challenge for this mode of immigrant church planting will be how they navigate transitioning from immigrant churches (often limited by linguistic barriers) to multigenerational ethnic churches that include those from the majority culture.

The strength of this model is akin to Paul discipling a young Timothy or Titus to reach the emerging demographic of Hellenized leadership, which could bridge both the Jewish and Greek cultures. I have seen this same dynamic at work in Latino-led and African-American-led congregations that are now multiethnic and multiclass, reflecting the diversity of the urban context. The leadership of people like José Humphreys and Mayra Lopez-Humphreys at Metro Hope in Harlem, Rich Villodas at New Life in Queens, Bryan Lorrits at Trinity Grace on the Lower East Side in New York, and David Anderson with Bridgeway in Washington, D.C., show that this is happening. These ministries are engaged in gospel-centered outreach to a kaleidoscope of urban dwellers. This is never a quick or simple process, but in the early part of the twenty-first century, it is showing significant fruit.

A similar immigration dynamic has occurred in the Netherlands. Large immigrant waves have arrived from Surinam and the Netherlands Antilles. Many of these immigrants have planted immigrant churches in the target language of their home country. Nevertheless, as the children of immigrants have come of age and have further integrated into Dutch society, there has been some cross-pollination. The tension between the missionizing impulse of these immigrant children and the secularizing inclination of the Netherlands provides an excellent case study in the gospel revitalization potential of immigrant waves in global cities.

Biblical Examples of Gospel Hybridity

What does all of this suggest as we consider our own approach toward discipleship and evangelism? As we conclude, I'll highlight a few biblical examples that provide a helpful framework for me in urban ministry.

The book of Acts is seminal for understanding gospel hybridity in urban ministry. Acts is a book of transitions. In Acts, as the early church became increasingly urban, it transitioned into a global and heterogeneous movement. These early believers had to navigate urbanization and globalization in faithful ways, and Acts is a primer on how they did this with gospel integrity. The early church transitioned from a Jerusalem-focused church to an ends-of-the-earth church, from a Galilean-focused leadership to a global church that included Hellenized-Jewish and Gentile leadership. Through these transitions, the guidance of the Holy Spirit and the commitment to the gospel helped them bear much fruit, no matter what the terrain.

The Pauline epistles call us to examine faithfulness in light of God's work in the world. As N. T. Wright posits, the faithfulness of Yahweh leads to the establishment of an iconoclastic global church that shuns ethnic and class divisions.[13] Saint Paul and his *missio Christi* understood the dynamic of a gospel that transcends parochialism in word and in deed. We begin with a particular worldview and locus, but then the gospel compels us to move beyond this to engage a broader, integrated global community. We do this for the sake of the gospel itself, not simply for sociological or pragmatic reasons.

Urban dwellers are a motley crew of humanity redeemed by Christ's cross and resurrection. Keller reminds us that the city is embodied in Acts 16 in all of its richness. We see Lydia the businesswoman, the nameless slave girl, and the blue-collar prison guard of Philippi. Though the method of gospel engagement is quite different in each case, all of these were called to belong to one new family—the church. Calling all three of these different types of people into gospel fellowship is the ongoing challenge we face today as well.

This has always been our Great Commission and our Great Commandment: preach the gospel and love our neighbors as ourselves. We must exercise discernment with the truth and grace of the gospel, a message that does not regard east or west, north or south, whether you are from the center or the margin. Calling all of these diverse groups of people to the gospel and to a new community is our mission.

RESPONSE TO GABRIEL SALGUERO

Timothy Keller

Grateful

Gabriel Salguero pays me a great compliment by likening some of my calls to the church to the challenges issued by writers like Reinhold Niebuhr and Dietrich Bonhoeffer, former teachers at Union Theological Seminary in New York City, where Salguero has done graduate study. He is right that my project to do practical gospel contextualization in the city is not new at all, and that I am largely trying to maintain what the older generation of evangelical authors such as René Padilla, Francis Schaeffer, and John Perkins initiated.

At Gordon-Conwell Seminary in the early 1970s, I took my basic course on "The World Mission of the Church" with Dr. Orlando Costas. Sadly, Costas died at a relatively young age and did not publish a great deal, but his instruction that year had a great impact on me. He introduced an understanding of church growth that looked beyond the numerical to the organic, conceptual, and "incarnational." Later, as their younger colleague at Westminster Seminary in Philadelphia, I came under the influence of Harvie Conn and Roger Greenway, who provided a rich theological grounding for this vision of city ministry very much in line with the writings of thinkers like Samuel Escobar and Costas. All of this is deep background to the material in the city vision chapters, which Salguero senses and affirms.

One of the theses that Salguero heartily endorses is that the city is "a complex topography." He does a brief survey of TV sitcoms—from

The Jeffersons to *Friends* and *Sex in the City*—to show they all are reductionistic simplifications of what urban life is like. It can't be reduced to stereotypes—crime and gang violence, yuppie playground, or ethnic enclaves. He therefore tweaks my statement that *The Bonfire of the Vanities* captured the spirit of 1980s Manhattan. It depends on which part of Manhattan you're talking about!

The account of his discovery of a church ministering to more than five hundred young people from the Fujian province who worked in the restaurants and hotels of Chinatown is a great example of the endlessly surprising character of the city. We can develop our categories, saying "there are seven types of people in the city" or "there are five kinds of neighborhoods in the city," but then we will continually discover things new and strange that don't fit into our neat categories.

On one of my first visits to New York City when I was considering whether to move my family there, I spoke with Barbara Benjamin Archilla, who had ministered in the city for many years. When I asked her what I should know, she responded, "You should know that the city is unmanageable." Salguero likewise warns against "the modern seduction of making the method the message" (p. 177). When people see a successful church in the city, "others are equally tempted to think these leaders have found the magic pill for fruitful gospel impact in cities. Keller rightly issues a clear warning here, one I am glad to echo. The complexity of cities cannot be reduced to any one model, no matter how successful or renowned."

Helpful

One of Salguero's helpful critiques is his response to my comment about churches using their resources to help the poor as an act of obedience to Jesus' command to do so and also as a testimony to the cultural elites who look on. Salguero responds, "This presentation of missional focus seems entirely too unidirectional to me" because it describes "ministry *to* the poor rather than *with* and *by* the poor" (p. 180). He goes on to briefly talk of the many ministries that treat the poor as objects, not as equals in Christ, not as members of the body of Christ from whom all can learn. He adds that he can't be too charitable here, because, he writes, "I don't see this as a minor point." This paternalism is perhaps the Achilles' heel of much of urban ministry.

This is an important warning and instructive to me as a teacher. Like other essayists in this series, Salguero feels keenly the lack in *Center Church* of much of the material that can be found in some of my other writings—in my book *Generous Justice*, for example. By design, *Center Church* does not try to reproduce all the content found in *Preaching*, *Generous Justice*, and *Every Good Endeavor*, all of which provide important instruction on a number of ministry topics in greater depth. Salguero's concerns about paternalism are absolutely right, but even though they are addressed well in *Generous Justice*, it is clear that some of the warnings need to be in the *Center Church* material as well.

A second area of milder critique has to do with the "homogeneous unit principle." I counsel in City Vision that we should stretch to be as inclusive and diverse as possible but also that we should know our limits. I say that no church can be all things to all people. Salguero thinks this kind of language does not encourage urban ministries to push hard enough to embrace a greater range of people. The biblical mandate to show Christ's power to unite people across cultural barriers is very strong (e.g., Eph 2). A church consisting of a variety of races and classes is not only a rich place to grow in Christ; it is a powerful testimony to the world. Using examples from his own life, Salguero urges us to never give up on this. He also is convicting about our deep inclination to "use culture as an excuse to isolate and separate ourselves from those God has called us to love and serve, namely, our neighbors" (p. 183).

I won't do anything to weaken this clarion call. He is quite right. My own statements should not be read as weakening this mandate. They reflect experiences I've had with churches and ministers who were deeply discouraged after years of frustrated efforts to become more multicultural. If I think they have done everything they could (and many have not), I'm likely to remind them of every church's limits. I point out that for every member of Group A that you can get into a multiethnic congregation, there is another member of Group A that will only be won to Christ in a more culturally familiar setting. That may be the case, but Gabriel Salguero is right that too many Christian leaders use such pragmatic arguments to undermine the Ephesians 2 mandate.

Intriguing

One final critique of the City Vision material is fruitful for reflection. It has to do with the question of where culture comes from. Salguero thinks I may be too dependent on the view of James Davison Hunter and others "that culture is formed primarily in the places of cultural elites and institutions." He calls this "idolizing the center." He counters that those at the margins of power also shape culture, and he points to the ability of social media to "democratize . . . cultural creation" (p. 178). He also points to influence points operating "*outside* the center" such as "the Harlem Renaissance, El Barrio's aesthetics movement, and the Dominican creativity of Washington Heights" (p. 179).

My first response is to ask some counterquestions: Why is it that the Harlem Renaissance and El Barrio's aesthetics movement didn't happen in the farmland of the Midwest? Why did they happen in New York City? Sociologists would point to "agglomeration"—the massing and accumulating of different kinds of talent and overlapping networks of capital in large urban areas that produce major social trends. It was because the artists of Harlem and El Barrio, despite their poverty, were near networks of business and media that their innovations had such impact. In other words, these movements *were* in the "center." Also, the ability of social media to democratize culture creation is not just the product of technology. In *A Secular Age*, Charles Taylor argues that the very power of "public opinion" in our culture (basically a new thing in history) is the result of two centuries of work by cultural elites to redefine the concept of authority and even of the self.[1]

Salguero's pushback here is good because it keeps us from lapsing into the simplistic idea that culture flows down, systematically and unimpeded, from elite institutions such as Harvard University, *The New York Times*, and major motion picture studios. However, I think it is just as reductionistic to think of culture as something that can be really redirected and reshaped by social media. Over the last two years, I've done much reading of Charles Taylor, who in various essays and books traces the development of secularity in Western culture. Our cultural journey to secularity was a "zigzag" journey—not a straight, linear process from one stage to the next, designed and planned by a small circle of elites. Rather, small movements and changes—whose makers did not envision the eventual outcome—coalesced and interacted with others to bring about slow, unforeseen changes in the direction of secular modernity.

Charles Taylor's history shows me that Salguero is right to say about cultural development, "None of this is fixed. Centers and margins are always moving" (though I think *A Secular Age* confirms Hunter's views more than those of his critics). But what is most confirmed by all of this is the power of cities to shape how human life is lived on the rest of the planet and the importance of Christians living and working in them.

Part 3

CULTURAL
ENGAGEMENT

Chapter 9

THE CULTURAL CRISIS OF THE CHURCH

The contemporary American church is pulsing with intramural debates. Within the church today, we see battles over the authority of the Bible, justification by faith, the atonement, gender roles in the family and the church, ways to conduct worship, and methods for evangelism, as well as innumerable disputes over the nature and ministries of the church. Then we have the more academic debates about the meaning of the kingdom of God, the character of God (e.g., "open theism" and "the social Trinity"), the "new perspective on Paul," the goals of the mission of the church, and questions surrounding issues of epistemology and the nature of truth.

On the surface these look like a diverse array of doctrinal disputes. But more often than not, lurking beneath these issues is the question of how Christians should relate to the culture around us. Some believe that the church's message is becoming incomprehensible to outsiders and therefore we should increasingly adapt it to the culture; while others believe that the church is already too influenced by the culture and we need to be more confrontational toward contemporary societal trends. Most church leaders are somewhere in the middle, but they can't agree on where we should confront or where we should adapt. As a result, the church is fragmenting even beyond its old divisions of denominational and theological traditions. Within each of the bodies of Baptists, Presbyterians, Anglicans, Lutherans, Methodists, and Pentecostals lie deep divisions over how to engage culture. In fact, there may be no more divisive issue in the contemporary American church today.

What has triggered this conflict?

Culture Shift

In the early part of the twentieth century, the fundamentalist-modernist controversy left much of the United States' educational and cultural establishment in liberal and secular hands, and conservative Christians in America responded by creating a massive network of their own agencies—colleges, periodicals, publishing companies, radio and television networks, and so on.[1] Nevertheless, the major cultural institutions of North America, although they rejected traditional Christian doctrine, continued to inculcate broadly Christian moral values. Most people in society continued to have views largely congruent with Christian teaching on respect for authority, sexual morality, caution about debt and materialism, and emphasis on modesty, personal responsibility, and family. Until the middle of the twentieth century, therefore, most conservative Christians in Western societies felt basically at home in their own cultures.

Sometime in the middle of the twentieth century, however, Western culture began to change rather dramatically. In Great Britain and Europe, church attendance fell precipitously after World War II.[2] And in the United States, while church attendance and religious observance rose initially after the war, by the late 1960s a major cultural shift was afoot. In their book *American Grace*, Robert Putnam and David Campbell call this a "shock" to American society's connection to Christianity and the church.[3] A "basic shift of mood" and crisis of confidence occurred, with regard not only to older ideals of patriotism and national pride but also to traditional moral values—particularly sexual mores. The very idea of moral authority began to be questioned.

In the United States, this new mood erupted with a vengeance and was widely transmitted through the youth culture of the 1960s. Popular music questioned all moral authority. Hollywood and television somewhat more slowly began to adopt the same tone. Two famous Westerns that came out in 1969—*True Grit* and *Butch Cassidy and the Sundance Kid*—represented the two clashing worldviews. The former expressed a traditional view of virtue, while the latter subverted traditional understandings of good, evil, and moral authority. In 1952, 75 percent of

Americans said that religion was "very important to them personally," but less than half of that percentage said so by the mid-1970s. Church attendance dropped from approximately 50 percent of the population in 1958 to about 40 percent in 1969, the fastest decline ever recorded in such a short span of time. Even more striking was the decline in church attendance among people in their twenties. In 1957, 51 percent of the members of that age group attended church; by 1971, that number had fallen to 28 percent.[4]

Most noticeable to Christians, however, was how the main public and cultural institutions of the country no longer supported basic Judeo-Christian beliefs about life and morality.[5] Before these changes, Americans were largely "Christianized" in their thinking. They usually believed in a personal God, in the existence of heaven and hell, and in the concept of moral authority and judgment, and they generally had a basic grasp of Christian ethics. A gospel presentation could assume and build on all these things in seeking to convict them of sin and the need for the redemption of Christ. Now, for more and more Americans, all these ideas were weakening or absent. The gospel message was not simply being rejected; it was becoming incomprehensible and increasingly hated. The world that Christians in the West had known—where the culture tilted in the direction of traditional Christianity—no longer existed. The culture had become a problem the church could no longer ignore.

Here is a personal case study illustrating this shift. My own parents—born in the 1920s—were evangelical Christians, while my wife's parents, who were born during the same decade and in the same U.S. state of Pennsylvania, were not. Yet if you had asked the four of them what they believed about the morality of sex outside of marriage, homosexuality, and abortion—or about almost any economic or ethical issue, such as going into debt or national pride and patriotism—you would have heard almost identical answers. Why? That era had cultural consensus about basic moral convictions. Yes, evangelicals often opposed smoking, drinking, profanity, and going to most movies—and those would not have been mainstream views. Nevertheless, evangelical churches could assume that the institutions of the culture went a long way toward giving citizens the basic "mental furniture" for understanding a gospel presentation. In the 1940s, a Christian minister could say to almost any young adult in the country, "Be good!" and they would know what he was talking about. By the late 1970s, if you said, "Be good!" the answer would be, "What's your definition of good? I might have a different one. And who are you to impose your view on me?"

Before this shift, nonbelievers did need to be persuaded of many doctrines in order to become Christians. They needed to understand that God was more holy than they had thought, but there was no need to convince them that God existed or that he got angry at disobedience. They needed to see they were more alienated from God than they thought, but there was no need to convince them that there is such a thing as sin or that there were moral, transcultural absolutes. People did need to see exactly what Jesus had done to save them, but there was less need to establish that Jesus lived and that he did the things the Bible said he did. People needed to learn that salvation was not by works but by faith; but virtually everyone had at least some idea of "salvation" and some type of belief in an afterlife. Finally, people needed to have the difference between faith and works explained to them, and how they had been relying on their works. They would often say to the gospel presenter, "Oh, I didn't realize that! How can I get it right?"[6]

In short, evangelicals could count on their listeners to at least be mentally able to understand the message of the Christian faith—a message largely seen as credible and positive. Their job was to convict people of their personal need for Christ and rely on the power of the Holy Spirit to urge them to make a personal commitment to Christ. Gospel presentations could be kept rather simple, stressing the importance of repentance and faith, without the enormous work of having to establish the very existence and character of the biblical God or the other parts of the basic framework of the Christian understanding of reality. In addition, it wasn't too difficult to bring people into church. It was generally understood that being part of a church was a good thing. In fact, those who wanted to be respected members of a local community understood that local church attendance would be part of the package.[7]

However, as the main cultural institutions stopped supporting Christianity, many Christians felt seriously out of place in their own society. In particular, younger adults became confused, resistant, and hostile to classic presentations of the gospel.[8] By the mid-1990s there was a growing sense that the conservative churches of the U.S. were fast losing contact with culture and society, despite the fact that in the late 1970s and early 80s the seeker-church movement had sought to make the church more appealing to contemporary people. The extensive study by Robert Putnam and David Campbell has shown this perception to be correct. While the mainline churches had begun their decline earlier, conservative churches were now in decline as well.

The reasons for this culture shift continue to be a subject of much debate, but one thing is certain: it became increasingly harder for evangelical Christians to be indifferent to culture.

The Stance of Pietism

How did most of the evangelical church in the United States relate to culture during the greater part of the twentieth century? The basic stance was to ignore culture and put all stress on conversions and on the spiritual growth of individuals. This was not, at its core, a particular model for relating Christ to culture. Some would say this was a form of cultural withdrawal or hostility, but I argue that this was not so much a negative view of human culture as one of indifference. Culture simply was not an issue. Too much attention to it was seen as a distraction. Young Christians had ministers and missionaries — not artists or business leaders — lifted before them as the ideals, not because involvement in culture was bad; it just wasn't the important thing. All were encouraged to enter full-time Christian ministry in order to evangelize the world.

Of course, in another sense this *was* a model for engaging culture, because this view often included a statement like this: "Yes, this society is not all that it ought to be. But the way to change the world is to change hearts one at a time through evangelism and discipleship. If we had enough real Christians in the world, society would be more just and moral."

I will call this approach "pietism." The word derives from a seventeenth-century movement within the church in German-speaking central Europe, in which the emphasis moved from doctrinal precision to spiritual experience, from clergy-led efforts to lay ministry, and from efforts to reform the intellectual and social order to an emphasis on evangelistic mission and personal discipleship.[9] Mark Noll argues that German pietism was one of the main sources (though not the only one) of contemporary English-speaking evangelicalism. Other sources included Puritanism and the revivalist Anglicanism of Wesley and Whitefield. These various strains or roots were not identical in their attitude toward culture. German pietism was greatly submissive to the state and culture, while much of Puritanism was not. So when American fundamentalism went into a more pietistic mode in the first half of the twentieth century, it was drawing more on one of its historical roots than on others.[10]

However, over the past fifteen years, many American evangelical Christians have abandoned the pietistic stance. Because of the (relatively abrupt) shifts in the West toward a post-Christian culture, many Christians were shaken out of their indifference. It became less possible for them to view the main cultural institutions as a favorable or even a benign force. They felt they needed to think about culture at the very least — and then to fight it, reclaim it, adapt to it, or deliberately withdraw from it.

Yet even if our social realities had not changed, there are several serious flaws in the pietistic indifference to culture. First, many have promoted the pietistic stance by arguing that increasing the numbers of Christians will somehow improve or change a society. But as James Hunter convincingly argues, numbers do not always equate to influence. Even if 80 percent of the population of a country are Christian believers, they will have almost no cultural influence if the Christians do not live in cultural centers and work in culture-forging fields such as academia, publishing, media, entertainment, and the arts.[11] The assumption that society will improve simply by more Christian believers being present is no longer valid. If you care about having an influence on society, evangelism is not enough.

Others who adopt a pietistic stance have argued that it is not a proper goal for Christians to try to improve culture at all, even indirectly. The nineteenth-century evangelist Dwight Moody was reputed to have said, "I look upon this world as a wrecked vessel. God has given me a lifeboat and said to me, 'Moody, save all you can.'"[12] This is a classic depiction of the pietistic mind-set. The argument is this: Who needs to engage culture when people are spiritually lost and dying? What should matter is evangelism and personal discipleship.

But this view is naive about culture's role in *preparing people for evangelism*. A pastor once explained to me how he became aware of this truth. He told me that for years he had encouraged the best and brightest in his church to enter full-time Christian ministry, not to enter secular vocations. Yet as the decades went by, he noticed that more and more people were not merely disagreeing with his gospel message; they couldn't even grasp the basic concepts of right and wrong, sin and grace. He confided, "I realized if all Christians only evangelize—if no Christians write novels or make movies or work in the culture at all—pretty soon the most basic concepts of Christianity will be so alien that no one will even understand me when I preach." It could be argued that this has indeed already happened. The culture's shift has exposed the significant problems with the pietistic stance of indifference toward culture.

The pietistic stance is also naive about culture's role in the process of *discipleship*. The reality is that if the church does not think much about culture—about what parts are good, bad, or indifferent according to the Bible—its members will begin to uncritically imbibe the values of the culture. They will become assimilated to culture, despite intentions to the contrary. Culture is complex, subtle, and inescapable, as we have seen in our treatment of contextualization. And if we are not *deliberately* thinking about our culture, we will simply be conformed to it without ever knowing it is happening. An interesting example is how churches in the evangelistic, pietistic tradition have readily adopted seeker-oriented models of ministry that use modern techniques of marketing and promotion without thinking about whether the very techniques themselves import the cultural values of consumerism and individualism.

The Emergence of Models

The movement away from the pietistic stance toward culture had humble beginnings. In the 1940s, a small handful of young men from fundamentalist churches began to pursue PhDs at Harvard and Boston Universities.[13] One of them, Carl F. H. Henry, recognized that while the culture still appeared to be largely based on Christianity, Christian morality was impossible to maintain over the long term in a society without Christian doctrine. In his seminal work *The Uneasy Conscience of Modern Fundamentalism*, he called Bible-believing Protestants to reenter major cultural institutions and engage as Christians "from a Christian worldview" in the public arena of scholarship, law, and art.[14] Twenty years later, Francis Schaeffer, who called Christians to relate to culture in this way, became the first popular figure to gain traction with an entire generation of evangelicals. He gave Christian perspectives on existentialism, the movies of Fellini and Bergman, the lyrics of Led Zeppelin, and the art of Jackson Pollack in an era when "Christian college students were not even allowed to go to Disney movies."[15]

As the pietistic stance faded, evangelicals began to search for models for relating Christ to culture, something they felt they hadn't needed previously.[16] One of the first alternatives that emerged out of the decline of the pietistic stance had its roots in the idea of "Christian worldview," especially as formulated by Abraham Kuyper of the Netherlands. Kuyper's views were perhaps most seminally expressed in "Sphere Sovereignty," the address he delivered at the opening of the Free University of Amsterdam in 1880. In his lecture, he argued that in the university, medicine, law, the natural sciences, and art would be studied and conducted on the basis of Christian principles, which had to be brought to bear on "every department, in every discipline, and with every investigator." "No single piece of our mental world is to be hermetically sealed off from the rest," he asserted, and then famously added, "there is not a square inch in the whole domain of our human existence over which Christ, who is Sovereign over *all*, does not cry: 'Mine!'"[17] All human activity and production are done for some end, with some vision, on the basis of some understanding of ultimate reality and the meaning of life—and this understanding will affect how the activity and production are carried out. Therefore, cultural production is something Christians should do, and they should do it in a way that accords with the glory of God. In other words, they should fully engage culture.[18]

In North America, this Kuyperian view of cultural engagement was first promoted by thinkers and institutions associated with certain strains of Reformed theology and has been dubbed "neo-Calvinism."[19] This movement called Christians to engage and change culture by carrying out their vocations from a distinctively Christian worldview. However, by the middle of the twentieth century, writers such as Gordon Clark, Carl F. H. Henry, and especially Francis Schaeffer had popularized the idea of worldview among American evangelicals, so that today the idea of Christian worldview as a basis for cultural engagement is widespread.[20] Through the writings of Schaeffer, James W. Sire, and authors of a host of other popular-level books and curriculum, the concept has spread broadly. It is fair to say it is a staple of Sunday school courses and youth ministry programs in the evangelical churches of North America. Joel Carpenter, in a paper delivered at Harvard Kennedy School, argued that the Kuyperian tradition of worldview has essentially captured most of evangelical higher education in North America.[21]

The original proponents of Kuyperian worldview engagement tended to be liberal in their politics — favoring European-style centralized economies and an expansive government with emphasis on justice and rights for minorities. However, another "wing" of Christian worldview proponents emerged in the 1970s and 1980s in the United States — the Religious Right. Many fundamentalist Christians such as Jerry Falwell, who had visibly championed the pietistic stance, abandoned it. Falwell and others came to believe that American culture was fast abandoning its moral values, and so he led conservative Christians to become a political force within the Republican Party.[22] The Religious Right made heavy use of the concept of worldview, as well as the notion of "transforming culture," but connected these ideas directly to political action in support of conservative policies. The expansive secularist state was seen to be an enemy that should be shrunk, and not only because it promoted abortion and homosexuality.[23] Conservative political philosophy believed that taxes should be low, the state shrunk to favor the private sector and the individual, and the military expanded. Those on the Religious Right often justified the entire conservative agenda on the basis of a biblical worldview. The movement claimed we needed political leaders who governed from a Christian worldview, which was defined largely as limited government, lower taxes, stronger military, and opposition to abortion and homosexuality.

A second response to the culture shift ascended around the same time as the Religious Right—the growth of the "seeker church" movement. Led by Willow Creek Community Church in the Chicago suburbs, the movement began in the late 1970s and grew to prominence in the 1980s.[24] One of the roots of this movement is the church growth trend that grew out of the thinking of missiologist Donald McGavran, who taught that non-Christians should not be asked to hurdle major cultural barriers in order to become believers. With this principle in mind, the seeker church movement detected the culture shift and recognized that Christianity was becoming increasingly culturally alien to nonbelievers. Its recommended solution was not "church as usual" (as with those who held on to the pietistic stance); nor was it "politics with a vengeance" (as with the Religious Right). Instead, this movement spoke frequently of the church's *irrelevance* and sought to "reinvent church"—principally by adapting sophisticated marketing and product development techniques from the business world—so it would appeal to secular, unchurched people.[25]

These two responses indeed represented major changes from the pietistic stance that essentially ignored or denounced culture. The Religious Right sought to aggressively change culture, while the seeker church movement called Christians to become relevant to it. It was not long, however, before Christians began to respond not only to the culture shift but also to these "responses." By the late 1990s, a new trend among young evangelicals appeared, known as "the emerging church."[26] The emerging church was yet another response to the ongoing cultural shift. Book after book was published, announcing the "death of Christendom" and "the death of modernity." Lesslie Newbigin had called on the churches of the West to have a "missionary encounter with Western culture,"[27] and by the end of the 1990s, a group of scholars had produced a book based on Newbigin's basic insights titled *Missional*

Church.[28] "Missional church" and "emerging church" became shorthand terms that described a new way of engaging culture.

But what is this new way? In reality, it is several different ways. Many young evangelical leaders agreed that both the Religious Right and the marketing techniques of the seeker church movement had failed to relate to culture rightly. They saw the Religious Right as evidence that the church had been taken captive by a naive loyalty to Americanism and free-market capitalism rather than to a truly biblical way of thinking and living. Others rejected the seeker church movement, perceiving it as a sellout to individualism and consumerism. To many Christians, both groups had become captive to Western, modern, Enlightenment culture. In response, those involved in the missional/ emerging church emphasized doing justice and rendering service in the broader human community—something that neither the Religious Right nor the seeker church (much less the older pietistic churches) had emphasized. Emerging church leaders also emphasized (as Francis Schaeffer did in his early years) involvement in culture making and the goodness of secular vocation. The movement's third emphasis was on spiritual formation and contemplative spirituality, often deploying spiritual disciplines that have historically been associated with Roman Catholicism and Eastern Orthodoxy.[29] These were offered as an alternative to the pro-consumerist seeker movement.[30]

However, the missional/emerging church has quickly fractured into numerous, semi-identifiable streams. Interestingly, much of the fragmentation is over the question of how to relate Christianity to culture. Emerging church proponents know what they *don't* want—the cultural obliviousness of pietism, the triumphalism of the Religious Right, and the lack of reflection and depth of most seeker churches. Yet they have not agreed on what the ideal model for relating to culture *should* be. Some of the churches in the emerging movement have been criticized as little more than seeker churches adapted to the more ironic sensibilities of younger generations. Others in the emerging stream have opted for a "neo-Anabaptist" perspective heavily influenced by such writers as Stanley Hauerwas and John Howard Yoder.

The dissension over different models continues through heated intramural debates within denominations and traditions. One example is within the community of conservative Reformed churches in which the Kuyperian "cultural transformation" point of view has reigned for decades. In recent years, a sharply different point of view has been advanced, often called the "Two Kingdoms" model for relating Christ to culture. Against the Kuyperian perspective, this group argues that "kingdom work" does *not* include transforming and redeeming culture, but only building up the church. In addition, those who hold to the Two Kingdoms model believe that Christians should live in the world as equal citizens with everyone else, appealing to commonly held intuitions about decency, right and wrong, and good order. In other words, Christians should not try to transform the culture to reflect Christian standards or beliefs.

● ● ●

What do we see today? Many of the historical models for relating Christ to culture are being rediscovered, tried, revised, and argued over. In the next chapter, we'll take a closer look at the most prominent current forms of these models. Usually I find it unhelpful to spend too much time critiquing the views of others; it is often better to move on quickly to constructing a positive plan for action. But in this instance I believe that thoughtful, compact critiques of the main streams of thinking and practice in the area of Christianity and culture will be helpful to you as a practitioner. Many find that seeing the models laid out side by side helps them both better situate and understand their own influences and "decode" the positions of those with whom they disagree.

In the end, my main aim in examining the models is to suggest that the way forward on how to best engage culture is a careful *balance* among several polarities. I believe the models we'll be examining each have a firm grasp of a particular important truth, yet they tend to downplay other important truths. As a result, in its purest form, each model is biblically imbalanced, finding itself on the edge of a precipice that we must take care not to plunge over—and none of them are, as D. A. Carson puts it, "compelling as a total explanation or an unambiguous mandate."[31] So in search of a more balanced approach, let's turn to the current landscape of models for relating Christianity to culture.

DISCUSSION QUESTIONS

1. Keller writes, "The contemporary American church is pulsing with intramural debates." Take a few minutes to list some of the deepest controversies that have taken up time and provoked debate within your own theological community or denomination. Which of these can be clearly attributed to culture shift and your community's views on Christ and culture?

2. Several causes are given for the shift in our culture away from traditional moral values (the rejection of authority, radical individualism, technological advances, etc.). Regardless of the cause, the gospel message has now become "increasingly incomprehensible" to people. How have you experienced this challenge as you communicate the gospel in your own cultural context? What aspects of the gospel do you find are most difficult for people to grasp?

3. Those who promote pietism argue that:

   - the way to change the world is to change hearts one at a time through evangelism and discipleship
   - increasing the numbers of Christians will somehow improve or change a society
   - it is not a proper goal for Christians to try to improve culture at all, even indirectly

   After reading this chapter, how would you respond to each of these objections? What are the strengths and weaknesses of the pietistic stance toward culture?

4. Which of the various religious responses to the culture shift described in this chapter (i.e., Religious Right, seeker church, emerging/missional church, etc.) have you been involved with? Did the historical overview in this chapter match your own experience?

Chapter 10

THE CULTURAL RESPONSES OF THE CHURCH

In response to the cultural crisis that has shaken so many evangelicals out of their pietistic stance, Christians (particularly in the United States) have been answering the question of how to relate to culture in four basic ways, which I will call the Transformationist model, the Relevance model, the Counterculturalist model, and the Two Kingdoms model.[1] In the previous chapter, we sketched out the historical emergence of these views and some of their animating ideas, and in the following chapters we will address them in greater detail. I believe that setting out these four basic categories is a clarifying and important preparation to developing a Center Church vision for cultural engagement.

The Problem with Models

Over the last three decades, the alternatives that have emerged to the pietistic stance roughly resemble many of the models laid out in H. Richard Niebuhr's classic book *Christ and Culture*.[2] Niebuhr lays out five basic ways of relating Christ to culture:

1. **Christ against culture:** a *withdrawal* model of removing oneself from the culture into the community of the church
2. **Christ of culture:** an *accommodationist* model that recognizes God at work in the culture and looks for ways to affirm this
3. **Christ above culture:** a *synthetic* model that advocates supplementing and building on the good in the culture with Christ

4. **Christ and culture in paradox:** a *dualistic* model that views Christians as citizens of two different realms, one sacred and one secular

5. **Christ transforming culture:** a *conversionist* model that seeks to transform every part of culture with Christ

Niebuhr considered the first model far too naive about the power of redemption and our escape from the effects of original sin. But he considered the second model far too untroubled by the cultural status quo and the ongoing reality of sin. He saw the third model as being at the same time too sanguine about both culture *and* Christ, lacking a sense of the importance of divine judgment, while he saw the fourth model as too pessimistic about the possibility for cultural improvement. Of all the models, Niebuhr considered the last model to be the most balanced — neither as pessimistic about culture as the sectarians and dualists nor as naively optimistic as the accommodationists and synthesists.

Still, even though Niebuhr presented these five models as distinct ways of understanding the relationship between Christ and culture, he acknowledged the "artificiality" of talking about models. He wrote, "When one returns from the hypothetical scheme to the rich complexity of individual events, it is evident at once that no person or group ever conforms completely to a type."[3] Niebuhr admitted that the sketching of models and categories has its pitfalls, namely, that some people conform well to a type, but many others do not.

Why use models at all then? I believe there are two reasons. The first one Niebuhr himself states: "The method of typology ... has the advantage of calling to attention the continuity and significance of the great *motifs* that appear and reappear in the long wrestling of Christians with their enduring problem. Hence it also helps us to gain orientation as we in our own time seek to answer the question of Christ and culture."[4] In other words, each of the models has running through it a motif or guiding biblical truth that helps Christians relate to culture. Each model collects people and groups who have stressed that motif, and by doing so, it helps us see the importance of that particular principle.

The second way the use of models helps us is by their very inadequacy. Many people and groups do not fit into any one category because they sense (rightly) that no one model can do justice to all of the important biblical themes. Within each model, then, there will be some who will be better at incorporating insights from other models, and some who conform exclusively to a type. So the fact that models often fail as descriptors is instructive in itself.[5] Through their limitations, models encourage church leaders to avoid extremes and imbalances and to learn from all the motifs and categories.

We can't make sense of what people do without relating them to others and noticing continuities and contrasts. This is the nature of modeling. Nevertheless, none of us like to be put into a category. Though I will show there are a variety of positions even within a particular model, some readers will still feel pigeonholed and should keep in mind that I am going to be expounding the sharpest and clearest versions of these positions. I realize that not everyone who identifies with a movement holds all its views in precisely the same way, and so I will necessarily have to flirt with overgeneralization. Yet if church and culture truly is the issue below the waterline of many of our struggles as the church, I believe it is critical to make and study maps of this particular landscape.

The Transformationist Model

The first model for cultural engagement is the Transformationist model, which engages culture largely through an emphasis on Christians pursuing their vocations from a Christian worldview and thereby changing culture. Since the lordship of Christ should be brought to bear on *every* area of life—economics and business, government and politics, literature and art, journalism and the media, science and law and education—Christians should be laboring to transform culture, to (literally) change the world. As we said earlier, this model is heavily indebted to the work and thought of the Dutch theologian and political leader Abraham Kuyper.

Kuyper contributed two fundamental insights to this debate. First, in every sphere of life Christians are to think and act distinctively *as* Christians. They do so because all cultural behavior presupposes a set of (at least implicit) religious beliefs. Everyone worships and is moved by some ultimate concern, and whatever this concern is will shape their cultural products. Kuyper's second basic insight is this: "Christians should articulate their way of thinking, speaking, and acting ... in the course of interacting with non-Christians in our shared human practices and institutions."[6] In other words, if as a Christian I am conscious of my Christian beliefs as I am living and working, these beliefs will affect everything I do in life. My culture making will move a society in a particular direction, and consequently I will be changing culture.

Though I am labeling as Transformationist those who center their engagement with culture on Kuyper's two key insights, it is important to note that the particular modes of application and implementation differ significantly among the various camps within this model. As we mentioned earlier, one of the groups is the Religious or Christian Right, who see cultural change effected primarily through political and issue-based activism. The language of the Religious Right includes calls for believers to penetrate cultural institutions, work out of a Christian worldview, and transform the culture in the name of Christ. The early architects of the movement (such as Francis Schaeffer, Chuck Colson, and others) based much of their work on Kuyper's insights. A 2008 article in *Perspectives*, a journal of politically progressive Calvinists, even lamented that the basic ideas of Kuyper—someone whom progressive neo-Calvinists consider their intellectual hero—had now become the basis for much of the Christian Right in the United States.[7] The Christian Right, of course, believes that a consistent biblical worldview leads to a conservative political philosophy.

Many have also pointed out the connections between Kuyper and a much smaller movement known as Christian Reconstructionism or theonomy.[8] This movement is based on the writings of Rousas Rushdoony, who advocated basing the modern state on biblical law, including much of the "civil law" portion of the Mosaic legislation.[9] Those in this camp envision a repristinated Christendom in which the government overtly supports the Christian faith and provides only limited tolerance for members of other faiths. Rushdoony often spoke of the "heresy of democracy."[10] Others outside of the United States have also made a case for a "confessionally Christian state."[11]

The original group in North America that invoked Kuyper for cultural engagement was comprised of neo-Calvinists. Yet this group differs sharply from the Christian Right and the Reconstructionists in several ways, most noticeably in their *politics*. The Christian Right is politically conservative, seeing low taxes and deregulated business as proper expressions of the biblical principles of individual freedom and private property. The neo-Calvinists, however, are center-left in their politics, seeing a progressive tax structure, strong labor unions, and more centralized economies as appropriate political expressions of the biblical principles of justice. And while those in the Christian Reconstructionist camp have taught that the civil government should be explicitly committed to biblical truth and standards, the neo-Calvinists speak instead of "principled pluralism"—the belief that Christians in government should seek principles of justice that can be recognized as such by nonbelievers because of natural revelation or common grace, and yet these principles clearly align with biblical principles as well.[12]

A second difference among the groups within the Transformationist model is in their overall strategy for *engagement*. The Christian Right typically seeks cultural change through targeted political activism against abortion and same-sex marriage and for the promotion of the family and traditional values. The strategy of the neo-Calvinists has focused primarily on education. A large network of Christian schools and colleges endeavor to produce students who "think Christianly" within every academic discipline and work in every field out of a Christian worldview. This view has influenced other evangelical colleges, publishing houses, and even a parachurch campus ministry—CCO (formerly Coalition for Christian Outreach).[13]

A third difference is *theological*. One of the main differences between the neo-Calvinists and the Religious Right has to do with neo-Calvinists' belief that Christians do not rely on the Bible alone when seeking guidance regarding business, art, and vocation. They teach that we can discern many of God's intentions for our life in the world by looking at creation, at "general revelation."[14] In other words, while neo-Calvinists believe there is a distinctively Christian way to carry out our cultural activity, they believe non-Christians can intuitively discern much of how God wants humans to live in culture. I believe this view helps neo-Calvinists make common cause with nonbelievers and adopt a far less combative stance in the public sphere.

Though we see clear differences among the various camps in the Transformationist model, all people working within this model share several commonalities.

1. They view "secular" work as an important way to serve Christ and his kingdom, just as is ministry within the church. They understand Christ's saving purposes as including not only individual salvation but also the renewal of the material world. Therefore, Christians should not only build up the church through Word and sacrament but also work to restore and renew creation.

Theologian Herman Bavinck taught that God's saving grace "does not remain outside or above or beside nature but rather ... wholly renews it."[15] Theologian Geerhardus Vos, following Bavinck, sees the kingdom of God operating in the world in two ways: first, *within the church* as it ministers in Word and sacrament, and second, when Christians live lives *in society* to God's glory. Vos writes, "There is a sphere of science, a sphere of art, a sphere of the family and of the state, a sphere of commerce and industry. Whenever one of these spheres comes under the controlling influence of the principle of the divine supremacy and glory, and this outwardly reveals itself, there we can truly say that the kingdom of God has become manifest."[16]

2. Even more than the other models we will examine shortly, Transformationists celebrate and assign high value to Christians who excel in their work and enter spheres of influence within business, the media, government and politics, the academy, and the arts.[17] This is due, I think, to the fact that Transformationists truly believe secular vocations are an authentic way of bearing witness to Christ's kingdom. In addition, those who embrace this model are more likely to see the importance of human institutions for shaping culture and therefore stress the importance of Christians living and working in them.[18]

3. All those in this category believe that the main problem with society is a secularism that has disingenuously demanded a "naked public square." In the name of tolerance and neutrality, secularist elites have imposed a particular worldview on society, forbidding believers from striving to see their beliefs and values reflected in culture. The assumption behind this is that Christians have been passive or that they have fallen into "dualism"—keeping their faith and beliefs strictly private and not letting them influence and change the way they live in public life. As I will show later, I believe this is largely a correct assessment and an important plank in the development of a faithfully biblical approach to culture.

Problems with the Transformationist Model

We can identify several significant problems with the Transformationist model, but I will begin by noting the movement of self-correction already going on within this model, especially within the neo-Calvinist part of the spectrum, and so my critique largely conforms to what members of the movement themselves are saying.[19]

1. The conception of "worldview" in Transformationism is too cognitive. The idea of "biblical presuppositions" is often understood as purely a matter of bullet-point beliefs and propositions. James K. A. Smith has written a book-length criticism of this aspect of "Christian worldview" movement titled *Desiring the Kingdom*.[20] Smith, a Calvin College professor, doesn't deny that ultimately everyone has a worldview. But he argues that a person's worldview is not *merely* a set of doctrinal and philosophical beliefs completely formed by reason and information. A worldview is also comprised of a set of hopes and loves—"tacit knowledge" and heart attitudes—that are not all adopted consciously and deliberately. They are more the result of experience, community life, and liturgy (or daily practices).

2. Transformationism is often marked by "an underappreciation for the church ... For [Transformationists], the implication is that the 'real action' is outside the church, not the church itself."[21] What really gets many Transformationists excited is not building up the church but penetrating the bastions of cultural influence for Christ. The problem here is twofold. First, just as pietism tended to lift up full-time ministry and denigrate secular vocations, Transformationism can lead to the opposite extreme. Much of the excitement and creative energy ends up focusing on cosmic or social redemption rather than on bringing about personal conversion through evangelism and discipleship. Second, as James K. A. Smith points out, worldview formation happens not just through education and argument (the neo-Calvinist emphasis) or mainly through politics (the Christian Right approach). Rather, it derives from the narratives we embrace, especially those that give us a compelling picture of human flourishing that captures our hearts and imaginations. These narratives are presented to us, not mainly in class-rooms, but through the stories we absorb from various sources.[22] Smith insists, therefore, that the liturgy and practices of church communities are critical for the formation of worldview. This is an important cor-rective. It balances the Kuyperian emphasis on penetrating the cultural institutions with the Counterculturalists' stress on the importance of Christians belonging to "thick" Christian communities (we will look at this in more detail shortly).

3. Transformationism tends to be triumphalistic, self-righteous, and overconfident in its ability both to understand God's will for society and to bring it about. One writer refers to a "hubris that one has both access to the power to get at the root of the problem and then the wisdom to know how to better the structures of society with insights from the gospel."[23] Part of this tendency to hubris is an overconfidence that we can glean from Scripture easily applied principles for economics, art, and government.[24] Neo-Calvinist philosopher Richard Mouw has joked that neo-Calvinists "seem to have an unusual facility for finding detailed cultural guidance in the biblical record."[25] This could read-ily be said of the Christian Right and the theonomists as well. The danger is that we may be tempted to think we can envision virtually an entire Christian culture. This is a failure to discern the Bible's redemptive historical story line. There is no book of Leviticus in the New Testament dictating what to eat, what to wear, or how to regulate a host of cultural practices. While there are important biblical values and principles that give guidance to Christians in business or public service—particularly a Christian vision of human flourishing—there are no detailed biblical plans for running a company or a government.

In addition, Transformationists can be overconfident about their ability to create cultural change. Slogans such as "taking back the culture" and the very phrase "transforming culture" itself lead to expectations that Christians can bring about sweeping changes. But as James Hunter masterfully shows, human culture is extraordinarily complex and not controllable by any one means. All changes that Christians can produce will be incremental.[26]

4. Transformationism has often put too much stock in politics as a way to change culture.[27] Hunter points out that government/politics is only one set of institutions in the cultural matrix, and he argues that the Religious Right, at least, has overestimated the influence of this institution. In general, he argues, politics is "downstream" from the true sources of cultural change, which tend to flow in a nonlinear fashion from new ideas produced in the "cultural centers"—the academy, the arts, the media companies, and the cities. Scholars generate new theories, some of which win the field and begin to hold sway. People influenced by the theories begin to act on them in other cultural institutions—teaching in schools, publishing books, producing plays and movies, using the narrative to cover the news—and slowly public opinion begins to shift. On the basis of this public opinion, laws begin to be passed.

An illustration is sexual harassment laws. Imagine trying to get harassment laws passed anywhere in America in 1910; it would have been impossible. A sea change had to come in our thinking about sex, gender roles, and human rights through all the various cultural institutions—all before laws could be introduced. Politics helps to cement cultural changes, but it typically does not lead them.

5. Transformationists often don't recognize the dangers of power.[28] As James Hunter points out, it is impossible for Christians to avoid the exercise of power in society.[29] Yet just as the pietistic stance underestimates the importance of human institutions, the activism of the Transformationist model often underestimates the danger of Christians becoming too absorbed in seeking and exercising power. Some Transformationists seem to think they cannot initiate any cultural changes unless Christians as a bloc gain political clout, but there are numerous examples of how the church loses its vitality when Christianity and the state are too closely wedded.[30] Miroslav Volf writes, "Christian communities [should be] more comfortable with being just one of many players, so that from whatever place they find themselves—on the margins, at the center, or anywhere in between—they can promote human flourishing and the common good."[31] Volf speaks of two "malfunctions" that a religious faith can exhibit in its relationship with culture. One he calls "idleness," and the other "coerciveness." Idleness—cultural withdrawal and passivity—is not a temptation for Transformationists, but coerciveness can be. Volf argues convincingly that Christianity, when true to its biblical self, is not a coercive faith. A proper understanding of the gospel, of the cross, and of Christian ethics would make it impossible for Christians to use power to oppress.[32] But it is not at all impossible to lose sight of these realities and to use power coercively in Christ's name. The Afrikaner supporters of Abraham Kuyper, for example, did so when justifying the brutal policies of apartheid in order to maintain a "Christian culture."[33] By setting our sights on gaining and retaining political influence, it is possible to miss the biblical themes of how God regularly works among the weak and the marginal and of how any truly Christian society must promote *shalom*—peace and justice for every citizen. One of the more worrisome aspects of the Religious Right to this point has been the apparent absence of concern for the poor.

The Relevance Model

The second contemporary model of cultural engagement we will call the Relevance model.[34] As with the Transformationist model, very different groups operate within it, and the spectrum here is even broader than that within the other categories. Indeed, many of these groups are pointedly critical of one another, and would cringe at the word *relevant* as a description of their ministry. Nevertheless, I think the word helps us identify a common thread connecting all of these movements and writers.

In H. Richard Niebuhr's scheme, his second and third models are the most positive toward culture. Niebuhr describes those of the second type—"the Christ of culture"—as being "equally at home" within the church and out in the culture.[35] This model sees Christianity as being fundamentally compatible with the surrounding culture. Those who embrace this model believe that God is at work redemptively within cultural movements that have nothing explicitly to do with Christianity. It sees Christ at work in all "movements in philosophy toward the assertion of the world's unity and order, movements in morals toward self-denial and the care for the common good, [and] political concerns for justice."[36] It is not just that these things are good in some general way—they are the work of God's Spirit. For Niebuhr, liberal theology was an example of this model. Liberal churches do not believe in an infallible Bible, an historical incarnation, an atoning sacrifice on the cross, or a literal resurrection. They reject any "once for all-ness" regarding Christian doctrine and salvation. They see God continually revealing new things and doing new things in history and culture.[37]

Another more recent expression of this approach is liberation theology, which grew out of the Roman Catholic Church in Latin America in the late twentieth century.[38] Liberation theology understood sin and salvation in radically corporate categories, so that Christian salvation is equated with liberation from unjust economic, political, and social conditions. Liberation theology fits the "Christ of culture" pattern because it sees movements of political liberation from oppression as God's work in the world—a work that the church should join. And so liberation theology "[obliterates] the distinction between the church and the world by identifying the purpose of God with the present historical situation."[39]

Niebuhr's third model is "Christ above culture" (also called the synthesist position). This approach has a stronger view of "the universality and radical nature of sin" than the second model, but nevertheless continues to have a very positive view of culture. The synthesists tend to be "both-and" people who feel no need to rethink and remake cultural products but rather to adopt them and supplement them with Christian faith. This model seeks to "build from culture to Christ."[40] Niebuhr names as the prime example of this model Thomas Aquinas, who sought to "synthesize the ethics of culture with the ethics of the gospel" rather than "transform" the ethics of culture with the gospel.[41]

The animating idea behind these approaches is that God's Spirit is at work in the culture to further his kingdom; therefore Christians should view culture as their ally and join with God to do good.[42] The primary way to engage culture, then, is for the church to adapt to new realities and connect to what God is doing in the world. Christians and churches that emphasize these ideas—those who embrace the Relevance model—share several common characteristics.

1. In general, they are optimistic about cultural trends and feel less need to reflect on them, exercise discernment, and respond to them in discriminating ways. Even one of the milder forms of the Relevance model—the seeker church movement—is much more sanguine about both modern capitalism and psychology than other models, and so it borrows heavily from the worlds of business and therapy without giving a great deal of thought to whether such methods import an underlying worldview and so reshape Christian ministry in the world's likeness.

2. People operating within this model put great emphasis on the "common good" and "human flourishing." They emphasize the modern church's failure to care about inequality, injustice, and suffering in the world. They call the church to work for justice in society, and they declare that only when it does so will it regain the credibility to speak to society about God. They see God at work outside the church, moving history toward greater reconciliation of individuals, races, and nations through various movements of liberation. Christians are to join in what is already happening—efforts to work against hunger, improve social conditions, and fight for human rights.

3. Those who hold to this model seldom speak of a Christian worldview. The very concept of "worldview" assumes a much greater gap or antithesis between Christian truth and human culture than this (more optimistic) model sees. Perhaps another reason Relevants do not talk much about worldview is that so many of them are sharply critical of the Religious Right. They intentionally avoid the negative rhetoric of "dying" or "declining" culture—or of "losing" or "winning" the culture—that characterizes that particular movement.

4. Relevants seek to engage culture by reinventing the church's ministry to be more relevant to the needs and sensibilities of people

in the culture and more committed to the service and good of the whole human community. While not condoning immorality and relativism, they locate the main problem in the church's incomprehensibility to the minds and hearts of secular people and its irrelevance to the problems of society. The church has lost touch with the people and the times, this group observes. It has failed to adapt to cultural changes. While others think Christians have become too assimilated to the world around them, this group assumes that, on the contrary, Christians are too withdrawn into their own subcultures, too hostile and condemning of nonbelievers, and too disconnected from them.

5. Adherents of this model make little distinction between how individual Christians should act in the world and how the institutional church should function. Every other model makes more of this difference, speaking of different "spheres" or "kingdoms," arguing that—no matter what individual Christians may do—there are some inappropriate ways for the organized church to engage culture. Relevants, however, issue a blanket call for the church to become deeply involved in the struggle for social justice. The mainline Protestant churches have for years seen their denominational agencies actively lobbying for legislation and engaging in direct political action. Many of the emerging churches also sense a mandate to become directly involved in justice issues in their locale without calling for any discriminating reflection on how politically involved they should be as an institutional body.

Whom, then, do we place within this category?

At one end of the spectrum, I put many of the older evangelical megachurches. Robert Schuller, a pioneer of the megachurch movement, was extremely open about how he applied the techniques of business and therapy to church ministry. In his book *Your Church Has Real Possibilities*, he lists "seven principles of successful retailing" and insists that any church that wants to grow must apply them directly to the church's ministry, including "excess parking."[43] Unfortunately, Schuller was just as open about reshaping doctrine along the lines of contemporary psychology, proposing that sin be redefined as a lack of self-esteem.[44] More doctrinally orthodox leaders such as Rick Warren and Bill Hybels have deliberately sought to be explicit about sin and judgment.[45] Nevertheless, churches that we could characterize as being in the seeker church movement still rather heavily rely on techniques of business, marketing, technology, and product development; have a strong emphasis on self-fulfillment and the practical benefits of faith to individuals; and use a language sometimes light on theological particulars.[46] They speak often about the need for the church to be "relevant" but little about Christian worldview or thinking out how to integrate one's faith with one's work and vocation.

Further along the spectrum, into the middle of this model, I would put many of the newer emerging churches, particularly those inspired by the old Emergent Village organization led by Brian McLaren and Tony Jones.[47] The emerging church strongly rejected the boomer-led megachurches as market driven, "canned," and "consumerist." They especially criticized the individualistic cast of these ministries and (at least in the 1970s and 1980s) their relative lack of involvement in care for the poor and in the struggle for justice in society. And yet their critiques have been more grounded in cultural analysis than in biblical and theological exegesis. That is, the main operating principle of the emerging church is its choice to adapt to the postmodern shift rather than to confront it.[48] An influential text that embodies this understanding of the church and mission is *Missional Church*, edited by Darrell Guder.[49] This book is a compendium of contributions that do not agree on all points. Some are more in line with the Counterculturalist model discussed below. But they agree on a couple of basic points, namely, that the kingdom of God is primarily a new social order of peace and justice that God is bringing about now in the world, and that the church's calling is to bear witness to it. The job of the church, in this view, is to discover what God is doing out in the world and to get involved with it.[50]

Finally, at the other extreme of the spectrum within this model, we might place those in mainline, liberationist theology groups. While many in the emerging church seek to blend doing justice with doing evangelism, many believe that doing justice essentially *is* doing evangelism. In this view, the gospel is the good news of the coming kingdom of peace and justice, and so, rather than calling for individual conversions, they invite individuals to join the church in order to work for justice. By the middle of the twentieth century, the World Council of Churches had interpreted the *missio Dei*—the mission of God—as God already at work in the world redeeming the whole creation by setting up a new social order of economic justice and human rights. It is not, they said, that the church has a mission and God blesses it, but that God has a mission already out in the world and the church must join it. "The world sets the agenda for the church" was their slogan.[51]

Problems with the Relevance Model

As with the Transformationist model, we can identify several significant problems with the Relevance model.

1. By adapting so heavily and readily to the culture, such churches are quickly seen as dated whenever the culture shifts or changes. The most visible case study is the fast decline of the mainline Protestant denominations. Ironically, it was their very adaptation to culture—their efforts to become relevant—that led mainline Protestantism to a place where it is now considered to be irrelevant and out of touch with the culture. Because they have removed the supernatural element and downplayed doctrinal beliefs, mainline churches appear to most people to be no different from any other social service institution. When a church becomes an organization that only offers social services, counseling, and other community activities, the questions many ask are, "Why does it exist? Why do we need this institution when it is doing, often somewhat amateurishly, what so many secular institutions are doing more effectively?" Many churches, in the name of adapting to the culture, have lost their distinctives and, consequently, the cultural power of Christianity.[52]

Even those in this category who are not theologically experimental—such as the evangelical seeker churches and many in the emerging church—place a heavy emphasis on adapting *methods* to new cultural realities. This often means such ministries look dated very quickly, unlike those in liturgical and traditional churches. Robert Schuller's church heavily adapted to the World War II generation and began graying by the 1980s, and the same is true of many seeker churches today.

2. A second critique has to do with the attitude this stance takes toward doctrine. Earlier, we discussed the need for contextualization, emphasizing that true contextualization begins with Scripture as a normative, nonnegotiable truth. But in this model—especially in its extreme forms—culture becomes normative over Scripture. **Of all the models, this one most often downplays the need for both theological precision and the insights of Christian tradition.** More than any other model, this approach encourages us to minimize or reengineer traditional doctrines in order to adapt to new cultural realities. Many young Christian leaders are moving in this direction, even though they are aware of the mistakes of the older liberal churches. Some raised in evangelical circles now call themselves "post-evangelical." They say they believe the ancient, orthodox creeds of the church, but beyond that, they do not wish to debate doctrine. They argue, for example, that the traditional evangelical belief in the inerrancy of the Bible is "rationalistic" and that the classic doctrines of substitutionary atonement and forensic justification are "individualistic." They are reluctant to speak of any doctrinal boundaries, of any inviolable beliefs that cannot be compromised.

3. Most of the different groups in the Relevance model share a significant emphasis on doing justice, on caring for the environment, and on carrying out various forms of social service. When these concerns are emphasized, evangelism and conversion may still be acknowledged and tacitly affirmed, but sometimes as no more than lip service. The main energy behind churches that follow this model is often directed not toward the teaching of the gospel and seeking conversions but toward producing art, doing service projects, or seeking justice. Churches that lose their commitment and skill for vigorous evangelism will not only neglect their primary calling, but will inevitably fail to reproduce themselves. It takes new converts and changed lives for churches to truly be of service to the community.

While the second and third criticisms are more appropriate to churches at the liberal end of the spectrum, the evangelical mega-churches are open to the criticism that by overly adapting to methods of secular management and therapy, the church has been diluted into a dispenser of spiritual goods and services and has turned its members into an audience of consumers. Traditional churches—with their emphasis on theological training, catechesis, and liturgical and ecclesiastical practices—produced real character and ethical change, but this kind of spiritual formation often does not occur in the typical evangelical megachurch.[53]

4. It is especially in this model that the distinctiveness of the Christian church begins to get blurry. Traditionally, the church has been seen as the only institution that ministers the Word and the sacraments; that determines what is the true, biblical preaching of the Word; and that brings people into a community governed and disciplined by called and authorized leaders. In the Relevance model, however, the importance of such distinct ministry fades. What matters is not what happens inside the church, but out in the world. If, as some propose, God's mission advances through historical processes moving toward increasing economic justice and social equality, this "removes the church from the equation of how God works in the world."[54]

The Counterculturalist Model

The third of our four models is what we will call the Counterculturalist model. I've given it this name because those within this model place their emphasis on the church as a *contrast society* to the world. And while other models of cultural engagement speak about the important concept of the kingdom of God, this model strongly emphasizes that the kingdom is manifest primarily as a church community in *opposition* to the kingdom of this world.

1. Those operating in this model do *not* see God working redemptively through cultural movements outside the church. Even the pietistic stance held hope that enough evangelistic work would eventually reform society, but this model does not agree. Human society will be what it has always been—the realm of "empire," of "the powers," of capitalistic markets, oppressive governments, and other social systems that crush people in order to increase the power of their leaders. Those in the Counterculturalist camp use the term *empire* to deliberately underscore how, even in a world of democracy and pluralism, oppression continues. They bluntly declare that we should not expect to see lasting improvements in society and harbor little hope that the culture can be transformed along Christian lines.[55] Their emphasis is on the dissimilarity between the kingdom of this world—a set of systems based on power and human glory—and Christ's kingdom, a community based on love, service, and the surrender of power. As Stanley Hauerwas and William Willimon have written, "The world, for all its beauty, is hostile to the truth."[56]

2. This model calls the church to avoid concentrating on the culture, looking for ways to become relevant to it, reach it, or transform it. In fact, the church should not be focusing on the world at all. If there is a cultural crisis today, they say, it is because the culture has invaded the church, and that consequently *the church is not truly being the church.* The church is to be a counterculture, an alternate human society that is a sign of the kingdom to the world. It should not try to turn the world into Christ's kingdom. Rather, the best thing the church can do for the world is to exhibit Christ's kingdom to it, largely through the justice and peace of its community.

3. This model levels sharp criticisms against the conservative evangelical church (particularly the Christian Right), the liberal mainline church, and the new evangelical megachurch. In their view, virtually all branches of the church in the West today have been corrupted by the "Constantinian error" of seeking to reform the world to be like the church. Counterculturalists predict that when Christians try to make the world more like the church, they succeed only in making the church like the world. Invariably, our attempts to influence or transform culture will become corrupted by power and dominated by the political economy of capitalism and liberal democracy. When this happens, the church will have prostituted itself and will no longer have anything of value to share with the world.

Those who adopt the Counterculturalist model look at the liberal mainline Protestants and note how they have become the "Democrat Party at prayer." They look at the Religious Right and see much the same thing—the "Republican Party at prayer." They believe that politicization—on both sides of the political spectrum—has alienated much of the populace and weakened the church's witness. Those who follow this model also criticize the evangelical megachurches as they try to be relevant and meet felt needs. This, they point out, only turns the church into a consumerist mall of services that reflects the reigning spirit of the world—the spirit of self-absorbed market capitalism. By simply giving people what they want, churches fail to confront the innate selfishness and individualism being nurtured by modern capitalism.

4. Counterculturalists insist that instead of trying to change the culture through this consumeristic narrative, the church needs to follow Christ "outside the camp" and identify with the poor and the marginalized. It needs to have thick, rich, liturgical worship that shapes Christians into a new society. The church does not "advance," "build," or "bring" the kingdom; it is to be a *sign* of the future kingdom to the world as it seeks to be a new human society ordered on the basis of God's law and salvation. Real Christianity, says the Counterculturalist thinker, is a life of simplicity, of material self-denial for the sake of charity, justice, and community. It means decreasing both geographical mobility (committing to a local church and a neighborhood) and social mobility (giving away large amounts of your income to those in need).

Who are the Counterculturalists? James Hunter has observed that of all the current Christian models for relating Christianity to culture, this approach has the most intellectual firepower behind it. Many Counterculturalists are scholars/writers who teach at or are associated with Duke University Divinity School, including Stanley Hauerwas, William Willimon, and Richard Hays. They are mainline Protestants dubbed by some as "neo-Anabaptists," who draw inspiration not so much from the magisterial Reformation (Lutheran and Calvinist) but the Radical Reformation of sixteenth-century Europe. The Radical Reformers demanded a sharp distinction between church and state, were often pacifists who refused to serve in the military, formed tight communities that were virtually or literally communes, and called on believers to avoid political entanglements.[57] In addition there are the actual Anabaptists—the churches that have descended directly from the original Anabaptist churches, especially the Mennonites and the contemporary Amish and Hutterites. John Howard Yoder's book *The Politics of Jesus* is an important guide to those who follow this model.[58] Another scholarly movement in this category is the "Radical Orthodoxy" of John Millbank and Graham Ward.[59]

Many who have been placed in the broad category of the emerging church also fall into this category, including evangelical thinkers such as David Fitch and Shane Claiborne. Claiborne is the most prominent member of a movement called the "new monastics." Like others influenced by the Anabaptists, they severely criticize capitalism and "empire."[60] They emphasize strong multiracial, cross class Christian community; a simple lifestyle; practical engagement with the poor; contemplative spirituality; and a prophetic stance against big corporations, the military, and consumer capitalism. The new monastics, though eschewing the idea of cultural transformation, tend to support liberal political policies, which puts them at loggerheads with the Religious Right and, typically, with evangelicals who remain in the pietistic stance. This also marks them out as different from seeker church leaders such as Bill Hybels and Rick Warren, who have tended to be more centrist or apolitical.[61]

The first two models we've examined (the Transformationists and Relevants) have typically contained a diversity of groups and thinkers whose practices and rhetoric differ quite widely. This is less true in this model. Of course, one could place the Amish at one end of the spectrum, representing those who take the spirit of a "counterculture" as literally as possible. In the middle of the spectrum are the new monastics, who live more within the mainstream culture than do the Amish but still create intentional communities and often live together in urban neighborhoods in direct contact with the poor. At the other end of the spectrum are those whose churches are not literally communal but whose theology is driven by the themes and motifs of the Counterculturalist model.

Problems with the Counterculturalist Model

As with the Transformationist and Relevance models, we can identify a number of significant problems with the Counterculturalist model.

1. Critics of the Counterculturalist model charge that it is more pessimistic about the prospect of social change than is warranted. To use a justly famous example, didn't Wilberforce accomplish a true and good social change when he and his allies worked to abolish slavery in the British Empire?[62] Was that an illegitimate project? It seems so, according to this model. A much subtler yet powerful example is the Christianization of Europe. Christianity permanently altered the old honor-based European cultures in which pride was valued rather than humility, dominance rather than service, courage rather than peace-ableness, glory more than modesty, loyalty to one's own tribe rather than equal respect for all individuals. Even though there is today some slippage in Western society back toward that pagan worldview, today's secular Europeans are still influenced far more by the Christian ethic than by the old pagan ones. And, by and large, Western societies are more humane places to live because of it. In other words, Christianity transformed a pagan culture.

The Counterculturalist model rightly warns us against triumphalism. But assuming we are willing to leave behind our utopian dreams of creating a Christian society or a "redeemed culture," history teaches us that it is indeed possible to improve and even transform some social structures. D. A. Carson writes the following:

> Sometimes a disease can be knocked out; sometimes sex traffic can be considerably reduced; sometimes slavery can be abolished in a region; sometimes more equitable laws can foster justice and reduce corruption ... Yet in these and countless other ways cultural change is possible. More importantly, doing good to the city, doing good to all people (even if we have special responsibility for the household of faith), is part of our responsibility as God's redeemed people.[63]

2. The Counterculturalist model tends to demonize modern business, capital markets, and government. There is a constant critique of capitalism (in almost all its forms) and a depiction of most business-people as greedy and materialistic. Also, its pacifism often goes beyond the simple refusal to engage in taking life in combat to the depiction of all human government as inherently violent. This view discourages Christians from getting involved in the business world (except for small entrepreneurial ventures with high social consciousness) or in politics (except at local levels in order to change neighborhood dynamics). James Hunter argues that, ironically, the Counterculturalists have in many ways been unintentionally shaped by late modern Western culture. In particular he refers to the movement's "neo-Nietzschean politics," which fuels resentment against power rather than appealing to truth, persuasion, and reasoned discourse. Hunter shows how, despite Counterculturalists' claim to eschew power and politics, this may be the most profoundly political of all the models:

> In some respects, neo-Anabaptists politicize their engagement with the world even more than the Right and the Left because they cast their oppositions to the State, global capitalism and other powers in eschatological terms. To literally demonize such powers as the State and the market as they do means that they draw much of their identity and purpose in the here and now through their cosmic struggle with them ... Their identity depends on the State and other powers being corrupt.[64]

Hunter then quotes Charles Matthewes as saying that neo-Anabaptists have a "passive-aggressive ecclesiology." That is, while claiming to refuse to be sullied by politics, they use the language of politics as much or more than any model, and while professing to avoid power, they use power language to demonize their opponents.

3. The Counterculturalist movement fails to give sufficient weight to the inevitability of contextualization, of a Christian community necessarily relating and adapting to the surrounding culture. As one writer observed, "The idea that the church can sustain itself as a discrete culture reflecting Christian values, isolating itself from the competing values of the secular world, is a problematic premise."[65] For example, Chinese Christians will certainly be shaped profoundly by their Christian faith. The current culture in China is the result of several traditions and worldviews—Confucianism, animism, and secular materialism. Christianity will certainly affect believers' "Chinese-ness." And yet, Chinese Christians are still Chinese. Think next of Finland. Finnish culture is the result of both Lutheranism and secularism. Orthodox Christians there will be quite different from much of Finnish culture and yet will still be Christian Finns, not Christian Americans or Christian Chinese. Their Christian Finnish-ness is not identical to Christian Chinese-ness. A pan-European/African multiethnic congregation in urban Germany will be different yet again.

Not only will Christians unavoidably be influenced by culture; they will unavoidably change the culture. All communities and individuals do, to some extent, shape the culture around them simply by living their lives. To give a specific example, when a group of new monastic, middle-class Christians moves into a poor community to serve it, they change it culturally by their very arrival. Their presence in the neighborhood changes property values, as well as the various flows of social, financial, and human capital in and out of the neighborhood. We can't avoid changing the culture. Speaking more generally, the way Christians choose to spend their time and money and how they do their work in the world will all necessarily be shaped by their Christian beliefs and priorities. These will in turn have an impact on how other people live their lives. James Hunter has noted that the separatism of the neo-Anabaptists stems in part from their almost wholly negative view of social power as evil. But everyone has social power, argues Hunter. So in the end, Counterculturalists are more involved in culture than their model admits.

4. A fourth criticism focuses on doctrine. Many in both the contemporary and the classic Anabaptist traditions are happy to affirm general evangelical statements of doctrine such as the Lausanne Covenant. However, because Anabaptist theology stresses the horizontal aspects of sin (e.g., abusing creation, violence in human relationships) and sometimes places less emphasis on the vertical (e.g., offending the holiness of God) in its understanding of Christ's work, **it tends to downplay the doctrines of justification and substitutionary atonement.** Often the primary understanding of the atonement is a form of *Christus Victor*, in which Christ defeats the powers on the cross. Some Anabaptist theologians strongly reject the notion of propitiation (that the cross satisfied the wrath of God) as a "violent" theory of the atonement.

5. Perhaps unintentionally, this model may undermine a church's emphasis and skill at evangelism—even more than the Relevance model may. The Counterculturalist advocates understand the Christian community itself—its unity and social patterns—as being *the* way of proclaiming the gospel to the world. They believe that "belonging precedes believing" and that evangelism consists of drawing people into an attractive community of love that is promoting justice in the world. This often means, practically, that the church puts little or no thought into how to clearly communicate verbally the gospel message in calling individuals to repentance. As we observed earlier, any element within a model that cuts off the motivation for vigorous evangelism can undermine the entire model. Without a steady stream of new converts and changed lives, the vitality and vision of the model cannot be fully realized.

The Two Kingdoms Model

Of the four models I am sketching, this final one—the Two Kingdoms model of cultural engagement—may well be the least-known among evangelical Christians in the United States. However, in its Lutheran form it has a long and venerable pedigree, as well as a place in Niebuhr's catalog of models (as "Christ and culture in paradox"). More recently, a number of conservative Reformed writers have undertaken a fresh articulation of this approach, claiming that it is the view John Calvin took of the relationship of Christ to culture and vigorously arguing for it on principles of Reformed theology, particularly as a counterpoint to the neo-Calvinist Transformationists who follow Kuyper.[66]

The name "Two Kingdoms" comes from the core teaching that God rules all of creation, but he does so in two distinct ways. First, there is the "common kingdom" (often called the earthly or even "left-hand" kingdom) established through the covenant with Noah in Genesis 9.[67]

In this realm, all human beings are members, and people know right and wrong through natural revelation or common grace. According to Romans 1:18–32 and 2:14–15, the light of nature and the human conscience give all human beings intuitions about God's standards of behavior, as well as wisdom and insight so that sin in the world is restrained. For example, even if someone does not believe the biblical teaching that God made man in his own image, nevertheless the sacredness and dignity of every human being can be known intuitively without belief in the Bible. Christians should be willing to work alongside non-Christian neighbors as co-citizens, sustained in their life together by God's common grace. Believers do not try to impose biblical standards on a society but instead appeal to common understandings of the good, the true, and the beautiful shared by all people. We love and serve our neighbors in this common kingdom.

In addition to the common or earthly kingdom, there is the "redemptive kingdom" (sometimes called the "right-hand kingdom"), established with Abraham in Genesis 12. Only Christians are members of this kingdom, and they are ruled not through common grace and natural revelation but through the special revelation of God's Word. They are nurtured within the church by means of preaching and the sacraments. In this view, building up the church—evangelism, discipleship, Christian community—is the only truly redemptive "kingdom work."

This twofold framework for the nature of God's rule is the animating principle of this model. Two Kingdoms advocates believe the main problem today is the confusion of these two kingdoms, whether by the liberal church striving for relevance or by newer conservatives trying to transform culture. From this conviction flow the following features of the Two Kingdoms model for relating Christ to culture.

1. Two Kingdoms proponents, unlike those in the Counterculturalist model (or those who take the pietistic stance), place a high value on Christians pursuing their work in "secular" vocations. We must not think we can only serve God within the church. All work is a way to serve God and our neighbor.

2. The Two Kingdoms model differs significantly from the Transformationists in their counsel on *how* Christians should do

their work in the world. While Christian work in the common kingdom has dignity and usefulness, Two Kingdoms advocates tell believers they are not to look for "uniquely 'Christian' ways of doing ordinary tasks."[68] A word that is conspicuously absent from Two Kingdoms discourse on secular work is the term *worldview*. As co-citizens in the common kingdom, Christians do not have unique ideas of the common good and human flourishing that non-Christians cannot intuitively know. There is no distinctively Christian civilization. Thus, according to the Two Kingdoms model, believers are not creating *distinctively* Christian culture.[69] They should not try to change culture so that it reflects Christian beliefs, nor should they think they are to "heal" creation. God's ruling power in the common kingdom is only to restrain evil—not to improve the culture by diminishing the effects of sin on human society. All that occurs in this realm is "temporal, provisional, and bound to pass away"—"not matters of any ultimate or spiritual importance."[70] When Christians are doing their work in the world, they are serving God and their neighbors, but they are not restoring creation or moving culture into a more Christian direction. Here Two Kingdoms thinkers join with the Counterculturalists in their criticism of Transformationism. The job of the church, they say, is not to change society but to simply be the church. There is no warrant for us to seek to create a Christian society.

3. **Two Kingdoms proponents part ways not only with Transformationists but also with Counterculturalists over their view of human government and the general world of commerce.** While Transformationists see the secular state as a huge problem, and Counterculturalists see it as a seat of violence and empire, the Two Kingdoms model sees a secular, neutral state as exactly what God wants, *not* a state coercively imposing religious values.[71] The Two Kingdoms view generally says the same thing about commerce and capital markets. These are not demonic (as the Counterculturalist says) or so fallen that they need to be redeemed (as the Transformationist says). They are spaces of common grace where Christians should pursue their callings with skillfulness and joy. Christians should not feel guilt and "unbiblical pressure" to establish Christian theories or practices of business or government.[72]

4. As a direct implication of everything we have said, Two Kingdoms advocates are very guarded about how much improvement, if any, Christians can expect to see in culture. They counsel us to avoid not only triumphalism but also great optimism. The Two Kingdoms model "demands limited and sober expectations ... The [common] kingdom, regulated by natural law, is severely limited in what it can attain."[73] As we have noted, God's common kingdom is predominantly a force for restraining disorder, not for building a new order. As VanDrunen argues, everything here on earth except for our souls and resurrection bodies is going to be destroyed. Nothing we do in the common kingdom, therefore, is of lasting importance. In the end, we should not expect too much out of this life — we should set all our hopes fully on the future hope of Christ's final salvation and return.

Is there a spectrum within this model, as we have seen to one degree or another in the others? Yes, there is. First, there is a distinction between the traditional Lutheran understanding of the Two Kingdoms and the recent version being promoted by conservative Reformed authors. Luther did not see the Two Kingdoms as the realm of the world and the church, but as the realm of the physical and the spiritual. For Luther, then, the visible, institutional church was actually part of the "temporal" kingdom in which even church government was ordered with a form of law, while the invisible church was the mystical communion of saints who live together under grace and in freedom.[74] Luther — and Lutheranism — did not believe, then, in as radical a disjunction between church and state as is set forth by contemporary Reformed Two Kingdoms advocates. Luther and Calvin called on kings and nobles to make Protestant reform the law of their lands.

There is also something of a spectrum within the Reformed Two Kingdoms camp. As we have seen, proponents of the Two Kingdoms view by and large resist the Transformationist idea that our worldview makes believers' work in the world profoundly different from that of nonbelievers. Two Kingdoms authors say that by means of common grace, not the Bible, God lets believers and nonbelievers know what they need to know to fulfill vocations in the world. Typical of this perspective is T. David Gordon, writing in *Modern Reformation*, where he strenuously argues that Christians out in the world do *not* do their work differently than nonbelievers do.[75] In his writings, Gordon insists that Christians do not labor in a "distinctively Christian" manner, nor do they seek to change the world or society.[76] David VanDrunen chimes in with this observation: "Generally speaking, believers are not to seek an objectively unique Christian way of pursuing cultural activities."[77]

However, Michael Horton, a prominent Two Kingdoms theologian and an editor of *Modern Reformation*, has taught that Christians *should* "pursue their vocation in a 'distinctively Christian' way."[78] This is a real difference, based perhaps on somewhat different views of the power of common grace or the purpose of Scripture, and yet with regard to Christian worldview, both thinkers are much more like each other than they are like Transformationists.[79] While Horton studiously avoids the term *worldview*, he has written that the form of Christians' work in the world *is* distinct from that of non-Christians, and that, while the institutional church should not be aiming to change the world, individual believers should be "salt" and should seek to reform society. He writes the following:

> The biblical drama, doctrines, and doxology yield a discipleship in the world that does indeed transform. It never transforms the kingdoms of this age into the kingdom of Christ (for that we await the King's bodily return); however, it does touch the lives of ordinary people every day through ordinary relationships. Not everyone is a William Wilberforce, but we can be glad that he was shaped by the faithful ministry of the Anglican Calvinist John Newton and committed his life to the extirpation of the slave trade.[80]

As we have seen, this is different in content and in spirit from what many other Two Kingdoms advocates have written. It gives more weight to the concept of worldview (without using the word), to the idea that the culture is fallen and distorted by sin, and to the hope that cultural reform is desirable and possible.

Problems with the Two Kingdoms Model

Several problems have been cited with the Two Kingdoms model.[81]

1. The Two Kingdoms model gives more weight and credit to the function of common grace than the Bible does. Two Kingdoms authors insist that Christians do not need to bring their understanding of the Bible and the gospel to bear on public life in order to strengthen it, because society is and can be kept healthy through the light of natural revelation given by God to all people. While this rightly highlights what the Bible says about the existence of common grace, it does not do equal justice to the biblical teaching that human beings suppress the truth they have (Rom 1:18–32) and therefore do *not* read natural revelation rightly. When John Calvin speaks of natural revelation in his *Institutes*, he strikes the balance perfectly. He writes the following:

> Let that admirable light of truth shining in [secular writers] teach us that the mind of man, though fallen and perverted from its whole-ness, is nevertheless clothed and ornamented with God's excellent gifts. If we regard the Spirit of God as the sole fountain of truth, we shall neither reject the truth itself, nor despise it wherever it shall appear, unless we wish to dishonor the Spirit of God ... Those men whom Scripture (1 Cor 2:14) calls "natural men" were, indeed, sharp and penetrating in their investigation of inferior things. Let us, accordingly, learn by their example how many gifts the Lord left to human nature even after it was despoiled of its true good.[82]

And yet, just before this passage Calvin writes that while it is true that "in man's perverted and degenerate nature some sparks still gleam ... [the light is nonetheless] choked with dense ignorance, so that it cannot come forth effectively ... [His] mind, because of its dullness ... betrays how incapable it is of seeking and finding truth."[83] Two Kingdoms advocates have often written as if natural law and common grace are enough to guide human beings—without the light of the Bible—to build a society that is peaceful and prosperous, one that fits human nature and destiny. But this seems to go beyond what the Bible teaches, namely, that human beings usually distort, suppress, and deny the natural revelation of God.

2. Much of the social good that Two Kingdoms people attribute to natural revelation is really the fruit of the introduction of Christian teaching—of special revelation, if you will—into world cultures. For example, Nicholas Wolterstorff has argued that the very idea of human rights came out of Christian teaching on the image of God. It did not develop, and perhaps could not have developed, out of other views of human nature.[84] Now, for highly complex reasons, the idea of human rights has gone global. Samuel Moyn has recently argued that human rights have filled the enormous vacuum left by the collapse of revolutionary socialism, as well as most other credible frameworks for grounding moral values and justice.[85] But we should still ask, "Where did the idea of human rights come from?" Since so many secular people support it, does this mean it is a product of natural revelation? No—it is the product of various factors. The world has been exposed to biblical teaching and has taken this insight of special revelation and given it a more universal, non-Christian meaning. But the basic ideas of inherent human dignity, the importance of forgiveness rather than vengeance, the importance of philanthropy and charity—all of these grew out of Christian civilization, for they were virtually absent in Western pagan and Eastern civilizations.[86] They now seem to have become permanent fixtures of contemporary Western life, even though the original basis for them, the Christian faith, has been largely abandoned by the culture.

Is it right, then, to strictly say that culture is ordered by natural revelation and hold that the Bible should not be brought to bear on public life? As Dan Strange observes, quoting Peter Leithart, the real condition in most Western societies is one of "middle grace"[87]—a complex interaction of concepts introduced from the Bible that get traction broadly for a host of other reasons, which we could eventually come to see as common grace.

A famous example is the abolitionist movement, led by evangelical Christians such as William Wilberforce and others. Christian leaders of the movement were inspired by views of human nature taken from the special revelation of the Bible. And yet they would have never been successful in their endeavors unless many non-Christian people had found the call to abolish slavery resonating in their hearts and consciences as well—the product of common grace. The question is whether non-Christian religions and people could have originally produced the idea that slavery per se is wrong. Historically, this idea grew out of Christian reflection on the idea of the *imago Dei*.[88] In other words, slavery could not have been abolished without common grace, but it would never have been abolished with *only* common grace.

3. The Two Kingdoms model implies or teaches that it is possible for human life to be conducted on a religiously neutral basis. This model wants the state to be secular and neutral. It denies the need for a Christian perspective on law, government, economics, and art. But it can be argued that the secular state is not only an undesirable goal. In the end, it is an impossibility. A secular state is really a myth—a disingenuous product of the Enlightenment.[89] As we observed in the chapters on contextualization, our practices are unavoidably grounded in fundamental beliefs about right and wrong, human nature and destiny, the meaning of life, what is wrong with human society, and what will fix it. All of these working assumptions are based on nonprovable faith assumptions about human nature and spiritual reality. Michael Sandel, who teaches a popular course on justice at Harvard University, states that all theories of justice are "inescapably judgmental." He goes on to observe that you cannot hold a position on financial bailouts, surrogate motherhood, same-sex marriage, affirmative action, or CEO pay without assuming some underlying beliefs about "the right way to value things." For example, when one person says women should have the right to choose an abortion while another says women shouldn't have that choice, each is valuing things differently—a valuation always based on moral beliefs that are not scientifically based. These implicit assumptions are acts of faith, and therefore there can ultimately be no neutral, secular state. All cultures and governments will be animated by certain of these acts of faith and not by others.[90]

Sometimes Two Kingdoms advocates will ask advocates of the Transformationist model, "What is the Christian form of auto repair? How should we do dentistry from a Christian worldview?" The fact that Christians and non-Christian dentists fill cavities in the same way shows that indeed we do share common intuitions about life and our common humanity in the *imago Dei*. And Two Kingdoms advocates are correct that the Bible is not a comprehensive handbook for running a business or doing plumbing. We quoted Two Kingdoms theologian T. David Gordon in a footnote earlier in this chapter: "The Bible is sufficient to guide the human-as-covenanter"—that is, as a Christian living in the covenant community—"but *not* sufficient to guide the human-as-mechanic, the human-as-physician, the human-as-business-man, the human-as-parent [or spouse] ... or the human-as-legislator."[91] Michael Horton has likewise written, "There is no difference between Christians and non-Christians with respect to their vocations ... If Christians as well as non-Christians participate in the common curse and common grace of this age in secular affairs, then there is no 'Christian politics' or 'Christian art' or 'Christian literature,' any more than there is 'Christian plumbing.'"[92]

The critics' response is that the Bible doesn't give a comprehensive handbook for *anything*, not even for being the church or living a Christian life. Gordon is right to say that the Bible does not give us all we need to know to be good parents or spouses. It leaves many details up to us—but what it does tell us is profound and powerful and makes Christian marriages different from those based on other worldviews and philosophies of life. The Bible speaks to an enormous range of cultural, political, economic, and ethical issues that have a marked impact on every area of life. Historian John Sommerville argues that Western society's most pervasive ideas—such as the teachings that forgiveness and service are more admirable than saving face and revenge—have deeply biblical roots that are very different from the shame-and-honor cultures in the pre-Christian Western Hemisphere.[93] Theologian Michael Allen reminds us that "Christian faith has [necessarily] cultural implications."[94] Many have argued that the very rise of modern science could have only occurred in a society in which the biblical view of a sole, all-powerful, and personal Creator was prevalent.[95] It seems naive to claim that Christian faith does not unavoidably shape culture in deep ways.

The issue of slavery provides an interesting example of how Christianity changes culture. While Christians are usually criticized for having waited so long to abolish slavery, Miroslav Volf points out how even in the New Testament the gospel was sounding its death knell. Paul told Philemon, a Christian slave owner, to receive and treat his slave Onesimus as a "beloved brother" not only "in the Lord" but "in the flesh" (Phlm 16 ESV). New Testament scholar Douglas Moo explains that Paul used the phrase "in the flesh" to refer to "that aspect of human life that is bound by earthly oriented interests (cf. NJB, 'on the natural plane')."[96] So Moo concludes that although Onesimus will technically remain Philemon's slave for the time being, "Paul is saying in effect, 'Your relationship with Onesimus will no longer be dictated by your legal relationship (master-slave) but by your spiritual relationship (brothers).'"[97] This is to so transform the use of power within the relationship that, as Volf states, "slavery has been abolished even if its outer institutional shell remains as an oppressive reality."[98]

As we reflect on these examples, we see that while the New Testament may not give believers direct calls to *transform society*, the gospel faith of Christians clearly had immediate and far-reaching impact on social and economic relationships, and not only strictly within the church. Indeed, then, Christian faith touches on and affects *all of life*, and to claim otherwise is to be less than fully faithful to the biblical or historical record.

4. The Two Kingdoms model produces a form of "social quietism." According to the Two Kingdoms approach, Christians should not be overconfident of our ability to improve or move the world to a greater reflection of Christian values. This approach, while it neutralizes the triumphalism of some elements of the Christian Right, can lead to the opposite error. As Kevin DeYoung states, this model shows an "unwillingness to boldly call Christians to work for positive change in their communities and believe that change is possible."[99] Michael Allen points to the uncomfortable case of the mid-nineteenth-century Southern Presbyterian Church in the United States and its doctrine of the "spirituality of the church." In his 1859 "Address to All the Churches of Christ," J. H. Thornwell laid out a classic Two Kingdoms view, insisting that "the provinces of church and state are perfectly distinct, and the one has no right to usurp the jurisdiction of the other ... The state looks to the visible and the outward; the church is concerned for the invisible and inward ... The power of the church is exclusively spiritual."[100] He goes on to defend the refusal of the Southern church to condemn slavery. Allen argues that the "spirituality of the church" teaching continued to affect Southern churches even into the civil rights era, where "many leaders and congregations objected to denominational support of social and political goals."[101]

5. The Two Kingdoms view contributes to too great a hierarchy between clergy and laypeople. While many adherents of the Two Kingdoms model encourage Christians to excel in their vocations and see them as a way to serve God, they do not view such work as "kingdom work."[102] The Two Kingdoms churches will in the end, then, be less celebrative of Christians in secular vocations than will the Transformationists. Not only that, but often within the church itself, the Two Kingdoms emphasis on the ordained ministry of the Word and sacrament can lead to "an exaggerated distinction between laity and church officers (e.g., evangelism is the responsibility of elders and pastors not of the regular church members)."[103]

Coming Together on Culture?

In late 2011, I wrote a blog post titled *Coming Together on Culture*. I noted that despite the division over Christ and culture in the Christian church today, I perceived that a percentage of people in each camp were listening to the critiques and were incrementally (and almost secretly) making revisions that moved them closer toward the other camps and positions.

In my blog post, I summarized the Transformationist and Two Kingdoms views, arguing that while each model had some imbalances, many were recognizing them and incorporating insights from various models:

> Transformationism is seen as too triumphalistic, coercive, naive about sin, and often self-righteous. It does not appreciate sufficiently God's common grace given to all people. It may not prepare Christians well to make common cause with nonbelievers

for the common good, or to appreciate the goodness of all work, even the most "menial" kind. It is criticized for putting too much emphasis on the intellect—on thinking out your philosophical worldview—and not enough on the piety of the heart and the reordering of our loves. It is critiqued for putting too much hope in and emphasis on Christians taking political power ...

The Two Kingdoms approach is seen as too pessimistic about the possibility of social change. Paradoxically, many holding this position are also too naive and optimistic about the role of common grace in the world. They argue that Christians can work beside nonbelievers on the basis of common moral intuitions given to all by natural revelation ... The Two Kingdoms approach gives too little weight to the fact that every culture is filled with idols, that sin distorts everything, that there can be no final neutrality, and that we need Scripture and the gospel, not just natural revelation, to guide us in our work in the world.[104]

The post generated some resistance. Michael Goheen, a noted author from the Kuyperian movement, countered that he and coauthor Craig Bartholomew (along with others), while solidly in the Transformationist camp, had "appropriated the work of Newbigin and would espouse a more missional Kuyperianism. That is, social engagement is not first of all to change society—that may happen but ... the goal ... is to witness to the lordship of Christ over all areas of public life and to love our neighbor as we struggle against dehumanizing idolatry."[105] Meanwhile, Michael Horton, a prominent Two Kingdoms theologian, wrote a post in response to mine, similarly objecting to the depiction of the Two Kingdoms position. Although six years ago he had written, "There is no difference between Christians and non-Christians with respect to their vocations" and "there is no 'Christian politics' or 'Christian art' or 'Christian literature,' any more than there is 'Christian plumbing,'"[106] he now wrote, "Nothing in the 2K [Two Kingdoms] view entails that 'Christians do not, then, pursue their vocation in a "distinctively Christian way"' or 'that neither the church nor individual Christians should be in the business of changing the world or society,'" and he added that Christian-led social reforms were good things.[107]

These two writers, however, despite their valid concerns about caricature, provide evidence that indeed there may be a "coming together on culture" among Christians. Mike Goheen's emphasis, still clearly within a Kuyperian model, has incorporated insights and critiques from other sources. And while many Two Kingdoms proponents indeed deny that (apart from their inner motivations) Christians do their work in a distinctive way or that they should be involved in trying to change society, Michael Horton's comments show an admirable facility to learn from the strengths and the critiques of other views. In the hope that I can contribute to this growing convergence, I turn now to some admirable examples of balance with regard to this issue, followed by an analysis of how the four models can relate more appreciatively to the insights of the others.

DISCUSSION QUESTIONS

1. This chapter summarizes four models of cultural response:

    - Transformationist model
    - Relevance model
    - Counterculturalist model
    - Two Kingdoms model

    Which of the four models most closely represents your own? Which models were you unfamiliar with? Which critiques did you particularly resonate with, and which (if any) did you find yourself objecting to?

2. Keller writes, "The fact that models often fail as descriptors is instructive in itself." Models are often inadequate, particularly when we are looking at the sharpest and clearest version of a position. Yet their very inadequacy can help us by revealing the limitations of a

particular view and encouraging us to avoid extremes. With this in mind, how would you summarize the greatest strength of each model? What do you believe is the biggest problem or weakness with each model?

3. Take some time to identify the various streams of theology that have shaped your thinking about the gospel and culture, noting the authors, mentors, traditions, articles, conferences, personal experiences, and biases that have influenced you. Has a particular stream of thought dominated your thinking about the church and culture, or have you been influenced by multiple streams? Which ones? Who were the key voices that shaped your practice into what it is today?

Chapter 11

WHY ALL THE MODELS ARE RIGHT ... AND WRONG

Earlier, we acknowledged the fact that dividing people into broad categories, or models, always has pitfalls. Some people conform well to the type, while others do not. Within a given model, we can find areas of pointed disagreement. And as we've seen in the case of the Christ and culture issue, people change; thoughtful proponents of certain models are always open to having their views tempered and enriched by insights from the others. We see also a growing body of work that appreciates and criticizes the various Christ and culture models and calls for a nuanced and balanced approach. I have cited several of these already—by Miroslav Volf, D. A. Carson, James Hunter, and Daniel Strange.[1] Perhaps the best reason for hope in a balanced Christ and culture model is the example of individuals whose thought and practice defy being contained within a single model.

Lesslie Newbigin, for instance, is often cited by Transformationists, Counterculturalists, and Relevants, even though they may not share all his doctrinal views. Counterculturalists respond to his stress on the church community itself as "the hermeneutic of the gospel,"[2] while Transformationists appreciate his emphasis on training Christians to integrate their faith with their work and influence culture.[3] For nearly everyone thinking about culture, Newbigin's analysis of the post-Christian character of the West is seminal. Most startling of all, Newbigin argues for the possibility of a government that is overtly based on Christian values. He contends that the logic of the cross should lead such a government to be noncoercive toward minorities, committed to the common good of all, and therefore could still allow a pluralistic society to flourish. It is an explicitly Christian political vision that does not sound quite like Christian Reconstructionism, with its claim that democracy is a "heresy," or like the principled pluralism of neo-Calvinism.[4]

Another hard-to-classify thinker is Jim Wallis, the author of *God's Politics*.[5] Wallis is a strong supporter of leaders of the new monasticism (part of what we are calling the Counterculturalist model). He wrote the foreword to Shane Claiborne's manifesto, *The Irresistible Revolution*, and yet he also calls Christians to invest in electoral politics, causing James K. A. Smith to ask whether Wallis promotes a "Constantinianism of the left."[6] He writes that Wallis focuses on "'people of faith' getting out the vote, lobbying congress, and doing everything they can to marshal the political process to effect prophetic justice." Wallis might be classified, then, as someone in the Relevance model, like mainline Protestants, or perhaps as a Counterculturalist. It is hard to say.

Yet another prominent example of a theologian who inspires reflection across the categories is N. T. Wright. Counterculturalists appreciate his reworking of the doctrine of justification so that salvation is not so much a matter of individual conversion as it is becoming part of a new community.[7] But Wright is not a Counterculturalist. He calls Christians to engage directly with the culture, suggesting that "through the hard work of prayer, persuasion, and political action, it is possible to make governments ... see that there is a different approach than unremitting violence." This he calls "restorative justice" and cites the example of Desmond Tutu in South Africa. He goes on to speak of calling governing authorities to keep in check those who through greed and force would otherwise exploit the poor and weak.[8] In this he sounds somewhat like the liberal political side of the Relevance model.

Wright sometimes sounds like a neo-Calvinist when he calls Christians to "advance the healing of the world" with "art, music, literature, dance, theater, and many other expressions of human delight and wisdom," and urges artists to "join forces with those who work for justice."[9] He concludes *Simply Christian* this way: "We are called to be part of God's new creation, called to be agents of that new creation here and now. We are called to model and display that new creation in symphonies and family life, in restorative justice and poetry, in holiness and service to the poor, in politics and painting."[10]

Finding a Way Forward

As we consider the various models and see thinkers who have learned from models other than their own, and as we witness those who have seemed to transcend or incorporate several models, how do we situate ourselves in the debate? How do we make choices about the proper way for Christians to relate to culture?

As we have seen, each of the four models has biblical support, and each effectively responds to a key problem the church faces in relating to culture. For example, is the lack of vibrant, courageous, effective evangelism a major problem that needs to be addressed? Certainly. But what about the failure of Christians to live out their worldview in the institutions of culture? Isn't it a major problem that Christians are vastly underrepresented in many sectors of the cultural economy? Absolutely. In the visual arts, literature and poetry, theater and dance, academic and legal philosophy, academic think tanks, major research universities, leading opinion magazines and journals, high-end journalism, most major foundations, public television, film, and high-end advertising agencies—there are few or no recognizably Christian voices.

And have we seen the church faithfully standing up for justice on behalf of those in need? Large segments of the Bible-believing church in the United States once supported the institution of slavery—supported by (flawed) biblical exegesis. This mistaken accommodation to cultural values led to an enormous loss of credibility for the church.[11] And this wasn't just a one-time event either. In the twentieth century, large segments of the church also supported segregation.

Yet we could also argue that the greatest problem for the church today is our inability to connect with nonbelievers in a way that they understand. Isn't it a major issue that the evangelical church exists as a subcultural cul-de-sac, unable to speak the gospel intelligibly to most Americans, and is perceived to be concerned only with increasing its own power rather than with the common good? Of course it is. Early Christian bishops in the Roman Empire, by contrast, were so well-known for identifying with the poor and weak that eventually, though part of a minority religion, they were seen to have the right to speak for the local community as a whole. Caring for the poor and the weak became, ironically, a major reason for the cultural influence the church eventually came to wield. If the church does not identify with the marginalized, it will itself be marginalized. This is God's poetic justice.

But perhaps the heart of the problem is our communal "thinness," the lack of distinctiveness in our own Christian communities. Isn't the church's real challenge today not only the views we hold but also our failure to practice a distinctly different way of life? Some evangelical Christians may refrain from drinking alcohol, but they are still as individualistic and consumeristic, as materialistic and obsessed with power pursuits, as everyone else. This is an enormous problem for our witness in the world.

Perhaps the problem, then, is in the ways we have repeatedly attempted to wield political clout and forcefully bring back a Christian-dominated society. Have our goals been misplaced? Have we been compromised by our focus on securing power and control through political means? Many, including sociologists Robert Putnam and David Campbell, have argued convincingly that this focus — this idol — is a real problem for the church today.

In short, the answer to all of these questions is *yes*. When we look at each of these models from some distance, it is clear that they all identify a real problem with the church and its witness in the culture. So it is not hard to see why each model has committed adherents. Each one is on to something — an essential truth about the relationship of the gospel to culture — that is extremely important. And yet none of them, taken alone, give us the full picture. None of them have been able to win the field. The core diagnoses of each model are correct and essential, yet incomplete. As a result, the core prescriptions are admirable and necessary, yet unbalanced. Is there a way forward?

Two Questions about Culture

I believe most of these concerns can be reduced to two fundamental questions. The first question deals with our attitude toward cultural change: *Should we be pessimistic or optimistic about the possibility for cultural change?* The second question exposes our understanding of the nature of culture itself and speaks to its potential for redemption: *Is the current culture redeemable and good, or fundamentally fallen?* Our answers to these questions reveal our alignments with biblical emphases as well as our imbalances.

Cultural Change: Pessimistic or Optimistic?

James Hunter argues that culture changes mainly (though not exclusively) from the top down rather than from the grass roots up.[12] Cultural changes tend to flow out of urban and academic centers. But these changes are typically not initiated by the innermost elites with the highest positions of prestige, for they have a vested interest in the status quo. Nor are they started by grassroots people at the periphery of cultural power, for they are often powerless to effect lasting change, being altogether shut out of institutions and cultural sectors that shape social life and thought. Instead, it is the "outer elites"—usually young men and women who are either low on the ladder of the highest-prestige institutions, or in the less influential or newer institutions—who initiate these changes.[13] In addition, the culture changes more readily when networks of common cause overlap different cultural fields, when the networks that initiate a change include people from the worlds of business, the academy, the arts, the church, and multiple other disciplines, all working together. Still, this is never a simplistic process or formula for effecting change. Because culture is a product of history, not merely of ideas, it has a kind of erratic inertia. It doesn't change easily or without a fight.[14] But it can, in the end, be changed.

This complex and rich understanding of cultural change throws a new light on each model. Each model has a tendency, especially among some of its more strident proponents, to be either *too optimistic* or *too pessimistic* about culture change. And within the groups that tend toward optimism, they tend to be too limited in their understanding of how culture can be changed. Some see the importance of arguing for truth claims, while others put more emphasis on the importance of communities and of historical processes—but any one of these can be the crucial factor in a culture shift. All of them can play a part, and none of the current models give equal or adequate weight to them all.

Culture: Redeemable, or Fundamentally Fallen?

D. A. Carson helps address the second question about the nature of culture when he points out how each of the models for cultural engagement fails to do justice to the fullness of the biblical story line or "metanarrative"—the great turning points and stages in the history of God's redemption: (1) creation, (2) the fall into sin, (3) redemption first through Israel and the law, then through Christ and the new covenant, and finally (4) heaven, hell, and the restoration of all things.[15] The Two Kingdoms model puts emphasis on the goodness of the material *creation*, the strength of the image of God in all human beings, and God's common grace to all people. Transformationists put greater emphasis on the pervasive effects of the *fall* into sin on all of life, on the antithesis between belief and unbelief, and on the idols at the heart of every culture. Counterculturalists stress the form of God's *redemption* throughout history, namely, by calling out and creating a new people, a new humanity, that exhibits to the world what life under Christ can and should look like. Finally, many of those in the Relevance category put great weight on God's *restoration* of this creation, on the healing of the nations, and on the resurrection from the dead.

All of these points on the biblical story line are covered well by the sum of the four models, and the implications of each point of the story line for relating Christ to culture are being faithfully thought out and applied. The problem, however, is that each model tends to overlook the implications of the points on the story line other than the one around which it finds its center of gravity. Two Kingdoms people are criticized for being naive about how people truly need the Scripture and the gospel, not just general revelation, to guide their work in the world. Transformationists are charged with being combative and triumphalistic, unable to appreciate the work and contributions of nonbelievers. Counterculturalists are said by critics to make such a sharp distinction between the world and the church that they end up missing some of the implications of both creation and fall—they underestimate the levels of sinfulness inside the church and of common grace at work in the world. The reality of sin that remains in believers means that the church is never nearly as good and distinctive as its right beliefs should make it; common grace in nonbelievers means that the world is never as bad as its wrong beliefs should make it. Finally, those in the Relevance category are often criticized for forgetting that the kingdom of God in the world is *both* "already" *and* "not yet." God is going to restore the creation, but he has not done it yet. To overlook the intransigence and darkness of human culture is to fail to take seriously enough the doctrine of the fall. To put more emphasis on serving the common good than on evangelizing the lost is to forget the "particularity" of redemption, of God's calling a people to himself. "In short," Carson concludes, "it appears that some, and perhaps all, of [these models] need to be trimmed in some way by reflection on the broader realities of biblical-theological developments."[16]

Biblical-Theological Resources

To move forward, we must seek theological balance, and by this I do not mean some midpoint between liberal and orthodox theology. Rather, D. A. Carson speaks of allowing the various points of biblical theology to "control our thinking *simultaneously and all the time*."[17] To flesh this out, we'll briefly survey the basic theological ideas that have special relevance for Christian cultural engagement and give initial direction about the specific balance we need to maintain in each area.[18]

Creation

The doctrine of creation tells us, first of all, that the material world is important. Unlike other ancient creation accounts, the earth is not the result of a power struggle between deities, but is a work of art and love by one Creator. A major part of God's work is his delight in continuing to sustain and cultivate creation (Pss 65:9–13; 145:21; 147:15–20). If God himself does both of these things—if he both cultivates and sustains the material creation *and* saves souls with his truth—how can one say that an artist or banker is engaged in "secular" work and that only professional ministers are doing "the Lord's work"?

In the Genesis creation account, Adam and Eve are called to be fruitful and multiply, to have dominion (Gen 1:26–28). Michael Allen writes, "Sandwiched as it is between divine declarations of creation's goodness, this calling suggests that familial, social, political, and economic activities are part of God's good intentions for the world."[19] The garden is given to human beings to care for and cultivate (Gen 2:15). A gardener does not merely leave a plot of ground as it is but rearranges the raw material so it produces things necessary for human flourishing, whether food, other materials for goods, or simply beautiful foliage. Ultimately, all human work and cultural activity represent this kind of gardening.

Fall

Michael Allen observes, "Death and sin limit the potential of culture, inasmuch as they skew the desires and abilities of cultural agents, who now pursue the wrong rather than the good."[20] Genesis 3:17–19 describes God's curse that falls after Adam and Eve sin. The text shows us that sin infects and affects every part of life. In a suggestive passage, Francis Schaeffer summarizes it this way:

> We should be looking now, on the basis of the work of Christ, for substantial healing in every area affected by the fall ...
>
> Man was divided from God, first; and then, ever since the fall, man is separated from himself. These are the psychological divisions ...
>
> The next division is that man is divided from other men; these are the sociological divisions. And then man is divided from nature, and nature is divided from nature ... One day, when Christ comes back, there is going to be a complete healing of all of them.[21]

So sin affects everything—not just hearts, but entire cultures, every area of life. The doctrine of sin cuts two ways. On the one hand, it means we must not think we can escape from sin and its effects by withdrawing into our countercultures; nor, on the other hand, can we forget that sin infects the way all work and culture making are done or that idols are at the core of every culture. Thus, under the category of "fall" we must take into account the complementary truths of God's curse and his common grace. Any goodness in the world—any wisdom or virtue—is an undeserved gift from God (Jas 1:17). Common grace is not special or saving grace; it is a restraining force that allows good things to come in and through people who do not know Christ's salvation.

A particularly important passage for this doctrine is God's blessing of Noah in Genesis 8–9, where God promises to bless and sustain the creation through means *besides* his redeemed people.[22] John Murray writes that common grace is "every favour of whatever kind or degree, falling short of salvation, which this undeserving and sin-cursed world enjoys at the hand of God."[23]

This biblical understanding of our fallenness—cursed yet still sustained by nonsalvific grace—is crucial for relating Christ to culture. The world is inherently good and sustained by common grace—yet it is cursed. Christians are redeemed and saved—yet they are still filled with remaining sin. The battle line between God and idols not only runs through the world; it runs through the heart of every believer. So the work and cultural productions of Christians and non-Christians will have both idolatrous and God-honoring elements in them. Cultural products should not be judged as "good if Christians make them" and "bad if non-Christians make them." Each should be evaluated on its own merits as to whether it serves God or an idol.

Against this background doctrine of the fall we remember Jesus' call to his disciples to be "salt of the earth" (Matt 5:13). Salt kept meat renewed so that it did not go bad. The salt metaphor does indeed call Christians to go out and be involved with the world—salt cannot do its work unless it is distributed. Christians are to penetrate all the arenas of society. But being salt means having a restraining influence on a society's natural tendencies to decline and fall apart. While social engagement is necessary and can be fruitful, we should not usually expect to see grand social transformations.

So while the doctrine of creation shows us the goodness of work and of so-called secular callings and gives us a vision for culture building, the doctrine of the fall warns us against utopianism and triumphalism.

Redemption and Restoration

The coming of Christ—his incarnation, life, death, resurrection, and ascension—holds great significance for cultural engagement. One of the most important aspects of the Christian understanding of Christ's salvation is that it comes in stages. As Francis Schaeffer has pointed out, sin has ruined and defaced every aspect of life, and so Christ's salvation must also renew every aspect of life—it must eventually free us totally from the curse on sin. As Isaac Watts wrote, "He comes to make his blessings flow *far as the curse is found.*"[24]

And yet Christ's saving and ruling power, often spoken of under the heading of "the kingdom of God," comes to us in two great stages. As Geerhardus Vos has observed, the kingdom of God is "the realm of God's saving grace," which is entered now through the new birth and faith in Christ (John 3:3, 5; Col 1:13). In this sense, the kingdom of God is already here (Matt 12:28; Luke 17:21; 21:31). But the kingdom is also, according to Vos, a realm of "righteousness and justice and blessing." It is a new social order (1 Pet 2:9) that shows itself especially in the church. The psalms vividly tell us that God's ruling power will heal not only human social problems but also nature itself, which is currently subject to decay (Rom 8:20–25). Psalms 72, 96, and 97 tell us that under the true king, grain will grow on the tops of mountains (Ps 72:16), and the fields, flowers, rocks, and trees will sing for joy (Ps 96:11–13). Herman Bavinck has noted that grace does not remove or replace but rather restores nature. Grace does not do away with thinking and speaking, art and science, theater and literature, business and economics; it remakes and restores what is amiss.[25]

To use Francis Schaeffer's terminology, the spiritual alienation between God and humanity is removed when we believe; we are justified and adopted into his family. But the psychological, social, cultural, and physical effects of sin are still with us. We can expect to see some healing now, yet full healing and removal of those results await the last day. So the kingdom of God, though "already" truly here, is "not yet" fully here (Matt 5:12, 20; 6:33; 7:21; 18:3; 19:23–24).[26]

Schaeffer suggests we can expect to see "substantial" healing now throughout the created order—but what does this really mean? Just how "already" and how "not yet" is the kingdom? Michael Allen puts it pointedly: "The real issue in the relationship of Christianity and culture, therefore, is … in what time and at what pace will these things happen?"[27]

Closely related to the question of *when* we see the fruit of the inaugurated kingdom is the question of the relationship between the church and the kingdom. Sometimes the Bible talks about the kingdom as though it operates inside the realm of the church alone; at other times it speaks as if it is outside the church, incorporating the entire world.[28] Just as the biblical teaching on our fallenness gives us complementary truths that we must resolve to hold in balance—the curse and common grace—so too does the biblical teaching on Christ's redemption. His saving power is already at work, but not yet fully here. This saving power is at work in the gathered church, but it is not exclusive to the church. Here again we see why the different models are correct—and yet how easily they can become reductionistic and unbalanced. We should expect healing from sin in all areas of life—private *and* public, within the church *and* out in culture. We must see the gathered church as the great vehicle for this restoration—and yet individual Christians out in the world can be said to be representatives of the kingdom as well. We cannot separate our spiritual or church life from our secular or cultural life. Every part of our life—vocational, civic, familial, recreational, material, sexual, financial, political—is to be presented as a "living sacrifice" to God (Rom 12:1–2).

The Landscape of Christian Cultural Engagement

What do we learn from this brief survey? The word *balance* thrusts itself on us yet again. The biblical material calls for a balance not of compromises but of "being controlled simultaneously and all the time" by all of the teaching in Scripture. A survey of the various Christ and culture models demonstrates precisely what D. A. Carson suggests — that indeed each of them fails to be controlled by all the biblical teaching *all the time*. Do those within the Two Kingdoms model do justice to the cultural mandate, the pervasive nature of idolatry, the insufficiency of natural revelation, and the reality of the kingdom outside the church? Does the Transformationist model do full justice to the "not-yet-ness" of the kingdom, to how much Christians participate with all humans in the common curse and common grace, or to the lack of clear calls to "take the culture" in the New Testament? Do those in the Relevance model do justice to the depth and pervasiveness of idolatry in all hearts and cultural products, to the particularity and offense of the gospel, and, again, to the "not-yet-ness" of the kingdom? Do the Counterculturalists do justice to the "already" nature of the kingdom or to their participation with the rest of the world in common curse and common grace? I think the answer to all these questions is, "Not sufficiently."

I have been making the case that each model is biblically unbalanced. That is, each has a pivotal theme that is true but insufficient, and the more we reductionistically apply that theme to cultural engagement without reference to other themes in the Bible, the more unbalanced the theological vision and the less fruitful the work. To visually represent this, I have created an illustration in which the four models are graphed against two axes. The vertical axis represents the *nature* of our cultural world ("Is the current culture redeemable and good, or fundamentally fallen?"). At the top is the belief that the world is full of strong common grace, that nonbelievers can readily understand natural revelation, and that God is at work in many ways in the world. At the bottom of the spectrum is the belief that the world is a dark and evil place, that God's natural revelation is hard to read, and that God's activity happens in and through the church alone. The horizontal axis represents the spectrum of views on our attitude toward cultural *change* ("Should we be pessimistic or optimistic about cultural change?"). On the left end of the spectrum is the belief that we should not actively try to change culture; on the right hand is the belief that we should be active in culture and optimistic about our efforts to change it.

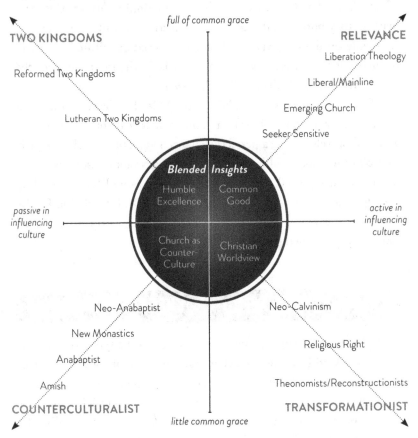

The Transformationist and Counterculturalist models are in the bottom half of the diagram because they share a lack of faith in common grace and a conviction of a radical antithesis between the world and the values of God's kingdom. As a result, they emphasize the need for a strong, prophetic critique of the idols of the culture. The Two Kingdoms and Relevance models are on the top because they are much more positive about finding common ground with nonbelievers in the culture.

The Two Kingdoms and Counterculturalist models are on the left because they both believe that strong Christian attempts to "engage" and "transform" lead to syncretism and compromise. Both call Christians to simply "be the church" rather than seek to change the culture. Meanwhile, the Relevants and Transformationists are on the right because they both spend much time reflecting on culture and enthusiastically calling Christians to become involved in culture in order to influence it for Christ. Each of the models on the right criticizes the two on the left for dualism and withdrawal.

If we ended this discussion here, it might lead to the conclusion that we can simply combine all the best of the models, leave out the extremes, and find ourselves with a perfectly balanced and faithful "über-model" that all of us should follow. To conclude this would be simplistic and incorrect. In my final chapter on this subject, I will lay out guiding principles for being faithful, balanced, and skillful in relating Christianity to culture in a fast-changing world—regardless of which model most shapes our own practice.

DISCUSSION QUESTIONS

1. Keller writes, "Some people conform well to the type, while others do not. Within a given model, we can find areas of pointed disagreement … Thoughtful proponents of certain models are always open to having their views tempered and enriched by insights from the others." What in this chapter challenged or provoked you? What did you find helpful? What did you disagree with?

2. This chapter provides two fundamental questions about culture to consider:

   • Should we be pessimistic or optimistic about the possibility for cultural change?

- Is the current culture redeemable and good, or fundamentally fallen?

How would you answer each of these questions? On a scale from 0 to 10 (0 = not at all, and 10 = highly), how optimistic are you about the ability of believers to change culture? On the same scale, how redeemable do you believe culture to be? Do you find yourself leaning in one direction or the other on each question? If so, why?

Possibility for Cultural Change

Pessimistic   Optimistic

0	1	2	3	4	5	6	7	8	9	10

Nature of Culture

Fundamentally fallen   Redeemable and good

0	1	2	3	4	5	6	7	8	9	10

3. D. A. Carson speaks of allowing the various points of biblical theology to "control our thinking simultaneously and all the time." How do the elements of the biblical story line affect your understanding and practice of cultural engagement?

   - creation
   - fall
   - redemption and restoration

4. Examine the illustration of cultural engagement on page 257. Where would you place yourself on this illustration? Where would you place each of your ministry colleagues and leaders? How can the different emphases within your team help to create a balanced, faithful perspective on cultural engagement?

Chapter 12

CULTURAL ENGAGEMENT THROUGH BLENDED INSIGHTS

As we have seen, the cultural situation in the West has forced every minister to adopt some model of relating Christ to culture. Many ministers, I believe, are largely unaware of the presuppositions, historical roots, or weaknesses of their model, or of the biblical merits of other models. Yet if you've come this far, I hope no one can say this of you. Nevertheless, you are still operating from within your own model. You have a personal history, temperament, church tradition, and ministry context that lead you to emphasize certain ways of relating to culture. In this chapter, I will offer practical counsel on how to operate faithfully and skillfully within the model you inhabit and with a balanced foundation.

Seek the Center

The first principle is that *proponents of each model should do their best to discern and incorporate the insights of the other models*. Referring to the illustration (p. 257), each of us should "seek the center"—i.e., to seek to face and operate close to the illustration's center. The main way to do this is to appreciate the seminal insights of each model, so we'll summarize them again here.

The Relevants are especially inspired by the coming shalom and restoration of all things. They emphasize the importance of a church that exists for others, *doing sacrificial service for the common good*. If the Christian faith is to have any impact on culture, the time must come when it is widely known that secularism tends to make people self-ish, while general religion and traditional morality make people tribal (concerned mainly for their own), but the Christian gospel turns people away from both their selfishness and their self-righteousness to serve others in the way that Jesus gave himself for his enemies. Just as Israel was told to "seek the peace and prosperity" of the great pagan city of Babylon (Jer 29:7), so Christians should be well-known as people who seek to serve people — whether they embrace Christianity or not.[1]

The Transformationists have a keen sense of the effects of the fall on human culture; their main focus is on *thinking and living in all areas of life in a distinctively Christian manner*. Most of our churches' discipleship models operate by drawing laypeople out of the world and into the life of the church — which can be unhelpful. D. Michael Lindsay's *Faith in the Halls of Power* shows that Christians who are deeply involved in cultural centers and institutions feel largely unappreciated by and alienated from the church.[2] Few churches actively support people to follow Christ in both their private and public lives, but the Transformationists are filling this gap.

The Counterculturalists point to God's redemptive strategy of calling out a distinct people for himself; their lead theme calls the church *to be a contrast community and sign of the future kingdom*, if we are to have any witness to the world. Those who advocate this model rightly argue that Christians who work as individuals dispersed within cultural institutions cannot give the world a Christian vision of human flourishing in the same way that a community can. The church can provide the best setting for shaping a Christian's worldview for work in the world.[3]

Those holding the Two Kingdoms view revel in the goodness of creation; their basic idea centers on the dignity of secular vocation and the importance of doing this work in a way *marked by an excellence that all can see*.[4] The distinctiveness of Christian work will have little impact, directly or indirectly, unless it is accompanied by excellence. Martin Luther is reported to have been asked, "How can I be a Christian shoemaker?" and to have answered, "Make excellent shoes for an excellent price" — in other words, be the best shoemaker you can be. The very act of honest work, even in its simplest forms, even when it is difficult to do out of a discernibly Christian worldview, is a wondrous good in and of itself. And therefore farming, police work, and other vocations in which we serve the common good are vehicles for God's love and care to the degree that they are done *very well*—with utmost skill and honesty.

These are the driving themes of the models. Each is represented as a line radiating out from the center of the grid. The farther you are from the center, the more you hold a particular model's theme reductionistically, with little regard for the insights of others, and therefore stand in great danger of failing to honor all of the biblical themes at the same time—creation, fall, redemption, and restoration. The center of the diagram, near the meeting of the axes, represents a place where there is a greater reliance on the whole cloth of biblical themes—marked by an effort to hold together the realities of creation and fall, natural revelation and special revelation, curse and common grace, the "already but not yet," continuity and discontinuity, sin and grace. The closer you are to the center of the grid, the more you hold your theme in balance with the other themes. This is a Center Church model for cultural engagement in which we seek to avoid the imbalances of triumphalism or withdrawal in the existing models and are equally loath to commit either cultural compromise or cultural withdrawal. A Center Church approach seeks to blend the cultural and biblical insights of all the models into our actual practice and ministry.[5]

For example, the Two Kingdoms model rightly lifts up the dignity and divine significance of *all* work done by all people. Regardless of who is doing it, any work done with excellence and skill that serves other people and the common good should be appreciated and celebrated by Christians. However, the Transformationist model points out the idolatries animating our lives, including our work, and therefore values work done from a distinctly Christian understanding of human flourishing. To combine both of these attitudes enables Christians to be both humble and appreciative of nonbelieving colleagues and yet not satisfied with doing work according to the reigning standards and philosophies in their field.

Miroslav Volf titles a section of his book *A Public Faith* "Two Noes and One Yes." This means, first, saying no to what he calls "total transformation"—to a goal of transforming the whole culture we inhabit. What Christians build culturally is not like the modern cities (Brasilia is the best example) that are built from scratch. It is like rehabilitating an existing city while living in it.[6] It means, second, saying no to what he calls "accommodation." Finally, we say yes to "engagement," which Volf describes as "expressing the middle between abandoning and dominating the culture ... what it might mean to assert one's difference while remaining within it," of "leaving without departing."[7]

Volf continues to spell this out by describing three stances that Christians can take to a particular element of culture. They can (1) adopt it as something acceptable, (2) take up the element but transform it from within, or (3) reject it and even work to abolish it in a society for the good of all.[8] By locating a large part of Christian difference in the unique biblical understanding of human nature and human thriving, Volf bridges a gap between the Transformationists and the Relevants. He makes shalom a critical goal of our culture making, yet insists that the common good be given biblical definition and content.[9]

I believe each model has at its core a unique insight about the world and a fundamental truth from the Bible that any professing Christian must acknowledge. And therefore, those within each model should seek in humility to find the genius and wisdom of the other approaches to better honor God's Word and his will.

Know the Season

So we should learn from all of the models, but does this mean the ideal position is one that does not fit into any of the models, that straddles the lines perfectly and balances all the insights and emphases of the models in perfect symmetry? I don't believe so, for two reasons.

First, H. Richard Niebuhr believed that Christianity's relationship to a culture went through a cycle.[10] He pointed to three stages of a historical cycle and how they follow one another.[11]

1. In the beginning, we have what Niebuhr calls the "converted church" in which the church and culture are sharply dissimilar and at deep odds with each other. The church is alien to the world. In this situation, the church emphasizes its distinction from the world and has strong standards for baptism and a high level of accountability within the community for Christian practice. It also engages in aggressive evangelism.

2. Next comes an "allied church" stage in which the church "enters into inevitable alliance with converted emperors and governors, philosophers and artists, merchants and entrepreneurs, and begins to live at peace in the culture they [these influential culture makers] produce under the stimulus of their faith." During this stage the church becomes far less rigorous in discerning signs of repentance and faith. Many people come into the church simply out of cultural pressure. The difference between the church and the world diminishes to near zero. At some point the culture itself begins to drift from its Christian roots because the church is no longer a spiritually dynamic force. Rather than the church shaping the culture, the culture shapes the church.

3. What happens then? A stage of renewal: "Only a new withdrawal [into the church as a contrast community] followed by a new aggression [of evangelism] can then save the church and restore to it the salt with which to savor society."

Niebuhr wrote in 1935 that this cycle has happened three times, and he was thinking of Western civilization when he laid out his stages.[12] Of course, to talk of three stages falls short of the complex reality. For example, Niebuhr is right that Christianity became corrupt, declined, and managed to come back. But did the reformers in the past face the hostile secularism of the modern West? I don't believe so; it is clear that to reengage a post-Christian society is not at all the same as evangelizing a pre-Christian society.

Here is one example. The pagans of the first and second century were astonished at the Christians' compassion for the sick and the poor. David Bentley Hart explains that Christians essentially invented orphanages and hospitals—no one had ever thought of them. Nicholas Wolterstorff makes the case that the idea of human rights came from Christian reflection on the *imago Dei*.[13] Christian compassion was therefore unique, attractive, and compelling to pre-Christian pagans. In our post-Christian society, this approach to human rights and commitment to compassion have been preserved, and therefore Christians' compassion and championing of human rights have a less dramatic effect on nonbelievers today. Indeed, because Christianized, European America committed genocide against Native Americans and allowed and promoted the African slave trade, the Christian faith is given little credit for the massive good that it has done for Western culture. Addressing post-Christian pagans is not at all the same as addressing pre-Christian pagans.

I want to adapt Niebuhr's proposal and suggest four seasons in the cycle of the church's relationship to a culture.

1. *Winter* describes a church that is not only in a hostile relationship to a pre-Christian culture but is gaining little traction; is seeing little distinctive, vital Christian life and community; and is seeing no evangelistic fruit. In many cultures today, the church is embattled and spiritually weak.
2. *Spring* is a situation in which the church is embattled, even persecuted by a pre-Christian culture, but it is growing (e.g., as in China).
3. *Summer* is what Niebuhr described as an "allied church," where the church is highly regarded by the public and where we find so many Christians in the centers of cultural production that Christians feel at home in the culture.
4. *Autumn* is where we find ourselves in the West today, becoming increasingly marginalized in a post-Christian culture and looking for new ways to both strengthen our distinctiveness and reach out winsomely.

At first glance, it seems that the Counterculturalist is most appropriate for "winter" (when there is a need to recover and nurture real Christianity); the Transformationist for "spring" (when cultural institutions are increasingly filled with Christians who need to be discipled for culture making); the Two Kingdoms for "summer" (when there is widespread cultural consensus on what human flourishing looks like); and the Relevance model for "autumn" (when many are still open to the gospel, but people are also beginning to question the relevance of faith for life).

This lineup is still too simplistic, however. For example, the American South and Sweden are both parts of post-Christian Western culture, but huge differences exist between them. In many parts of the

American South, the church still has a great deal of public influence and positive regard—it's still summer there. In addition, the models in their most unbalanced forms are never fully fruitful in any time or place. So for example, many champion the Counterculturalist model as the proper response to a post-Christian culture. It is often pointed out that the original monastic orders saved Christian civilization and evangelized pagan Europe. But is the new monasticism as effective and aggressive in its personal evangelism as were the original monastics? Many in the Counterculturalist model are in such a pitched reaction against the individualism of seeker churches and church growth movements that the message "you must be born again" is lost. Instead, they say, we should simply be a loving community that carries out justice and seeks peace. Often those with a Two Kingdoms mind-set place an emphasis on evangelism and discipleship, which, as we have seen, is especially crucial for a season in which the church is marginal within a culture.[14]

So there are no simple answers to the question, "What season is it?" Yet it is a question that we must ask. If all these models in their balanced formulation have biblical warrant, where will we situate ourselves? The answer is not simply an attempt to hit on the perfect balance between all four all of the time. As we have seen, each model has a "tool kit" of biblical themes and approaches, and our present cultural season helps us better understand which tools we need to take out of the kit and use.[15]

Follow Your Convictions

The second reason we cannot simply call for a perfect union of all of the models is that each one tends to attract people on the basis of their different ministry gifts and callings. As the apostle Paul has famously told us, while all Christians must have all the Spirit's "fruit" (or character virtues), no Christian has all of the Spirit's gifts. Paul indicates in such places as 1 Corinthians 12–14; Ephesians 4; and Romans 12 that God gives each Christian one (or perhaps more) spiritual gift that equips him or her to serve others in the name of Christ. So the model we embrace will likely be influenced by the temperament and spiritual gifts we possess. How, then, do we discern what our spiritual gifts are?

As a pastor helping people answer this question over the years, I have noticed that people's differing gifts are often revealed by the different human needs with which they resonate. Evangelizing is a duty of a Christian, as is helping the poor. But these ministries are also gifts — some people are especially gifted to do evangelism, and others to show mercy to those in need.[16] I often encountered people in my church who pressed me about particular ways that our church was failing in ministry. Some were passionate about evangelism; some were insistent we reach out to the needy; others bewailed how disorganized we were whenever we tried to do evangelism or mercy! I came to realize that some had the gift of evangelism, some of mercy, and some of administration, and their gifts made them particularly sensitive to certain kinds of problems. As their pastor, I needed to warn them that their gifts were giving them a bit of tunnel vision, but mainly I needed to train and release them into the area of ministry the Spirit was calling them through the distribution of his gifts.

I believe something similar (and related) is happening when it comes to these models of Christ and culture. As I read books by people who have thought through these matters, it seems that virtually no one can be neutral, unbiased, and uncommitted to a particular model. I have quoted from the works of Daniel Strange, Miroslav Volf, James Hunter, and many others — but as balanced and nuanced as these writers are, they usually show they are most comfortable with one particular model and most conversant with one model's set of tools. Michael Goheen has done deep reading for years in the "missional" writings of David Bosch, Lesslie Newbigin, and others; has incorporated much of what we call Counterculturalist thinking; and yet considers himself a Kuyperian.[17] Kevin DeYoung wrote a blog post in which he critiqued both the Transformationist and the Two Kingdoms models. He drew this conclusion:

> Perhaps there is — I can't believe I'm going to say it — a middle ground. I say, let's not lose the heart of the gospel, divine self-satisfaction through self-substitution. And let's not apologize for challenging Christians to show this same kind of dying love to

others. Let's not be embarrassed by the doctrine of hell and the necessity of repentance and regeneration. And let's not be afraid to do good to all people, especially to the household of faith. Let's work against the injustices and suffering in our day, and let's be realistic that the poor, as Jesus said, will always be among us. Bottom line: let's work for change where God calls us and gifts us, but let's not forget that the Great Commission summons us to go into the world and make disciples, not to go into the world and build the kingdom.[18]

Nevertheless, DeYoung wishes to identify most with what he calls the "careful two kingdoms theology."[19]

Why do each of us tend to feel most comfortable with one of these models? My view is that it has to do largely with our gifts and calling. There is little doubt that people with gifts and a personal calling to serve the poor tend to be attracted to forms of the Relevance or Counterculturalist models. People with the greatest passion for evangelism will tend to appreciate the Two Kingdoms or perhaps the Transformationist model. Many have charged Transformationism with being the Christ and culture model that only college-educated people with an intellectual or academic bent can love or even understand. All of these observations are correct to some degree.

So what does this mean? I believe it indicates we should inhabit the model that fits our convictions, whose "tool kit" best fits our gifts. Once we know our model, we should be able, depending on the cultural seasons and context, to use tools from the other kits. On this point, Andy Crouch's distinction between postures and gestures is a vivid and elegant way to express this flexibility. Crouch sees our basic model or stance toward culture to be a "posture" — our "unconscious default position" — but a "gesture" is an ad hoc move that briefly seems to come out of another model. A person whose posture is highly antagonistic to culture in general might still in a gesture accept some particular cultural trend, while a person whose posture toward culture is mainly friendly may still in a gesture feel a particular cultural element must be completely condemned.[20]

Remember the Difference between
Organized and *Organic*

One of the greatest points of tension between the models is in the way they understand the *mission* of the church. The traditional understanding of the Great Commission is that the church has been given the mandate to go into all the world to preach the gospel in order to make disciples of men and women from all nations.[21] But three of the four models seem to add significantly to this mission. Many fear that emphasizing mercy and justice, or political and cultural engagement, will displace or at least severely erode the church's capacity for evangelism and discipleship. In reaction to this emphasis, many are adopting a Two Kingdoms model, which clearly insists that the mission of the church is only and strictly to preach the Word, evangelize, and make disciples. While warnings about the "social gospel" are warranted, I believe we must still come to grips with the Bible's call to the Christian community to do justice and love mercy. But how?

At this point it is important to remind ourselves of the critical distinction between the "church institutional" and the "church organic." Abraham Kuyper taught that the church institutional was the gathered church, organized under its officers and ministers. It is called to do "Word and sacrament" — to preach the gospel, baptize, and make disciples. This he distinguished from the church organic, referring to all Christians living in the world who have been discipled and equipped to bring the gospel to bear on all of life. We should not think of Christians out in the world as merely distinct and detached individuals. They are the body of Christ, the church. As Christians in the world, they are still to think and work together, banding together in creative forms, being the church organic that the church institutional has discipled them to be. Theologian John Bolt writes the following:

> In Kuyper's view, Christians who go out into their various vocations
> do so neither as direct emissaries of the institutional church nor as
> mere individual believers ... Christian social, cultural, and political
> action does not flow directly from structures and authorities of the

church, but comes to expression organically in the various spheres of life as believers live out the faith and spirituality that develops and is nurtured in the church's worship and discipline.[22]

Michael Allen points out that H. Richard Niebuhr himself failed to distinguish between the rights and responsibilities of the Christian and those of the church, and this oversight has been deadly to mainline churches. Allen contrasts the mistake of the "spirituality of the church" doctrine that led to the Southern U.S. churches' support of slavery with the opposite error of mainline Protestant denominations that have become deeply and institutionally involved in politics. "One story shows a church that will not address any social ills, even the evils of chattel slavery, while the other tale portrays a church speaking authoritatively, even lobbying, with regard to very detailed political action plans."[23] Kuyper's distinction solves this dilemma well. A church that is educating and discipling people to do justice in the public sphere will have to be sensitive to social issues and ills in its teaching and preaching, and yet it will not make the fatal mistake of becoming a lobbying group and losing sight of its main mission.[24]

This distinction helps to bridge the gaps between the Christ and culture models. If it is maintained, then those becoming enamored with justice and cultural engagement will avoid falling into the error of the older mainline churches that lost their vision for evangelism and discipleship. On the other hand, faithful churches concerned to maintain the mission of the church as disciple making will disciple people to evangelize — but also to engage culture and do justice.

Act, Don't React

I've become convinced that one of the reasons we have not seen more balanced cultural engagement "near the center" is that many of us are not choosing our Christ and culture model in the right way. Instead of looking at Scripture, the culture, and our own gifts and calling, we tend to form our views in visceral reactions to the behavior of other Christians. In other words, we stand here and not there because *those* people are there and not here. While it is true that all of these models draw on older antecedents and patterns that have been in the church for centuries, there is a tendency for their contemporary versions to be defined in reaction and hostility to one another. The various groups are like large tectonic plates along which major and minor eruptions and quakes happen constantly. Each camp is calling the church to do different things, and they regularly attack one another for the ways they emphasize their differences. Indeed, they can most easily raise money from donors by depicting themselves as the faithful antidote to the other groups.

This tendency—to react rather than act—lies behind the reductionistic impulse at the extreme of each model, an impulse that becomes self-defeating in the end, leading to imbalance and unfaithfulness to the full biblical witness. So what should we do about this problem? I end with some practical exhortations.

1. Avoid arrogance. It is extremely easy to believe that the culture model that has helped you the most is the best one for everyone. It is especially easy to feel superior if you compare the strengths of your favorite model with the weaknesses of the others. Don't do that. Do not think that your particular tradition is "the new thing God is doing" and all the others are fading away. A balanced assessment shows that none of these particular traditions are dying. Each has serious weaknesses but also great strengths.

2. Avoid blame. If you have grown by adopting another culture model, you may feel angry or betrayed by the former one. You may have had good or bad personal experiences at the hands of cultural elites, which may have influenced you unduly. You may blame a certain model for all the troubles of the church because rabid proponents hurt the last congregation of which you were a member. Forgive, and look for places where you can repent. Try to remove the personal histories as you think about culture. Look at the Bible, the cultural moment, and your gifts.

3. Avoid frustration. If you are in a church or denomination that does not share the cultural model you feel is best, it can have a radicalizing effect on you. Opposition can push you into more extreme forms of your position. Don't let conflict make you too rigid a proponent for your approach.

4. Avoid naïveté. Some people say "a plague on all your houses" and insist that one church transcend all models or incorporate them all. Because every church and Christian has history, a temperament, and a unique take on various theological issues, every church and Christian will be situated in some tradition and model. It is inescapable. The gospel should give us the humility both to appreciate other models and to acknowledge that we have a model of our own. So enjoy the strengths of your position, admit the weaknesses, and borrow like crazy from the strengths of the others.

DISCUSSION QUESTIONS

1. Keller writes, "If all these models in their balanced formulation have biblical warrant, where will we situate ourselves? The answer is not simply an attempt to hit on the perfect balance between all four all of the time." We must also learn to discern the current "season" in the cycle of the church's relationship to a culture.

   - *Winter*—a church that is hostile to culture, seeing little fruit; embattled and spiritually weak.
   - *Spring*—a church that is embattled, possibly persecuted by the culture, but is seeing growth.
   - *Summer*—an "allied" church, highly regarded by the culture with Christians in the centers of cultural production.
   - *Autumn*—a church that is increasingly marginalized in a post-Christian culture, looking for new ways to reach out winsomely.

   In which of these four seasons do you and your ministry peers find yourself right now? To which signs or factors can you point as proof? Does this change when you consider your context nationally or regionally? How is this current season of cultural engagement different from that of the previous generation of church leaders?

2. Andy Crouch's distinction between postures and gestures is "a vivid and elegant way to express this flexibility" needed for balanced cultural engagement. Crouch sees our basic model or stance toward culture to be a "posture"—our "unconscious default position"—but a "gesture" is an ad hoc move that briefly seems to come out of another model. Can you cite an instance when you embraced a gesture that didn't match your typical posture? What were the reasons that led you to do this?

3. What do you think of the distinction between the role of the church as an organized institution and the church as an organic body of individual believers? How does this distinction aid in thinking about cultural engagement and the mission of the church? Do you believe it is a biblical distinction?

4. Keller writes, "Many of us are not choosing our Christ and culture model in the right way. Instead of looking at Scripture, the culture, and our own gifts and calling, we tend to form our views in visceral reactions to the behavior of other Christians." This chapter closes with four practical suggestions.

   - Avoid arrogance.
   - Avoid blame.
   - Avoid frustration.
   - Avoid naïveté.

   How can you seek to avoid reacting to the extremes of other models? Which of these four concerns is most relevant to you?

REFLECTIONS ON
CULTURAL ENGAGEMENT

Andy Crouch, author of Culture Making *and
executive editor at* Christianity Today

There are many ways to get the relationship between the church and culture wrong, and most of them involve getting it partly right. As Tim Keller points out in this section on cultural engagement, Christians have gravitated toward models that each preserve some important truth about culture, but each of these models neglects other important truths.

Models are helpful, but we human beings often think best in stories and images. Is there a story or image that can help us stay centered—aware of original sin but also aware of common grace, active but not overconfident in our cultural endeavors, engaged but also counter-cultural, relevant but also radical?

I believe there *is* a story *and* an image that can help us a great deal in holding together these various tensions. It is, in fact, *the story of the Image*—the biblical theme we sometimes call by its Latin name *imago Dei*, the image of God.

Once you understand the story of the *imago Dei*, you not only have our cultural calling in summary form, you also have a compact version of the gospel itself. The four chapters in the story of the divine image tell us who we were meant to be, what went wrong, how we were rescued, and what we are meant to do in light of our salvation: (1) image bearing, (2) image breaking, (3) image revealing, and (4) image restoring. And at each point they illuminate how the church can faithfully approach its cultural context, however hostile or friendly that culture may be to faith.

Image Bearing

On the very first page of Genesis we find human beings created in the "image" and "likeness" of God. What exactly does this mean? Christians reflecting on the *imago Dei* have tended to focus on various *capacities* that might especially image the Creator. Augustine saw *rationality* as the most distinctive quality of human beings. Contemporary theologians like John Zizioulas call attention to our *relationality* (seen, among other ways, in the creation of human beings as male and female), which reflects the life of the Trinity. Others draw parallels between divine and human *creativity*—no other creature seems able to transcend and transform its environment in anything resembling the way we human beings do.

Yet while all our remarkable human capacities may indeed be part of bearing the image, the *imago Dei* cannot be just the sum of our abilities. Otherwise, we will end up excluding many human beings from the circle of the image bearers. If rationality is the essential quality of the divine image, what about those in the last stages of Alzheimer's disease? If the divine image requires relationality, what about sufferers from severe autism who struggle to communicate or bond with other human beings? If creativity is essential, are especially innovative and artistic personality types more "like God" than the rest of us? Indeed, since all these capacities occur in greater and lesser degrees in different people, does that mean the most rational, the most relational, the most creative, are the most godlike?

No—when we lack, or lose, even our most distinctive human capacities, we are still image bearers. The youngest, the oldest, and the most infirm all bear the image. Somehow, bearing the image is possible even in seasons of great *incapacity* and vulnerability. This is good news, given that every human being (at the beginning of life, at its end, and often in its midst) will experience extreme vulnerability.

Our vulnerability is not just acute at certain seasons of life; it is also routine throughout our lives. Genesis 2:25 describes the first man and woman as "both naked, and they felt no shame." Nakedness is a very distinctive sort of vulnerability toward the world and one another, and it is the basic state of human beings—and only human beings. Other creatures are born with everything they need to make their way in the world; human beings are born naked. The very creature that possesses greater capacities than any other creature also has vulnerabilities greater than any other. Vulnerability is so essential to being human that it may be essential to bearing the divine image as well.

It is these odd creatures, possessed of authority and capacities that no other creature is given but also deeply vulnerable, who are given an extraordinary calling: to have dominion over the very good world that God has made. And the way human beings have dominion is through culture—the collective, cumulative human effort to "make something of the world," to paraphrase journalist Ken Myers. It is culture, the accumulation of human capacity to transform and interpret the world, that has allowed us to shape and steward (as well as, alas, exploit and destroy) the rest of creation far more decisively than any other species.

All the capacities associated with the image of God are essential for culture to flourish. Our *reason* allows us to learn about the world around us and pass on what we learn to future generations, so that human culture can be profoundly cumulative and adaptive in ways that animal behaviors are not. Our *relational* nature allows us to collaborate and bond with one another in spite of our differences. Gender and sexuality, one of the most powerful expressions of relationality, is at the root of the family, the most basic unit in which culture is expressed and transmitted. Our *creativity* allows us to transcend instinct, and even previous human experience, in response to new challenges and possibilities.

At the same time, culture is essential for caring for human beings in their vulnerability. The first human beings are placed in a garden—a cultivated environment—even before they know disease and death. When they are ejected from the garden in Genesis 3, God mercifully provides protective culture in the form of leather garments (in the place of their inadequate fig leaves) to shield them from the wildness of the world. Many other creatures flourish with little more than instinct to guide and protect them in the world; human beings need rich and extended cultural environments even to survive, let alone thrive. Culture is the most basic expression of care for human beings at their most vulnerable, creating what Peter Berger calls a "sacred canopy" that holds at bay the potential chaos of the cosmos.[1]

We are culture makers, then, because we are image bearers — and we fulfill our image-bearing commission by being culture makers. This leads to several crucial insights:

1. Every human culture contributes to fulfilling God's original commission to human beings. The original instructions to humanity — "be fruitful and increase in number; fill the earth and subdue it" (Gen 1:28) — cannot be fulfilled without culture, and indeed, they cannot be fulfilled without multiple cultures. Cultural diversity is necessary for full image bearing. A monoculture (of the sort that the men of Babel seem to have sought to create, with one language and one fixed city for their home) could never answer the divine call to "fill the earth," a call that could only be answered with cultural adaptation to the earth's vast range of ecological and geographical contexts. (The kind of culture that allows human beings and all other creatures under their stewardship to live and flourish amidst the fjords of northern Europe is quite different from the kind that enables flourishing on the islands of the Caribbean.) Cultural homogeneity is insufficient for the fulfillment of the image-bearing call — only cultural diversity is sufficient to reflect and refract the divine image into every possible place and time. This is true not just because of the diversity of creation; it also reflects the infinite depths of being in the Creator himself, depths that can only be captured in the most fragmentary and partial way by any given individual.

2. All beneficial culture, not just "Christian" culture, answers our image-bearing call. Image bearing helps address a perennial problem for Christians trying to make sense of culture — the "problem" of the "good pagan." What do we make of the virtues we find in resolute nonbelievers? What about the excellence of much of non-Christian, pre-Christian, and post-Christian cultural production, from the epics of Homer to the architecture of Frank Gehry? Indeed, how do we account for the admirable culture created by adherents of what Christians believe are false religions — the glories of Islamic calligraphy, the literary beauty of the Bhagavad Gita, the measured calm of a Zen monastery?

Image bearing gives us a clear way to understand this common cultural inheritance and its excellence: every human being and every human culture, not just Christians and the culture they create, are subject to God's call to bear his image in the world. So we are not surprised to find truth, beauty, and goodness in the cultures around us. The Reformed tradition speaks of this goodness outside of Christian revelation as "common grace," and indeed, it is rooted in the very first act of grace, the investing of mortal creatures made of dust with the capacity to bear the image of God.

3. Image bearing makes a powerful case for pluralism. The Bible does not reserve image bearing just for God's chosen people. The world is not divided, as so many ancient (and even modern!) people have divided it, into true human beings (people like us) and barbarians (subhuman outsiders). So healthy societies do not privilege one cultural or religious group over others, coercing belief or suppressing cultural difference. Far from having fantasies of cultural dominance that would enforce Christian beliefs or morality on others, Christians should be in the vanguard of ensuring that the freedom of image bearers is respected, even the freedom to be wrong. The Creator himself seems to have granted this freedom to the first image bearers, walking in the garden only "in the cool of the day" (Gen 3:8) and leaving them to their cultural task, and their temptation, at other times. Recognizing the divine image in all their neighbors, Christians have every reason to be exceptionally good and respectful citizens in our pluralistic cities and nations.

In this section on cultural engagement, Keller presents four dominant models for engaging culture. Of all these models, our image bearing may be best reflected in those who recognize "Two Kingdoms." Rooted in our original creating and calling, culture is worthwhile in itself and does not require Christian control or transformation to be a worthy setting for human activity. But separated from the other three chapters in the story of the image, the theme of image bearing can lead us to neglect a darker truth about human beings and their cultures. The image is still borne by every human being, but every human being now arrives in a culture where the image has been fatally distorted by sin.

Image Breaking

One of the most powerful ways to understand the fall — the corruption of human beings and the whole cosmos by sin — is to see it as an act of *image substitution*. The image bearers listen to the serpent's promises that if they eat the fruit, they will be like God, knowing good and evil, and will not die. The serpent holds out the promise that the fruit, consumed apart from God, will grant what only God can actually grant, namely, godlikeness and eternal life. It is a substitute for relationship with and dependence on God. The biblical name for created things that substitute for relationship with and dependence on God is *idols*, and the fruit in the garden is just the first of many idols that the image bearers embrace.

An idol is an "image of god" — a created thing that purports to represent some aspect of ultimate reality. Every idol promises to extend the *capacities* of human beings — to give us more authority over the world than we had before. And every idol promises to minimize the *vulnerability* and dependence that are equally part of being human and bearing the image of God. Indeed, every idol promises benefits that the true God wants us to have; the first man and woman already had access to the tree of life, ensuring they would not die, and they were already made in the image of God, designed to grow in knowledge and wisdom.

But the fruit of the garden, like all idols after it, promises the benefits that come from God *without relationship with God*. It is a "god substitute." And the great irony and tragedy of the human story is that by turning from the true God to idols, the image bearers convince themselves that the truest image of God is found not in one another — human beings in all their authority and vulnerability — but in inanimate, created, and cultivated things.

So idols end up being not just "god substitutes" but "human substitutes" as well. They not only displace God from his proper place as the center of our worship; they also displace us from our proper place as his image bearers in the world. This act of image substitution is not a mere case of mistaken identity. Its consequences are much worse than that. The idols to which human beings turn for blessing, protection, and power cannot keep their promises. The more the substitute images convince us that they, rather than we, bear the divine image, the more power they have to demand our worship and allegiance. The end result of worshiping false images is that the true image bearers are destroyed. Our freedom turns to bondage; our identity and security turn to fear and shame. Instead of relational and cultural diversity, human beings now seek domination and uniformity. Instead of using our reason to celebrate and care for God's world, we use it to exploit the world. And instead of caring for one another in our vulnerability, we began to take advantage of one another's vulnerability.

The worship of false images ends up breaking the true image. The image bearers become image breakers.

Idolatry is the story of every human culture. Every culture takes some good created thing and by elevating it to godlike status becomes enslaved to it, at the price of the dignity of the image bearers. Many of the cultures around ancient Israel offered human sacrifice to their most powerful idols, literally sacrificing true image bearers on the altars of the false image. Our modern cultures refrain from explicitly sacrificing human beings in religious rituals, but they are full of image breaking all the same. Think about the way the idol of beauty, expressed in literally unattainable bodily proportions in advertising images, leads some young women to starve their bodies and some older women to subject themselves to gruesome and ineffective cosmetic procedures; or the way that the idol of work and productivity can so easily lead successful executives to neglect their spouses and children. The human sacrifice in these cases is by no means merely metaphorical.

Idols always lead to the exploitation and destruction of image bearers. A culture that prizes sexual autonomy ends up gratuitously exploiting human bodies, violating intimacy, and terminating "unwanted" unborn lives. A culture that values international peace and domestic security ends up stockpiling enough weapons to destroy the planet and incarcerating nearly one in one hundred men.

Idolatry is intrinsically linked to injustice as well. Idolatry's price is always highest for those who are the weakest in a society—slaves, women, the poor, foreigners and immigrants, and children. Indeed, the biblical writers draw an indelible connection between idolatry and injustice, because the fruit of idol worship is always systems of exploitation, and the root of injustice is always the pursuit of good things apart from trust and dependence on God.

So we must be alert to idolatry and injustice in every culture—and in the church. The true divine image has been lost—both among the poor who bear the brunt of false-image worship, but also among those who benefit from it for the time being. So while we can celebrate the remnants of image bearing in the cultures of the world, we also can never treat any culture as simply an uncomplicated expression of the divine image. This is the advantage of a posture like Keller's, of a "critical enjoyment and an appropriate wariness" toward our culture's mixture of image bearing and image breaking. And that posture also helps prevent us either from uncritically identifying with culture or un-*self*-critically distancing ourselves from it. God's own people can become deeply complicit in idolatry and injustice. Image breaking is not just "out there," but it is also "in here"—no Christian community can rest in self-satisfied cultural congruence, but must always be alert for the prophetic call to repent of idolatry and injustice.

Of the models Keller presents in this section, it is those who advocate the "Counterculturalist" model of Christianity and culture who are most keenly aware of the way that culture, this side of the garden, perpetuates idolatry and injustice. Keller notes the strengths (and weaknesses) of the Counterculturalist vision for the church as a "contrast culture," but arguably the most important contribution of the Counterculturalists is in keeping the church fully alert to its potential complicity in the service of false gods, even when those gods are military, economic, or technological rather than explicitly religious. Still, by itself, the Counterculturalist model can tend to miss the ongoing goodness of image bearing even in very broken cultures, as well as the hope the whole biblical story holds out for the restoration of the image in the midst of history.

Image Revealing

The story of culture is, of course, a story about us—human beings fulfilling the divine commission to be fruitful and multiply, but also denying the true God in favor of false gods of our own creation, false gods that corrupt and destroy the image bearers. But the story of culture is also a story about God, who has graciously intervened to prevent the divine image from being entirely lost. Not only has God kept alive the spark of the divine image in every human culture through common grace; even more dramatically and decisively, God has entered into history to reveal the true Image once again.

Of course, Christians identify the "image revealing" chapter of the story with the incarnation, in which the "image of the invisible God" (Col 1:15) becomes flesh in Jesus of Nazareth. But it is important to remember that in many important respects, this act of image revealing began not with the individual named Jesus but with his ancestors Abraham and Sarah and the creation of an image-bearing *nation* that is named Israel. Israel, the people God calls to be a blessing to the nations, is the first great step toward the revealing of God's image. Israel will worship the true God rather than the idols of the other nations; Israel will uphold a standard of justice far more comprehensive than the injustice of her neighbors. Above all, Israel is meant to find its blessing, protection, and identity in relationship with God, demonstrating true image bearing to the world east of Eden.

Indeed, you cannot understand Jesus' mission without understanding Israel's. Because image bearing is thoroughly cultural, God reveals his plan for image bearing first through a *nation*—a people who embody a cultural tradition extended through time. Yet this holy nation fails in its commission to bear the image. Israel, like the other nations, gives itself over to idolatry and injustice, bringing down on itself the wrath of God, spoken through the prophets, against those who destroy the true image. In the ruins of exile, it seems that Israel's image-revealing role is fatally compromised, even though alongside the story of national failure are individual stories of redemptive faithfulness like Daniel's and Esther's. But the true fulfillment of Israel's image-bearing vocation seems remote as the New Testament opens, with Israel under the thumb of the greatest empire yet devised, an empire rooted in pagan idolatry and whose own emperors are claiming greater and greater divine status.

It is at this point that Jesus appears in the story—his mission inaugurated by the words, "You are my Son, whom I love; with you I am well pleased" (Mark 1:11). He is the true image bearer. His brief but supremely consequential life is marked by the faithfulness and flourishing that was meant for Adam and Eve—and for Israel too. Indeed, the early church quickly came to identify Jesus as the "second Adam," whose obedience bore, redeemed, and reversed the curse that had fallen on the first.

So in Jesus we see what "human flourishing" truly entails—not our shallow idea of flourishing that is drawn mostly from Western technological affluence, but the fullness of being that comes when a human being, constantly dependent on God, speaks truth, heals the sick, drives back the powers of darkness, bears the full weight of idolatry and injustice, and overcomes death itself. That which Adam and Eve failed to obtain through their disobedience—the quest to become like God and conquer death—Jesus, who is in very nature God, obtains through his obedience, even unto death.

And all this happens, it is crucial to see, *in the midst of history*, which is to say, *in the midst of culture*. It happens in the midst of the story of Israel, the nation that was meant to bear the image among the nations of the world; it happens at the apex of the Roman Empire's power, creating a powerful counternarrative to that empire's pagan promise of peace through strength; and it unleashes vast and enduring cultural effects, not only leading to the official conversion of Rome within three centuries but converting the imagination of people from every nation under heaven then and now—most recently in our time, spreading with astonishing speed in the theoretically atheist nation of China.

The calling of Israel, and the fulfillment of that calling by Jesus, is the key to history. This radical belief means that as much as Christians are citizens of their nations and their home cultures, they have a much deeper allegiance to the church and to the kingdom that Jesus announced and inaugurated. As much as we can learn from the rich tapestry of cultural diversity and the many strands of human history, the church takes its bearing from the singular figure of Jesus, who challenges so many of our assumptions about true human flourishing. And the church believes that only in joining God's story in history can any human being, or any human people, find and fulfill their purpose.

Returning again to the models laid out by Keller, we see that the Transformationist model, which emphasizes the total and powerful claim of Jesus on every other story, preserves something important about the radical nature of God's image-revealing act. There is a real discontinuity between God's self-revelation and every human culture. Apart from Israel and its Messiah Jesus, we cannot reason or intuit our way to true flourishing. Jesus is the indispensable solution to our alienation from God and one another, the only one in whom the divine image is fully known, and his gospel generates a worldview that will always be at odds with every human culture. Ultimately every knee will bow before the only one worthy to represent God and exercise his dominion.

I should add that the more extreme forms of Transformationist thinking, such as Reconstructionism, err in assuming too much about the church's ability to faithfully rule in Jesus' place in the kingdoms of the earth—but they do keep alive the crucial claim that only in Jesus do we find the image truly, finally revealed.

Image Restoring

We are now in the fourth act of this extraordinary story—the act where the image once imparted to human beings, broken through idolatry, and revealed in Jesus Christ is now being restored in the world. Just as the first Adam's disobedience contaminated the whole world with death, the second Adam's obedience unto death is now working renewal in the whole cosmos. Israel was called to bear the image in the midst of the nations, but only in rare moments did Israel imagine it could decisively influence the nations. The church, the "new Israel," has an audacious mission: to *restore* the image wherever it has been lost, throughout the world and throughout time. The divisions and inequality wrought by idolatry and injustice are now to be overcome by the cross—between different nations and between men and women, young and old, even (as unimaginable as this was in the Roman context) between masters and slaves.

As Peter celebrates on the day of Pentecost, he quotes the prophet Joel: "In the last days, God says, I will pour out my Spirit on all people. Your sons and daughters will prophesy, your young men will see visions, your old men will dream dreams. Even on my servants, both men and women, I will pour out my Spirit in those days, and they will prophesy" (Acts 2:17–18). The book of Acts narrates how, with breathless speed, the good news burst out of Jerusalem into the wider Roman world, sweeping up men and women, those of high status and low, Jews and Gentiles, Africans like the Ethiopian eunuch (Acts 8) and Europeans like the Roman centurion (Acts 10).

In the church's commission of restoring the image, evangelism and doing justice are both central. Evangelism not only delivers the best possible news we could ever hear—the true Image has been revealed, and the true Image Bearer gave himself to rescue us from our broken images—but it also leads to the incomparably empowering gift of the Spirit, the indwelling, image-restoring presence of God. We cannot repair our broken image by our own well-intentioned efforts—that just repeats the self-sufficient idolatry of Eden. The first Christians had to stay in the city until they were "clothed with power from on high" (Luke 24:49). Only when we know the name of the true Image Bearer and have his Spirit bearing witness with our spirits that we are children of God do we have any hope of living his dependent, obedient, faithful, and fruitful life.

At the same time, it is inconceivable that there could be evangelism—proclamation of the good news and invitations to conversion and baptism in the Spirit—without action in the world to make culture and especially to set victims of idolatry and injustice free from their captivity. We share the general call to cultivate and create in the world with all of our fellow image bearers, but the specific call to do justice and love mercy is addressed with particular urgency to God's "holy nation," now drawn from every language group and people, who have been freed from their own captivity and now are sent into the world on an image-restoring mission.

So every Christian has a dual cultural calling. First, we have been rescued from idols and injustice to *bear* the image afresh — to participate in every domain of culture as stewards of the good creation. But second, we have been sent to *restore* the image where it has been lost. To focus on the second mission without the first would be to abdicate our own culture-making and culture-keeping calling. It is good (indeed, "very good") when Christians make excellent culture, whether shoes, songs, or apps, and Christians do not need to apologize for or seek to justify doing good work as image bearers.

But it is not enough for Christians to be simply good culture-making citizens; we also have a mission — a mission that attends especially to the lost and the least — to confront the makers of idols and the perpetrators of injustice. We go to forgotten corners of culture that others shun and invest in cultural institutions that others might well find too costly or risky. It is right that Christians practice every specialty of medicine — and it is right that Christians are overrepresented in medical callings that serve the poor, taking tremendous risks to care for the victims of infectious diseases like Ebola. It is right that Christians practice as attorneys — and it is right that Christians set aside high-paying legal careers to ensure that the rule of law actually works for the poor and oppressed. It is right that Christians start businesses that harness the abundant goodness of creation to create wealth and opportunity — and it is right that many Christians seek to do so in countries where conventional missionaries cannot go.

So Christian activity in culture has an inescapable bias toward the marginal, disadvantaged, and disempowered. This does not mean we disdain the wealthy and powerful — they too are image bearers and suffer from being image breakers, and they are equally loved by God and worthy of the gospel. But the image-distorting effects of idolatry and injustice are not distributed equally — they fall hardest on the most vulnerable. And the odd truth is that if one seeks to primarily serve the powerful, one is very unlikely to ever meaningfully serve the poor; but when one serves the poor, the powerful also end up being attracted, intrigued, and ultimately converted and blessed.

Evangelism and justice go together in the restoration of the image.

Any attempt to do justice without evangelism underestimates both the power of idolatry and the power of the Spirit. And any attempt to do evangelism without attending to issues of justice misses the glorious goal of salvation, to restore to human beings the freedom and dignity they were always meant to have.

The model that Keller refers to as "Relevance" is the one that most readily joins this image-restoration project. It emphasizes that a church that is not on a restorative mission in the world is not a church at all. The image that has been revealed in Jesus Christ is meant to make a difference in history, and God has gone ahead of us into every culture, preparing the way for both evangelism and the work of justice. But it is crucial that we not allow our understanding of image restoration to be diluted or reduced to secular understandings of human rights and freedoms. Relevance-oriented Christians are often tempted to take for granted their host culture's own conceptions of what is wrong and how it can be remedied. In fact, the work of image restoration always goes deeper and further than any secular program of social concern.

It is not easy to hold together these four chapters of the image story—image bearing, image breaking, image restoring, and image revealing—and that may explain why we tend to sort ourselves into the four major models that Keller describes. Perhaps it is inevitable that at different times and in different places, church leaders find themselves needing to emphasize one or another theme. But ultimately, all four themes are essential to understanding the whole story. If we find ourselves feeling strongly drawn to one model over the others, that is probably because the context where we live and lead has neglected one of the key biblical themes. The ardent Counterculturalist has probably lived in church contexts that were far too naive about idolatry and injustice; the proponent of Relevance has probably seen too many churches withdraw into complacent communities to the extent of ignoring the mission field right outside their doors. It is not wrong to develop forms of church life that recover and emphasize neglected themes—as long as we keep the whole story in mind.

The image-bearing story helps us understand how much we differ from our neighbors, and how much we have in common with them. The idea that human beings bear the divine image, though an idea shared with our Jewish neighbors and to some extent our Muslim neighbors as well, is implausible, though not unattractive, to elites in the secular West. The claim that injustice is rooted in idolatry, and that even very good features of culture can become idols with destructive, demonic power, is an affront to the materialism of Marx.

And yet this story also gives us remarkable common ground with our non-Christian neighbors. We can approach them with reverence (because they are image bearers), forbearance (because they are in the grip of idols, whether they know it or not), sacrificial love (because this is how Jesus extended himself), and hope (because God is working in the world to restore image bearers to himself and to their true calling).

And the story of the image given, broken, revealed, and restored gives us the deepest possible reason to participate seriously in culture. Culture is where God's story with us began, investing us with the commission to make something of his very good, abundant world. And because the biblical story ends in a city full of "the glory and honor of the nations" (Rev 21:26), we have hope that culture—redeemed, transfigured, and glorified—will also be the image bearers' offering of praise at the story's end.

RESPONSE TO ANDY CROUCH

Timothy Keller

Andy Crouch's essay does not adopt the typical form of the book review, listing some things to affirm, some things to critique, and some things to propose or suggest. Instead, he looks at the cultural engagement section and proposes grounding the whole of it in a particular biblical story and image, namely, that of the *imago Dei*. His is not exactly a review or a response paper but a constructive project and proposal for a new way to frame cultural engagement biblically.

I outline four basic models of relating Christianity to culture: Transformationist, Relevance, Counterculturalist, and Two Kingdoms. Using some of D. A. Carson's work in his *Christ and Culture Revisited*, I argue that each of them has some biblical support from the plotline of the Bible: creation, fall, redemption, and restoration.

The Two Kingdoms approach has the highest view of creation and common grace. It views culture making by nonbelievers as filled with much wisdom and goodness. Christians work in the world as full participants. The Counterculturalist approach, on the other hand, takes very seriously the fall and the deeply distorted nature of human culture. Any direct attempt to "change culture" will only end up infecting and entangling the church in the culture's idols. It counsels the church instead to simply be a "contrast community" to the surrounding society. The Transformationist approach, however, believes culture can to a degree be healed of and redeemed from its idolatrous nature but only in Christ and only by those operating out of a Christian worldview. Finally, the Relevance approach believes it is possible to restore the kingdom of God in the world now by changing social structures toward greater inclusion and justice.

Having laid out the biblical grounding of each of the models, yet indicating that none of them can claim to be the approach that holds all of the biblical themes and truths in perfect balance and completeness, I conclude that the models constitute a tool kit to be deployed in different proportions of emphasis in different times and places, and that when using one model, we should always incorporate insights from the other approaches to avoid the imbalances of our own.

Crouch seems to rightly find this schematization—this "model of models" with its grid of pluses and minuses for each one—somewhat stale. It looks a bit like a slide deck showing the whiteboard results of a strategic planning event. He looks for a single biblical-theological theme that is also a metaphor to sustain a way of "holding together these various tensions." And he finds it. "It is, in fact, *the story of the Image*—the biblical theme we sometimes call by its Latin name *imago Dei*, the image of God." If Crouch is right, this does not simply hold the tensions together but more positively gives us "our cultural calling in summary form" (p. 274). He then proceeds to expound the "story of the Image" and fold in much of the data I gathered on models.

I need to recap this project in order to assess it.

1. Image Bearing. The first stage in the story of the Image is human beings as image bearers. What is the image of God? Crouch does not reduce the image of God to capacities such as rationality and creativity, as well as our moral sense and need for relationship. He rightly warns that to do so might lead to the conclusion that a person with Alzheimer's disease, someone in a coma, or an infant would not possess as much of God's image. The *imago Dei* means not less than those capacities but *more*—being related to and dependent on God. An aspect of this is human vulnerability. Unlike animals, which come into the world virtually self-sufficient, human beings can't even live without clothes. Which is to say, we really can't live without culture. Crouch writes, "Many other creatures flourish with little more than instinct to guide and protect them in the world; human beings need rich and extended cultural environments even to survive, let alone thrive.

Culture is the most basic expression of care for human beings at their most vulnerable" (p. 276). Since human beings are made to image or reflect God and therefore are intrinsically relational and dependent, not self-sufficient, we are inherently culture makers.

I think this helps answer an age-old question: Is humanity's stewardship of creation, the "cultural mandate," a part of God's image in us? Crouch's analysis leads us to see that it essentially is, not as a discrete office or "assignment," but as a seamless extension of being made in the *imago Dei*. (And as Louis Berkhof points out, the divine image and the stewardship of creation are introduced in the same breath in Genesis 1:26.[1]) "We fulfill our image-bearing commission by being culture makers," writes Crouch (p. 277). He goes on to argue that, since all human beings, Christians and non-Christians, are in the image of God, we have a case for seeing all human "culture [as] worthwhile in itself" and that it "does not require Christian control or transformation to be a worthy setting for human activity" (p. 278). This is especially well grasped by the Two Kingdoms model as I outline it in the cultural engagement chapters.

2. Image Breaking. The second stage in the story of the Image is humanity's fall into sin, which Crouch calls image substitution. Physical idols were literal, false images of God, but he draws this idea out and says that sin fundamentally is putting something in the place of God, creating "god substitutes." Crouch explains how "idols always lead to the exploitation and destruction of image bearers," as well as to injustice (p. 280). Idolatry, then, is a crucial way to understand what is wrong with any particular culture. Every culture is sinful and will lift up and absolutize things like individual freedom (or alternatively the family and tribe), or beauty and sexual autonomy, or moneymaking and wealth, or national solidarity and racial pride, and so on. This stage in the story of the Image is especially well understood by the Counterculturalists.

3. Image Revealing. Jesus Christ comes into the world to reveal the true image of God (Col 1:15). Crouch helpfully points out that before the coming of Christ, the redeemed community of Israel, with its divinely ordered life, had begun to reveal to the world what the real image of God looks like. Human life not dominated by "god substitutes" of sex, money, and power should have been evident in Israel to the degree that it followed God's laws fully. (Christopher Wright's books on the Old Testament make this case well.) But it is in Jesus himself that we can see what true human life in the image of God should look like. This stage in the story is well represented in the approach of the Transformationists, who insist that only through the revelation of Jesus can human culture be to some degree repaired from its sinful brokenness.

4. Image Restoring. The church is the "new Israel." Though Crouch doesn't mention the text, Paul in Ephesians 4:22–24 writes that saving grace is restoring the image of God in Christians. This supports Crouch's contention that Christians are not merely to do evangelism and build up disciples inside the church; they are to exhibit to the world the restored image of God in human beings—which means "action in the world to make culture and especially to set victims of idolatry and injustice free from their captivity" (p. 285). He goes on to say that "it is right that Christians are overrepresented in medical callings that serve the poor, taking tremendous risks to care for the victims of infectious diseases," and "it is right that Christians set aside high-paying legal careers to ensure that the rule of law actually works for the poor and oppressed" (p. 286). Why? This shows the world the restored image of God, human life undistorted by slavery to god substitutes of wealth, power, and material safety and comfort. He points out that those using what I call the Relevance model are usually the most engaged in this kind of work.

Does Crouch succeed in his effort to draw together the diverse data points of "Christ and culture" models into a biblical-theological story that helps us make sense of our cultural callings? Indeed, he does. In fact, I think his last point about image restoration makes one of the best brief and compelling cases of Christians' engagement in culture making and justice that I've heard. "Repairing the world" is a slogan of which the Counterculturalist and Two Kingdoms folks are rightly suspicious. Likewise they deplore the slogan "Transforming the culture for King Jesus." But thinking of our work in the world in terms of image restoration is a more compelling argument for culture making, avoiding both utopianism and triumphalism.

I need to strongly consider the importance of the story of the Image for future teaching and training in this area. This is a great essay. My only parting observation is that the particular understanding of the *imago Dei* that Crouch deploys throughout his work is not so much the Lutheran, Roman Catholic, or traditional Arminian version as it is that of the Reformed churches. Though he doesn't identify himself as Reformed in his theology, Andy Crouch gives one of the clearest and most practical expositions of the Reformed doctrine that I have ever seen (and I'm Reformed). Thanks (and I don't mean this ironically) for the basic training in how to use my own theological resources, Andy!

ABBREVIATIONS

Bible Books

Gen	Genesis	Joel.	Joel
Exod	Exodus	Amos	Amos
Lev	Leviticus	Obad	Obadiah
Num	Numbers	Jonah	Jonah
Deut	Deuteronomy	Mic	Micah
Josh	Joshua	Nah	Nahum
Judg	Judges	Hab	Habakkuk
Ruth	Ruth	Zeph	Zephaniah
1–2 Sam . . .	1–2 Samuel	Hag	Haggai
1–2 Kgs . . .	1–2 Kings	Zech	Zechariah
1–2 Chr . . .	1–2 Chronicles	Mal	Malachi
Ezra	Ezra	Matt	Matthew
Neh	Nehemiah	Mark	Mark
Esth	Esther	Luke	Luke
Job	Job	John	John
Ps/Pss	Psalm/Psalms	Acts	Acts
Prov	Proverbs	Rom	Romans
Eccl	Ecclesiastes	1–2 Cor . . .	1–2 Corinthians
Song	Song of Songs	Gal	Galatians
Isa	Isaiah	Eph	Ephesians
Jer	Jeremiah	Phil	Philippians
Lam	Lamentations	Col.	Colossians
Ezek	Ezekiel	1–2 Thess . .	1–2 Thessalonians
Dan	Daniel	1–2 Tim . . .	1–2 Timothy
Hos	Hosea	Titus	Titus

Phlm . . . . . . Philemon
Heb . . . . Hebrews
Jas . . . . James
1–2 Pet . . . . 1–2 Peter

1–2–3 John 1–2–3 John
Jude . . . . Jude
Rev . . . . Revelation

General

cf. . . . . *confer*, compare
ch(s). . . . . . . chapter(s)
ed(s). . . . . . . editor(s), edited by, edition
e.g. . . . . *exempli gratia*, for example
esp. . . . . especially
et al. . . . . *et alii*, and others
ff. . . . . and the following ones
ibid. . . . . *ibidem*, in the same place

idem. . . . . . . that which was mentioned before, same, as in same author
i.e. . . . . *id est*, that is
n. . . . . note
p(p). . . . . page(s)
rev. . . . . revised
trans. . . . . . . translator, translated by
v(v). . . . . verse(s)

NOTES

Series Introduction

1. Richard Lints, *The Fabric of Theology: A Prolegomenon to Evangelical Theology* (Grand Rapids: Eerdmans, 1993), 9.

2. Ibid., 82.

3. Ibid., 315.

4. Ibid., 316–17.

5. These three areas correspond roughly to Richard Lints's four theological vision factors in this way: (1) *Gospel* flows from how you read the Bible; (2) *City* flows from your reflections on culture; and (3) *Movement* flows from your understanding of tradition. Meanwhile, the fourth factor—your view of human rationality—influences your understanding of all three. It has an impact on how you evangelize non-Christians, how much common grace you see in a culture, and how institutional (or anti-institutional) you are in your thinking about ministry structure.

6. It can be argued that the Gospel axis is not like the other two. In the other two axes, the desired position is a midpoint, a balance between extremes. However, Sinclair Ferguson (in his lectures on the Marrow Controversy) and others have argued that the gospel is not at all a balance between two opposites but an entirely different thing. In fact, it can also be argued that legalism and antinomianism are not opposites but essentially the same thing—self-salvation—opposed to the gospel. So please note that putting the gospel between these two extremes is simply a visual shorthand.

Chapter 1: Intentional Contextualization

1. Today, by God's grace, this story is changing, and we see a vibrant movement of new churches in the city.

2. In scholarly discussions of contextualization, many words have been infused with technical meaning by various writers. So the words *adaptation*, *indigenization*, *translation*, *Contextualization*, and *praxis* are all given specific and distinct meanings (see A. Scott Moreau, "Evangelical Models of

Contextualization," in *Local Theology for the Global Church: Principles for an Evangelical Approach to Contextualization*, ed. Matthew Cook et al. [Pasadena, CA: William Carey Library, 2010], 165–93). Often "adaptation" is used for a method of missiological engagement that is not as deep or thorough as "contextualization." This chapter, however, is written for pastors and practitioners. I write with some awareness of the scholarly debates, but I will not seek to observe the very fine distinctions some missiologists make between methods. Besides, as Moreau states on p. 172, there is no consensus among scholars about how each term is defined. Therefore, I will use the terms *adapt*, *translate*, and *contextualize* as synonyms here. I will refer to the widely accepted distinction between indigenization, syncretism, and contextualization below.

3. These cultural narratives can change in a society over time. Andrew Delbanco (*The Real American Dream: A Meditation on Hope* [Cambridge, MA: Harvard University Press, 1999]) explains the three baseline cultural narratives of American society: "God" (seventeenth to the mid-eighteenth century), "Nation" (mid-eighteenth century to the twentieth), and now "Self." The first narrative is a religious one—religious freedom and faithfulness to God. It yielded to the idea of being "the greatest nation on earth." Today the main narrative of our culture is self-fulfillment. For another interesting way to analyze cultural narratives, see Leslie Stevenson, *Seven Theories of Human Nature* (New York: Oxford University Press, 1974).

4. The idea of cultural narrative is well expressed by Andrew Delbanco (*The Real American Dream*, 1–3): "Human beings need to organize the inchoate sensations amid which we pass our days—pain, desire, pleasure, fear—into a story. When that story leads somewhere and thereby helps us navigate through life, it gives us hope. And if such a sustaining narrative establishes itself over time in the minds of a substantial amount of people, we call it a culture." Cultural narratives are necessary to create meaning in life. "We must imagine some end to life that transcends our own tiny allotment of days and hours if we are to keep at bay the 'dim, back-of-the-mind suspicion that one may be adrift in an absurd world' … [We must overcome] the lurking suspicion that all our getting and spending amounts to nothing more than fidgeting while we wait for death."

5. Barney's ideas are discussed in David J. Hesselgrave, *Planting Churches Cross-Culturally: North America and Beyond*, 2nd ed. (Grand Rapids: Baker, 2000), 145; see Bruce J. Nicholls, *Contextualization: A Theology of Gospel and Culture* (Downers Grove, IL: InterVarsity, 1979), 11–12.

6. Nicholls (*Contextualization*, 11–12) writes, "Perhaps a better model would be a sphere of which each segment is in proximity to the others, or again of a pyramid with the worldview as the unseen base, and values, institutions, and observable behavior as the three sides each interacting with the other." But the pyramid model may still not be dynamic enough. It implies that changes in behavior, values, and institutions can interact with one another but cannot shape the underlying worldview.

7. David Wells, "The Painful Transition from Theoria to Praxis," in *Evangelicalism and Modern America*, ed. George Marsden (Grand Rapids: Eerdmans, 1984), 90. Compare this with Richard Lints's definition: "By 'contextualization of the gospel' I mean the manner in which the expression of the biblical message is shaped in and by the native conceptuality of a given culture" (*The Fabric of Theology: A Prolegomenon to Evangelical Theology* [Grand Rapids: Eerdmans, 1993], 101 n.19).

8. Ray Wheeler, "The Legacy of Shoki Coe," *International Bulletin of Missionary Research* 26.2 (April 2002): 78.

9. Ibid.

10. Nicholls (*Contextualization*, 26–28) gives two examples of contextualization done by theologians in the ecumenical movement of the 1970s.

11. Craig Blomberg, "We Contextualize More Than We Realize," in *Local Theology for the Global Church*, 37 n.2.

12. J. Gresham Machen, *Christianity and Liberalism*, new ed. (1923; repr., Grand Rapids: Eerdmans, 2009), 5–6.

13. Ibid., 2.

14. Ibid., 121.

15. Natee Tanchanpongs, "Developing a Palate for Authentic Theology," in *Local Theology for the Global Church*, 110. Tanchanpongs makes an excellent case that personal sanctification should be one of the tests of whether we have moved from contextualization into syncretism. Syncretism nullifies some part of biblical teaching in order to reshape Christianity into the image of a particular culture. The result of religious syncretism can be seen in the lives of the people who believe it. Syncretism does not produce people whose lives match the descriptions of Christian character—"the fruit of the Spirit"—or Christian behavior in the Bible.

16. Harvie Conn (*Eternal Word and Changing Worlds: Theology, Anthropology, and Mission in Trialogue* [Grand Rapids: Zondervan, 1984], 176–78, 184–90, 194–95) makes this point.

17. D. A. Carson, "Maintaining Scientific and Christian Truths in a Postmodern World," *Science & Christian Belief* 14.2 (October 2002): 107–22, www.scienceandchristianbelief.org/articles/carson.pdf (accessed January 13, 2012).

18. For a full essay making this argument from a conservative, evangelical point of view, see Craig Blomberg, "We Contextualize More Than We Realize," in *Local Theology for the Global Church*.

19. For example, J. Gresham Machen, who founded Westminster Seminary, followed B. B. Warfield and others at Princeton Seminary in their approach to defending the faith through the use of rational proofs and historical evidences. Cornelius Van Til and other younger faculty at Westminster later made a sharp critique of this use of reason in apologetics, arguing that the Warfield/Machen approach gave too much authority to unaided human reason and therefore was unwittingly being too influenced by the Enlightenment. More recent scholarship by Mark Noll and others has brought to light how much old Princeton was

shaped by the Scottish Enlightenment and "common sense realism." In summary, Machen was criticized by some of his own successors as being too adapted to the rationalism of the Enlightenment, and there is some warrant for that charge. Some blindness to one's own culture is inevitable, but it may also be that if you spend a great deal of energy, as Machen did, combating illegitimate contextualization, you may be unconscious of the fact that you are doing it.

20. Nicholls, *Contextualization*, 31.

Chapter 2: Balanced Contextualization

1. John R. W. Stott, *Between Two Worlds: The Challenge of Preaching Today* (Grand Rapids: Eerdmans, 1982).

2. Bruce J. Nicholls (*Contextualization: A Theology of Gospel and Culture* [Downers Grove, IL: InterVarsity, 1979], 8) writes, "Evangelical communicators have often underestimated the importance of cultural factors in communication ... Some have been unaware that terms such as *God, sin, incarnation, salvation*, and *heaven* convey [very] different images in the minds of the hearer from those of the messenger."

3. See Natee Tanchanpongs, "Developing a Palate for Authentic Theology," in *Local Theology for the Global Church: Principles for an Evangelical Approach to Contextualization*, ed. Matthew Cook et al. (Pasadena, CA: William Carey Library, 2010), 116ff., for a discussion of tacit knowledge, Michael Polanyi's proposals about the nature of it, and the relationship of tacit knowledge and belief to contextualization.

4. D. A. Carson (*Biblical Interpretation and the Church* [Carlisle, UK: Paternoster, 1984], 22–23) writes, "Suppose, for instance, that a pastor wishes to encourage people to accept his authority and to follow his leadership almost without question. This might arise because he is a demagogue; or it might arise because in his cultural setting people naturally reverence leaders and eschew iconoclasm. He can foster what he regards as healthy spirituality in this respect by citing passages such as Heb. 13:17 ... but he will probably be less inclined to cite 1 Pet. 5:11ff or Matt. 20:24–28 ... [He may be] very concerned to get across to his congregation the responsibility for the church to pay good teachers with 'double honor' ... while the church leaders themselves may be very exercised about those passages which insist that spiritual leaders must be free from greed and covetousness and love of material goods."

5. See Carson's detailed case for various biblical teachings on God's love in his *The Difficult Doctrine of the Love of God* (Downers Grove, IL: InterVarsity, 2000).

6. Carson, *Biblical Interpretation and the Church*, 23.

7. It is true, of course, that the biblical authors themselves wrote out of a particular culture. In order to understand a biblical writer's intended meaning—and therefore what a particular biblical text is actually teaching—it is critical to

understand the historical, linguistic, and cultural setting of both the writer and the original readers. However, this does not mean we can somehow discover some inner kernel of timeless truth in the Bible to hold on to while discarding many less "essential" teachings as culturally conditioned. An evangelical theology of Scripture acknowledges that the Bible is a thoroughly human book, each author being embedded in human culture, but it believes that God specifically chose each author's culture and even the very life circumstances so that God's overruling providence sovereignly determined every word to be written just as it was. See J. I. Packer, *"Fundamentalism" and the Word of God* (Leicester: Inter-Varsity, 1958), ch. 4, "Scripture"; Nicholls, *Contextualization*, 45–52.

8. See John Stott and R. Coote, eds., *Down to Earth: Studies in Christianity and Culture* (Grand Rapids: Eerdmans, 1980), esp. the appendix "The Willowbank Report."

9. See Anthony Thiselton, *The Two Horizons: New Testament Hermeneutics and Philosophical Description* (Grand Rapids: Eerdmans, 1980), 104, 439; J. I. Packer, "Infallible Scripture and the Role of Hermeneutics," in *Scripture and Truth*, ed. D. A. Carson and John D. Woodbridge (Downers Grove, IL: InterVarsity, 1983), 348–49; Grant R. Osborne, *The Hermeneutical Spiral: A Comprehensive Introduction to Biblical Interpretation* (Downers Grove, IL: InterVarsity, 1997).

10. For the sake of clarity, we won't enter into the complex details of Contextualization through a hermeneutical spiral. In reality, there are at least *two* spirals and *three* horizons. First, you must go back and forth between the biblical text and your own cultural setting in order to let the text correct your understanding (i.e., you must seek to fuse your own horizon of understanding with the horizon of understanding of the text). After that, you must bridge the gap between your own understanding of the truth (now instructed by the biblical text) and that of the people you are trying to reach (see D. A. Carson, "A Sketch of the Factors Determining Current Hermeneutical Debate in Cross-Cultural Contexts," in *Biblical Interpretation and the Church*, 17.

11. Richard Lints, *The Fabric of Theology: A Prolegomenon to Evangelical Theology* (Grand Rapids: Eerdmans, 1993), 101–3.

12. Lints (*Fabric of Theology*, 102) quotes David Wells: "In the one understanding of contextualization, the revelatory trajectory moves only [one way] from authoritative [text] into contemporary culture [context]; in the other, the trajectory moves ... from text to context and from context to the text." In the first view, the communicator assumes he has no cultural involvement himself. He can simply read the text, understand it, and then bring it home to the new culture without adapting to the new culture at all. In the latter view, the context and text relate in an endless circle, which ultimately means we can never conclude what the text "really" says.

Chapter 3: Biblical Contextualization

1. Francis Hutcheson, an eighteenth-century moral philosopher, uses a famous illustration to demonstrate this. He asks us to imagine that we hear of a man who discovers buried treasure in his backyard worth millions of dollars. But then we hear that he gives it all away to the poor. Even if we would never do so ourselves, and even if we swagger publicly that such an act is stupid, we cannot help but admire what was done. There is an indelible sense of the moral beauty of the act itself.

2. J. Alec Motyer, *The Prophecy of Isaiah: An Introduction and Commentary* (Downers Grove, IL: InterVarsity, 1993), 235.

3. D. A. Carson, *The Cross and Christian Ministry: Leadership Lessons from 1 Corinthians* (Grand Rapids: Baker, 2004), 122. We have said we cannot choose between essentials and nonessentials in Scripture. However, in a culture there are things that do not directly contradict Scripture and therefore are neither forbidden nor commanded by the Bible. Carson is saying that, in general, the Christian in mission should adopt such cultural features to avoid making gospel communication unnecessarily strange.

4. See David G. Peterson, *The Acts of the Apostles* (Grand Rapids: Eerdmans, 2009), 40; see also Jay E. Adams, *Audience Adaptations in the Sermons and Speeches of Paul* (Nutley, NJ: P&R, 1976), esp. 61–64.

5. See Adams, *Audience Adaptations*, esp. 61–64.

6. Peterson, *Acts of the Apostles*, 44.

7. Ibid.

8. Another helpful survey of the gospel presentations in Acts is found in John R. W. Stott, *The Message of Acts: The Spirit, the Church, and the World* (Downers Grove, IL: InterVarsity, 1994), 79–81. Stott seems to be looking more at the speeches of Peter early in the book. Peter does not address pagan audiences; nevertheless, Stott (p. 81) comes up with a gospel outline similar to the one we discern in Paul: "Here, then, is a fourfold message. Two events (Christ's death and resurrection), as attested by two witnesses (the Bible and historical witnesses to resurrection), on the basis of which God makes two promises (forgiveness and the Spirit), on two conditions (repentance and faith) ... We have no liberty to amputate this apostolic gospel."

9. D. A. Carson, "Pastoral Penseés: Motivations to Appeal to in Our Hearers When We Preach for Conversion," *Themelios* 35.2 (July 2010): 258–64, www.the gospelcoalition.org/publications/35–2/ (accessed January 19, 2012).

10. Carson's final point is important: "All of the biblically sanctioned motivations for pursuing God, for pursuing Christ, say complementary things about God himself, such that failure to cover the sweep of motivations ultimately results in diminishing God." As we have seen in this chapter, contextualization must roll out biblical truths in an order that is adapted to culture, but faithful gospel ministry must not hide from people any part of the whole counsel of God, lest the picture of God we give people be less than true and full.

11. See Sherwood G. Lingenfelter and Marvin K. Mayers, *Ministering Cross-Culturally* (Grand Rapids: Baker, 2003), 37–50.

12. Richard F. Lovelace, *Dynamics of Spiritual Life* (Downers Grove, IL: InterVarsity, 1979), 198–99.

13. Biblical principles about thrift and modesty must be applied here, but we must also recognize that terms such as *modesty* and *respectful*, while not infinitely elastic, will look different in different cultures.

14. Francis Schaeffer, *The Church at the End of the Twentieth Century* (Downers Grove, IL: InterVarsity, 1970), 67.

Chapter 4: Active Contextualization

1. See David F. Wells, "An American Evangelical Theology: The Painful Transition from Theoria to Praxis," in *Evangelicalism and Modern America*, ed. George Marsden (Grand Rapids: Eerdmans, 1984), 90, 93. Wells writes, "Where is the line between involvement and disengagement, acceptance and denial, continuity and discontinuity, being 'in' the world and not 'of' the world? Contextualization is the process through which we find answers to these questions. The Word of God must be related to our own context ... The preservation of its identity is necessary for Christian belief; its contemporary relevance is required if Christians are to be believable."

2. Richard Cunningham, director of University Colleges and Christian Fellowship (UCCF) in Great Britain, gives practical training on how to give an evangelistic talk. He advises that every speaker *identify, persuade*, and *invite* (Alex Banfield Hicks and Richard Cunningham, "Identification, Persuasion, and Invitation," Christian Persuaders Podcast #1, www.bethinking.org/what-is-apologetics/introductory/identification-persuasion-and-invitation.htm [accessed January 20, 2012]). These three stages (though they overlap too much to be called true "stages") correspond closely to my three steps of *enter, challenge*, and *appeal*.

3. Francis Schaeffer, *2 Contents, 2 Realities* (Downers Grove, IL: InterVarsity, 1975), 17–18.

4. Of course the Westminster Confession and catechisms treat the commandment "Honor your father and mother," but the answers it draws from Scripture show it was not searching the text with ancestor worship in mind. The Confession tends to generalize the command to mean respect for all in authority, such as civil magistrates.

5. In Acts 17:26–28, Paul quotes pagan poets. If you are speaking biblical truth to those who are skeptical of the Bible's authority, it is good to reinforce your points with supplemental, respected authorities. So, for example, if you are teaching what the Bible says about something, and (in our Western society) you have some empirical, scientific study that confirms the Bible's statement—use the study. It gradually strengthens the skeptical listener's trust in the Word.

Contextualization includes learning which supplemental authorities are credible to the listeners.

6. See David J. Hesselgrave, *Communicating Christ Cross-Culturally* (Grand Rapids: Zondervan, 1978), 198–236.

7. See the sermons from this period, with illuminating commentary by the editor, in *The Works of Jonathan Edwards: Sermons and Discourses, 1743–1758*, vol. 25, ed. Wilson H. Kimnach (New Haven, CT: Yale University Press, 2010).

8. I believe this principle is implied in 1 Peter 2:12, a striking verse that assumes the world will in some respects praise and admire Christian faith and practice and yet in other respects will hate and persecute it; see Miroslav Volf's article on 1 Peter, "Soft Difference," www.pas.rochester.edu/~tim/study/Miroslav%201%20Peter.pdf (accessed December 1, 2015). I am not arguing that this verse proves the principle—a principle more readily seen in Paul's actual reasoning with listeners, as in Acts 17.

9. David G. Peterson, *The Acts of the Apostles* (Grand Rapids: Eerdmans, 2009), 496.

10. Thanks to Rochelle L. Cathcart for this insight.

11. C. S. Lewis, *The Problem of Pain* (New York: Macmillan, 1973), 29, 34–35.

12. Alexis de Tocqueville, *Democracy in America* (New York: HarperCollins, 1988), 296.

13. Ibid., 538.

14. Emily Bobrow, "David Foster Wallace, in His Own Words" (taken from his 2005 commencement address at Kenyon College), http://moreintelligentlife.com/story/david-foster-wallace-in-his-own-words (accessed January 4, 2012).

15. Ibid. When Wallace says we should worship "some sort of god or spiritual-type thing," he then lists "JC or Allah, be it YHWH or the Wiccan Mother-Goddess, or the Four Noble Truths, or some inviolable set of ethical principles." So he is counseling religious pluralism with a vengeance! But just as Paul in Acts 17:28 was careful—in the early stage of his argument—to express commonality between pagan poets and God, it is possible to accept Wallace's description of the *problem* as sound (i.e., that we need to build our lives around something that transcends this world).

16. See Martin Luther's comments on the first commandment in his Large Catechism (Birmingham, AL: CreateSpace, 2011), 1–3.

17. For an in-depth treatment of this subject, see chs. 1 and 3 of my book *The Meaning of Marriage* (New York: Dutton, 2011), esp. 80–82.

18. Richard Kearny, moderator, "On Forgiveness: A Roundtable Discussion with Jacques Derrida," in *Questioning God*, ed. John Caputo, Mark Dooley, and Michael Scanlon (Bloomington: Indiana University Press, 2001), 70.

19. Jean-Paul Sartre, "Existentialism Is a Humanism," in *Existentialism from Dostoyevsky to Sartre*, ed. Walter Kaufmann (New York: Meridian, 1989), 352–53, www.marxists.org/reference/archive/sartre/works/exist/sartre.htm (accessed January 20, 2012).

20. It can be argued that belief in human rights makes far more sense if there is a God than if there is not. Nicholas Wolterstorff makes this case in "Is a Secular Grounding of Human Rights Possible?" and "A Theistic Grounding of Human Rights," in *Justice: Rights and Wrongs* (Princeton, NJ: Princeton University Press, 2008), chs. 15–16. See also Christian Smith, "Does Naturalism Warrant a Moral Belief in Universal Benevolence and Human Rights?" in *The Believing Primate: Scientific, Philosophical, and Theological Reflections on the Origin of Religion,* ed. Jeffrey Schloss and Michael Murray (New York: Oxford University Press, 2009), 292–317; Timothy Keller, *Generous Justice: How God's Grace Makes Us Just* (New York: Dutton, 2010), ch. 7; Timothy Keller, *The Reason for God: Belief in an Age of Skepticism* (New York: Dutton, 2008), ch. 9.

21. Andrew Delbanco, *The Real American Dream: A Meditation on Hope* (Cambridge, MA: Harvard University Press, 1999), 103.

22. Ibid., 103–4.

23. Ibid., 106–7.

24. Theologian Dan Strange writes that non-Christian systems of thought are both antithetical to, yet practically "parasitic" on, Christian truth. That is, they must affirm some aspects of reality, of God's truth, even when they resist other parts of his truth. Strange concludes that ultimately the gospel is the "subversive fulfillment" for non-Christian systems. That is, the gospel challenges their aspirations and yet in another sense fulfills them (see "Perilous Exchange, Precious Good News: A Reformed 'Subversive Fulfillment' Interpretation of Other Religions," in *Only One Way? Three Christian Responses on the Uniqueness of Christ in a Religiously Plural World,* Gavin D'Costa, Paul Knitter, and Daniel Strange [London: SCM Press, 2011], 93).

25. Blaise Pascal, *Pensées* (New York: Collier, 1910), 68, #187.

26. See Roger Nicole, "Postscript on Penal Substitution," in *The Glory of the Atonement,* ed. Charles E. Hill and Frank A. James III (Downers Grove, IL: InterVarsity, 2004), 445–52.

Reflections on Gospel Contextualization

1. Those in the majority may often forget they are as distinctively "ethnic" as those they label "ethnic minorities." For an illuminating and challenging exploration of ethnicity, see Dewi Hughes, *Ethnic Identity from the Margins: A Christian Perspective* (Pasadena, CA: William Carey Library, 2012).

2. The distinction between magisterial and ministerial authority is Francis Turretin's in his *Institutes of Elenctic Theology* (Phillipsburg, NJ: P&R, 1992), 1:90.

3. Chip and Dan Heath, *Made to Stick: Why Some Ideas Die and Others Survive* (London: Arrow, 2008), 57.

4. One reviewer cheekily states, "To read Keller, after all, is to be trained in the art of the Aristotelian mean. This is his m.o." (Jonathan Leeman, "Book

Review: Center Church," http://9marks.org/review/center-church-doing
-balanced-gospel-centered-ministry-your-city/ [accessed March 11, 2015]).

5. Michael Horton makes this point in "Does Anybody Really Know What
Time It Is?" in *Planting, Watering, Growing*, ed. Daniel R. Hyde and Shane Lems
(Grand Rapids: Reformation Heritage Books, 2011), Kindle ed. loc. 5973. As
does Keller, Horton refers to Machen: "In the 1920s … Machen was already
issuing a complaint that the obsession with 'applied Christianity' was so pervasive
that soon there would be little Christianity left to apply" (loc. 5983).

6. Sitting squarely on the shoulders of an older generation of Dutch missiologists, particularly J. H. Bavinck.

7. See Daniel Strange, *Their Rock Is Not Like Our Rock: A Theology of Religions*
(Grand Rapids: Zondervan, 2015). The term *subversive fulfillment* is not my
own but Hendrik Kraemer's in "Continuity or Discontinuity," in *The Authority
of Faith: International Missionary Council Meeting at Tambaram, Madras*, ed.
G. Paton (London: Oxford University Press, 1939), 5.

8. In terms of application, I note four aspects in gospel communication:

1. ENTER: Step into the worldview and discern the story.
2. EXPLORE: Search for elements of grace and the idols attached to
   them.
3. EXPOSE: Show up the idols as destructive frauds.
4. EVANGELIZE: Show off the gospel as "subversive fulfillment."

9. For example, Ted Turnau, *Popologetics* (Phillipsburg, NJ: P&R, 2012); Tim
Chester and Steve Timmis, *Everyday Church* (Nottingham: Inter-Varsity, 2011).

10. Christopher Robert Flint, "How Does Christianity 'Subversively Fulfil'
Islam?" *St. Francis Magazine* 8.6 (December 2012): 776–822.

11. Tim Chester, *Unreached: Growing Churches in Working-Class and Deprived
Areas* (Nottingham: Inter-Varsity, 2012).

12. J. H. Bavinck calls the perennial questions that human beings ask
"magnetic points." See Strange, *Their Rock Is Not Like Our Rock*, 249–54.

13. J. H. Bavinck, *An Introduction to the Science of Missions*, trans. David H.
Freeman (Phillipsburg, NJ: P&R, 1960), 136–37.

14. See J. Daryl Charles, "Engaging the (Neo)Pagan Mind: Paul's Encounter
with Athenian Culture as a Model for Cultural Apologetics (Acts 17:16–34),"
Trinity Journal 16:1 (Spring 1995): 47–62.

15. Ted Turnau, "Reflecting Theologically on Popular Culture as
Meaningful," *Calvin Theological Journal* 37 (2002), 279.

16. As this relates to desire, see Ted Turnau, "Popular Culture, Apologetics,
and the Discourse of Desire," *Cultural Encounters* 8.2 (March 2013): 25–46.

17. Bavinck, *Introduction to the Science of Missions*, 140.

18. Acts 17:27 is negative in its connotation (see Ben Witherington, *The Acts of
the Apostles: A Socio-Rhetorical Commentary* [Grand Rapids: Eerdmans, 1998], 528).

19. Greg Bahnsen, *Always Ready: Directions for Defending the Faith* (Nacogdoches, TX: Covenant Media Press, 1996), 261.

20. Bavinck, *Introduction to the Science of Missions*, 138.

21. D. A. Carson, "Athens Revisited," in *Telling the Truth: Evangelizing Postmoderns*, ed. D. A. Carson (Grand Rapids: Zondervan, 2000), 394–95.

22. Bavinck, *Introduction to the Science of Missions*, 169.

23. See David K. Clark, *To Know and Love God* (Wheaton, IL: Crossway, 2003), 99–131.

24. D. A. Carson, *The Gagging of God* (Leicester: Apollos, 1996), 552. I suggest, though, that such a glorious vision does not mean the cross-cultural communicator has no role to play in new fledgling situations. To me at least, it does not seem overbearing, patronizing, or, worse still, imperialistic to recognize a distinction between gospel immaturity and maturity in these areas. Isn't such mutual support both necessary and loving? For more on this, see Bavinck, *Introduction to the Science of Missions*, 191–99.

25. What Carl R. Trueman calls "the creedal imperative." See his *The Creedal Imperative* (Wheaton, IL: Crossway, 2012).

26. Richard Lints, *The Fabric of Theology: A Prolegomenon to Evangelical Theology* (Grand Rapids: Eerdmans, 1993), 112.

27. John Piper, "Preaching as Concept Creation, Not Just Contextualization," April 10, 2008, www.desiringgod.org/articles/preaching-as-concept-creation-not-just-Contextualization (accessed March 11, 2015).

Response to Daniel Strange

1. See Lausanne Committee for World Evangelization, "The Willowbank Report: Consultation on Gospel and Culture" (Lausanne Occasional Paper 2, 1978), www.lausanne.org/content/lop/lop-2 (accessed August 31, 2015).

Chapter 5: The Tension of the City

1. Cities have a glamorous attraction to young adults today, and some Christians may imbibe the depiction of cities as consumer heavens. See "Is London a Luxury Resort?" and "The Consumer City: Vancouver," in Edward Glaeser, *The Triumph of the City: How Our Greatest Invention Makes Us Richer, Smarter, Greener, Healthier, and Happier* (New York: Penguin, 2011).

2. The *Dictionary of Biblical Imagery* (ed. Leland Ryken, James C. Wilhoit, and Tremper Longman III [Downers Grove, IL: InterVarsity, 1998], 150) speaks of the city as "humanity *en masse*" and therefore "humanity 'writ large.'"

3. The *Dictionary of Biblical Imagery* (p. 150) defines *city* as a "fortified habitation."

4. See Frank Frick, *The City in Ancient Israel* (Missoula, MT: Scholars Press, 1977), 79.

5. Translation by Leslie C. Allen, *Psalms 101–150*, rev. ed. (Word Biblical Commentary 21; Nashville: Nelson, 2002), 210.

6. See Frick, *City in Ancient Israel*, 79.

7. See Franklin E. Zimring, *The City That Became Safe: New York's Lessons for Urban Crime and Its Control* (New York: Oxford University Press), 2011. Across all categories, New York City's crime rate is down 80 percent from twenty years ago. The drop came without an increase in prisoners incarcerated (the traditional conservative solution for crime) or a decrease in poverty (the traditional liberal solution for crime). Smarter law enforcement only accounts for about half of the drop. Zimring concludes that many of the factors that changed attitudes and behavior are simply being missed because social theorists—both conservative and liberal—simply don't know what to look for. He writes (p. 204), "The specific mechanisms at work in New York City [that have led to decreased crime] ... are unknown." Nevertheless, he states (p. 202) that this twenty-year decline essentially proves the "inessentiality of crime to urban life," thus putting to rest one of the deepest fears generated in the last century about cities. At the end of his book, he writes (p. 217), "We now know that life-threatening crime is not an incurable urban disease in the United States." It is interesting to note that Zimring does not consider as one possible factor the growth of evangelical churches, adding somewhere between a half million to one million Christians to the NYC population over the past generation (see Michael Luo, "In New York, Billy Graham Will Find an Evangelical Force," *New York Times*, June 21, 2005, www.nytimes.com/2005/06/21/nyregion/21evangelical.html?ref=billygraham; see also the website www.nycreligion.info/).

8. See, e.g., Philip Bess, "A Realist Philosophical Case for Urbanism and against Sprawl: Part One," www.thepublicdiscourse.com/2011/07/3379 (accessed January 23, 2012).

9. The classic text describing and celebrating the density of population, mixed-land use, and street life is Jane Jacobs, *The Death and Life of Great American Cities* (New York: Vintage, 1961), esp. part 1 "The Peculiar Nature of Cities," and part 2, "The Conditions for City Diversity."

10. Glaeser, *Triumph of the City*, 6.

11. It should be noted there is some scholarly debate about who actually builds the city: Is it Cain, or is it his son Enoch? The issue has to do with the name of the city. The name of Enoch's son, Irad, sounds like Eridu, generally regarded in Mesopotamian tradition to be the first city to be founded (see Gordon J. Wenham, *Genesis 1–15* [Word Biblical Commentary 1a; Nashville: Word, 1987], 110–12).

12. Robert Alter, *Genesis: Translation and Commentary* (New York: Norton, 1997), 19.

13. Henri Blocher, *In the Beginning: The Opening Chapters of Genesis*, trans. David G. Preston (Downers Grove, IL: InterVarsity, 1984), 199.

14. Geerhardus Vos, *Biblical Theology: Old and New Testaments* (Grand Rapids: Eerdmans, 1948), 294.

15. Genesis 18:16–33; 19:16–36; see 2 Peter 2:7–8.

16. Vos, *Biblical Theology*, 295. It should be noted that Geerhardus Vos generally saw the power of the city to create and influence culture as being a negative influence in human history. Meredith Kline in his *Kingdom Prologue* is more balanced, saying the city is a "divine ordinance" (p. 101). However, Kline sees the city as an instrument of God's common grace. Its effect on culture when used well is only "remedial," a way to resist the tendencies of human evil and is not a way to bring in the kingdom of God, contrary to those in the Kuyperian school (pp. 105–6). For more on the related debate about Christ and culture, see part 3 of this volume.

17. J. Alec Motyer, *The Prophecy of Isaiah: An Introduction and Commentary* (Downers Grove, IL: InterVarsity, 1993), 16.

18. Ibid., 17.

19. Note the idea of the two cities worked out in Isaiah 13–27. The theology is worked out most thoroughly in Augustine's *The City of God* (*De Civitate Dei*).

20. Augustine, *City of God*, 14:13.

21. Revelation 11:8, 13; 16:19; 17:18; 18:10, 16, 18–19, 21; see also 2:13—Pergamum, "your city—where Satan lives."

22. Revelation 3:12; 11:2; 20:9; 21:2, 10, 14–27; 22:2–3, 14.

23. Jerusalem, as history has shown, was not the city of God per se. The prophets showed how far short the earthly Jerusalem fell from its future antitype (Jer 13:9–14; Mic 3:11–12). It was only a mixture of the city of man and the city of God, at its best pointing beyond itself to that ultimate city (see Jer 3:16–17).

24. See 2 Kings 24:14, where "all the officers and fighting men, and all the craftsmen and artisans" were exiled. The professional classes were taken and the poor left behind. Daniel 1:3–5 describes how the nobility and cream of Israel's ruling classes were to receive instruction in Babylonian ways and culture. Tremper Longman III (*Daniel* [NIV Application Commentary; Grand Rapids: Zondervan, 1999], 47) observes that Nebuchadnezzar wanted to assimilate conquered people groups into Babylonian culture so they would lose their distinct cultural identities and thus become compliant.

25. While Jeremiah 28 calls the Jews to invest in the life of the city, Daniel 1 warns them against defiling themselves through overassimilation to the pagan culture. Both of these texts were given to the exilic community for guidance. Thanks to Richard Coekin for this insight.

Chapter 6: Redemption and the City

1. Note the references to "Pauline Christianity" in Wayne A. Meeks, *The First Urban Christians: The Social World of the Apostle Paul*, 2nd ed. (New Haven, CT: Yale University Press, 2003); see also Todd D. Still and David G. Horrell, eds., *After the First Urban Christians: The Social-Scientific Study of Pauline Christianity Twenty-Five Years Later* (Edinburgh: T&T Clark, 2009).

2. Leland Ryken, James C. Wilhoit, and Tremper Longman III, eds., *Dictionary of Biblical Imagery* (Downers Grove, IL: InterVarsity, 1998), 153, emphasis mine.

3. John R. W. Stott, *The Message of Acts: The Spirit, the Church, and the World* (Downers Grove, IL: InterVarsity, 1994), 293.

4. Ibid., 314.

5. Ibid., 305.

6. Ibid., 314.

7. J. A. Alexander, as quoted in ibid., 293.

8. Ibid., 292–93.

9. I recognize that other human factors were used by God to bring about the astonishing growth of the early church in its first three centuries. There was a cultural crisis in the Greco-Roman worldview, and the worship of the old pagan gods was dying out. Nevertheless, historians now realize how important it was for the influence and spread of the church that it first took root in the urban areas.

10. Richard Fletcher, *The Barbarian Conversion: From Paganism to Christianity* (Berkeley: University of California, 1999).

11. See Harvie Conn, "Christ and the City: Biblical Themes for Building Urban Theology Models," in *Discipling the City*, ed. Roger Greenway (Grand Rapids: Baker, 1979), 222–86. Conn writes (p. 237), "The city is the fulfiller of the paradise of God ... This eschatological strand repeatedly ties the future of the city with the original, sinless past of Eden and its restoration in Christ. Even under the curse, man's cultural calling will be maintained." In other words, the garden of Eden, had Adam not fallen, would have developed into the city seen in Revelation 21. It would have been a perfect city under God. In his essay, Conn explains that the city has the same three functions as the garden of God did, namely, it is (1) a place to cultivate the earth and "mine the cultural riches of creation," (2) a place to live in safety and security, and (3) a place to meet God.

12. Gordon J. Wenham, *Genesis 1–15* (Word Biblical Commentary 1a; Nashville: Word, 1987), 61.

13. Gordon Spykman, *Reformational Theology: A New Paradigm for Doing Dogmatics* (Grand Rapids: Eerdmans, 1992), 256.

14. Harvie Conn and Manuel Ortiz, *Urban Ministry: The Kingdom, the City, and the People of God* (Downers Grove, IL: InterVarsity, 2001), 87.

Chapter 7: The Call to the City

1. This is true whether one takes a stricter view of population within legal "city limits" (see www.worldatlas.com/citypops.htm) or larger "metropolitan areas" (see www.citypopulation.de/world/Agglomerations.html).

2. See Edward Glaeser, *The Triumph of the City: How Our Greatest Invention Makes Us Richer, Smarter, Greener, Healthier, and Happier* (New York: Penguin, 2011), 1. Other statistics in this paragraph (and the preceding one) are taken from the *Economist* article "The Brown Revolution" (May 9, 2002), www .economist.com/node/1120305 (accessed January 24, 2012).

3. A good, up-to-date source of information on cities is the special report issued by *Financial Times* in early 2010 titled "The Future of Cities," www.ft .com/cities (accessed January 24, 2012).

4. See Thomas L. Friedman, *The World Is Flat 3.0: A Brief History of the Twenty-First Century*, rev. ed. (New York: Farrar, Straus and Giroux, 2007).

5. See comments on the effects of agglomeration in chapter 8.

6. Edwin Heathcote, "From Megacity to Metacity," *Financial Times* (April 6, 2010), http://on.ft.com/Ihh7RT (accessed January 24, 2012).

7. Noted urban sociologist Saskia Sassen and economist Edward Glaeser list the most influential city-networks in the world: (1) New York–Washington, D.C.–Chicago, (2) Beijing–Hong Kong, (3) Frankfurt–Berlin, (4) Istanbul–Ankara, (5) Brasilia–Rio de Janeiro–Sao Paulo. Each network combines the strengths of finance, government, and the creative arts ("16 Global Cities to Watch," Foreign Policy 190 [2011]: 72-85).

8. Neal Peirce, "The 'Citistates' Are on the Rise, and the Competition Is Fierce," *Philadelphia Inquirer* (July 26, 1993), A11, http://articles.philly .com/1993-07-26/news/25975949_1_citistate-nation-states-world-population (accessed January 24, 2012).

9. The dynamics outlined in this section are especially pronounced in American cities, but they characterize many European cities as well.

10. Redeemer Presbyterian Church in New York City came into existence at the very beginning of this renaissance—in 1989. At that time, moving into the center city to begin a church seemed to be a fool's errand. The year we moved to New York City, a highly publicized poll revealed that most of the residents of NYC would move away if they could. Indeed, in the 1970s and into the 1980s, nearly everyone was trying to leave cities—well-off and poor, white, black, and immigrant. Those were bad times! Yet, within a few years of our founding, I began to get calls from churches, denominations, and leaders who had begun to notice the renaissance in nearby cities. They realized it was time to plant churches to reach the new residential communities that were growing in cities.

11. Glaeser, *Triumph of the City*, 131–32, 238–41, 259–60.

12. See Ariella Cohen, "Cities in Crisis," *Next American City* (Spring 2009), available at www.citymayors.com/economics/us-cities-crisis.html (accessed January 24, 2012).

13. See David Owen, *Green Metropolis: Why Living Smaller, Living Closer, and Driving Less Are the Keys to Sustainability* (New York: Riverhead, 2009). For a shorter survey, see "Is There Anything Greener than Blacktop?" in Glaeser, *Triumph of the City*, 199.

14. "In the absence of evidence that a reduction or increase in crime can be tied to economic or environmental variables, Mr. Bloomberg said he concluded the success is due to 'a better police department than ever before.' 'We have looked for every kind of relationship and correlation to the weather, the economy, or whatever,' he said. 'It's not there'" (Tamer El-Ghobashy, "Mayor Touts 'Safest Decade,'" *Wall Street Journal* (December 29, 2011).

15. In the *Wall Street Journal* article "Mayor Touts 'Safest Decade,'" James Alan Fox, a professor of criminology, states that policing is just one of several factors that contribute to precipitous crime reductions. "There's no one reason why crime falls." Fox cites, in addition to better policing, an aging population, an increase in incarceration, and the stabilizing of illegal drug markets. But Franklin Zimring, in *The City That Became Safe*, states that New York City's crime reduction happened despite no significant changes in the population age or incarceration or even illegal drug use. He shows that many of the reasons for precipitous crime reduction are yet unidentified or hard to measure. He does conclude, however, that the last twenty years proves that crime is not a necessary fact of life in major cities.

16. See Peter Berger and Richard John Neuhaus, *To Empower People: From State to Civil Society* (Washington, D.C.: American Enterprise Institute, 1985).

17. S. Mitra Kalita and Robbie Whelan, "No McMansions for Millennials," *Wall Street Journal* (January 13, 2011), http://blogs.wsj.com/developments/2011/01/13/no-mcmansions-for-millennials/; Jordan Weissmann, "Why Don't Young Americans Buy Cars?" *The Atlantic* (March 25, 2012), www.theatlantic.com/business/archive/2012/03/why-dont-young-americans-buy-cars/255001/#.T3H8uIuSBoQ.twitter (accessed April 5, 2012).

18. See Harvie Conn, *The American City and the Evangelical Church* (Grand Rapids: Baker, 1994), 181–82.

19. We estimate there are 322,000 Christian churches for a United States population of 311 million—a bit more than one church for every 1,000 residents (see the website of the Hartford Institute for Religious Research, http://hirr.hartsem.edu/research/fastfacts/fast_facts.html). The average size of a congregation in the U.S. is 75, which means that if there is one church for every 1,000 residents in a city, 7.5 percent of the population will be going to church. Note that these are median figures; actual numbers vary greatly from region to region.

20. See Philip Jenkins, *The Next Christendom: The Coming of Global Christianity*, rev. ed. (New York: Oxford University Press, 2007); idem, *The New*

Faces of Christianity: Believing the Bible in the Global South (New York: Oxford University Press, 2008); Lamin Sanneh, *Whose Religion Is Christianity? The Gospel beyond the West* (Grand Rapids: Eerdmans, 2003).

21. These statements are based on numerous examples I have witnessed firsthand in New York City over the past twenty years.

22. See Mark Galli's interview of Bob Roberts, "Glocal Church Ministry," *Christianity Today* 51.7 (July 2007), www.christianitytoday.com/ct/2007/july/30.42.html (accessed January 24, 2012).

23. It should be said that this is not the only way to reach out to the world. There is still a need for Christians in every country to consider the call to relocate to distant lands to accomplish the global mission of the church. To my surprise, in recent years I have seen that domestic urban church planting has almost become romanticized among young evangelicals in the same way overseas missions was romanticized among former generations. We should avoid all rose-colored idealizations. My point is that cities—at home and abroad—are far more important now to the accomplishment of the world mission of the church than they were fifty years ago.

24. David Brooks, "I Dream of Denver," *New York Times* (February 16, 2009), www.nytimes.com/2009/02/17/opinion/17brooks.html (accessed January 24, 2012).

25. Jenkins, *Next Christendom*, 93.

26. Ibid., 94.

Chapter 8: The Gospel for the City

1. I am thinking of a sermon by Francis A. Schaeffer titled "No Little People, No Little Places," in *No Little People: Sixteen Sermons for the Twentieth Century* (Downers Grove, IL: InterVarsity, 1974); see www.sbts.edu/resources/files/2010/02/sbjt_062_schaeffer.pdf (accessed January 24, 2012).

2. Thanks to Richard Coekin for convincingly emphasizing this point to me.

3. Edward Glaeser, *The Triumph of the City: How Our Greatest Invention Makes Us Richer, Smarter, Greener, Healthier, and Happier* (New York: Penguin, 2011), 36.

4. Ibid.

5. For a thorough but highly technical study of this subject, see Edward L. Glaeser, *Cities, Agglomeration, and Spatial Equilibrium* (New York: Oxford University Press, 2008).

6. Ibid., 1.

7. See Elizabeth Currid, "How Art and Culture Happen in New York: Implications for Urban Economic Development," *Journal of the American Planning Association* 73:4 (Autumn 2007): 454–67.

8. Ibid., 454.

9. Ibid.

10. Ryan Avent, *The Gated City: How America Made Its Most Productive Places Ever Less Accessible* (Amazon Digital Services, Kindle Single, 2011).

11. Some have pointed out to me that when Jonah was rebuked for not "loving the city" as God did (Jonah 4:10–11), he was being challenged to love the *people* of the city—not "city living" or the city as social structure. And this certainly is true for the Jonah text. Nevertheless, as we have shown in chapter 5 ("The Tension of the City"), the Bible *does* see the city as a positive social arrangement, and many Bible scholars (e.g., Henri Blocher, Meredith Kline) even argue that the Bible sees the city as God's creation. Speaking practically, Christians who want to be fruitful in cities must have at least a positive appreciation for the strengths and advantages of city life as outlined in this part of the book.

12. Full disclosure: global city church planting is one of my greatest passions. It is the primary focus of our affiliated global missions agency, Redeemer City to City (visit www.redeemercitytocity.com).

13. Glaeser, *Triumph of the City*, 126. See also p. 259, where Glaeser carefully critiques the view of Richard Florida, namely, that cities flourish when they attract the young and hip, artists, the avant-garde, and people who have alternative lifestyles. Glaeser believes that cities should instead concentrate on "core public services"—safe streets, good schools, and so on.

14. Jane Jacobs, *The Death and Life of Great American Cities* (New York: Vintage, 1961), 117.

15. See also part 7 ("Integrative Ministry") in *Center Church* (pp. 291–336); this material can also be found in *Serving a Movement* (pp. 103–68).

Reflections on City Vision

1. Dietrich Bonhoeffer, *Letters and Papers from Prison: The Enlarged Edition*, ed. Eberhard Bethge (New York: Simon & Schuster, 1973), 279.

2. While Keller draws deeply from some of the writings of Francis Schaeffer and Lesslie Newbigin, the inclusion of the voices of people like Samuel Escobar, C. René Padilla, and John Perkins may have strengthened his argument about moralists' idolization of culture through a methodological consistency. In short, his theological and cultural canon could have exemplified the universal and particular tensions he says are ever-present in culture.

3. James Emery White, *The Rise of the Nones: Understanding and Reaching the Religiously Unaffiliated* (Grand Rapids: Baker, 2014).

4. "The Shifting Religious Identity of Latinos in the United States," Pew Research Center: Religion and Public Life, May 7, 2014, www.pewforum.org/2014/05/07/the-shifting-religious-identity-of-latinos-in-the-united-states/ (accessed March 16, 2015).

5. Homi Bhabha, *The Location of Culture* (New York: Routledge, 1994).

6. For a fuller treatment of power and agency from a postmodernist perspective, see Michel Foucault, *The History of Sexuality: The Will to Knowledge* (London: Penguin, 1998) or his *Discipline and Punish: The Birth of a Prison* (London: Penguin, 1991).

7. Dietrich Bonhoeffer, *Life Together: A Discussion of Christian Fellowship* (New York: HarperCollins, 1954).

8. Jorge Lara-Braud, *Church & Society Magazine*, March/April 1986, 20.

9. Martin Luther King Jr., "An Address before the National Press Club," in *The Essential Writings and Speeches of Martin Luther King Jr.*, ed. James M. Washington (New York: HarperCollins, 1991), 101.

10. Manuel Ortiz, *One New People: Models for Developing a Multiethnic Church* (Downers Grove, IL: InterVarsity, 1996), 108.

11. Bruce J. Nicholls, *Contextualization: A Theology of Gospel and Culture* (Downers Grove, IL: InterVarsity, 1979), 31, as quoted by Keller, p. 37–38.

12. I know well the polemics and controversies around this term, particularly around contemporary global ministries studies and postcolonial theorists. The term, of course, is really an attempt to categorize how the migration of Christians from the global South is impacting faith in the global North.

13. For a fuller description of the iconoclastic implications of a global church in light of the faithfulness of God to the covenant, see N. T. Wright, *Paul and the Faithfulness of God* (Minneapolis: Fortress, 2013).

Response to Gabriel Salguero

1. Charles Taylor, *A Secular Age* (Cambridge, MA: Harvard University Press, 2007).

Chapter 9: The Cultural Crisis of the Church

1. This story is told well in Joel A. Carpenter, *Revive Us Again: The Reawakening of American Fundamentalism* (New York: Oxford University Press, 1999).

2. A strong reaction against traditional cultural values in general and Christianity in particular came to Britain and Europe more quickly after World War II than it did in the United States. It may be that the culture shift happened faster in Europe than in the U.S. because evangelical Christianity in the U.S. is populist—appealing to the masses—while evangelicalism in the UK is not (see Alister Chapman, "The Educated Evangelicalism of John Stott," http://blogs. westmont.edu/magazine/2009/11/09/the-educated-evangelicalism-of-john-stott/ [accessed January 30, 2012]). In other words, the broad appeal of populist evangelical Christianity among the poor and working classes has probably served to keep American society more traditional. Some observers believe this may be changing,

however (see, e.g., Robert D. Putnam and David E. Campbell, *American Grace: How Religion Divides and Unites Us* [New York: Simon and Schuster, 2010]).

3. This social shift actually happened in two stages, according to Putnam and Campbell. In the 1960s, many in the mainline Protestant churches identified with the ideas of 1960s counterculture, which led to a backlash so that many Americans during the late 1970s through the early 1990s moved from mainline churches into more evangelical and conservative churches and swelled their ranks. This helped fuel the rise of the Christian Right, which vigorously opposed the views of 1960s radicals. However, according to Putnam and Campbell, just as mainline churches became associated with the extreme Left, so the evangelical church by the 1990s had come to be identified with the hard political Right, thus causing a similar move away from the conservative church and its values, particularly by those under the age of thirty-five. Meanwhile, many of the young 1960s radicals had completed their "long march through the major cultural institutions," especially the American academy, and the entertainment/media world. The result is that United States society—in particular in its large cities and on the coasts—has finally begun to approximate Europe and Canada in the disdain with which Christian doctrine and Christian morality is held in the public culture (see Putnam and Campbell, *American Grace*, 91–133).

4. Figures cited in Putnam and Campbell, *American Grace*, 97–99.

5. For example, in the 1950s, the movie studio producing Cecil B. DeMille's *The Ten Commandments* sent monuments of the biblical Ten Commandments to hundreds of public buildings—parks, courthouses, etc. These monuments were accepted and set up everywhere, and no one even raised an eyebrow. In the last twenty years, of course, such monuments are the subject of intense litigation and debate.

6. The preceding paragraphs are based on my own experience of doing personal evangelism in the homes of a small town in Virginia during the late 1970s and early 1980s. There the population had been "Christianized" by the culture, as had been done in the West for centuries, though few people understood the gospel or had a vibrant personal faith.

7. I once heard a lecture by the management pioneer Peter Drucker. He told how surprised he was when he moved to the New York City area in the 1950s (to teach at New York University) and tried to take out a mortgage in order to buy a house. At the bank he was asked if he went to church or synagogue. He was surprised to be asked this (Drucker was from Austria) and asked why it was relevant. He was told something along the lines of, "Why would we trust a man who didn't go to church or synagogue?"

8. See Putnam and Campbell, *American Grace*, 124–25.

9. See Philip Jacob Spener, *Pia Desideria*, trans. Theodore G. Tappert (Minneapolis: Fortress, 1964).

10. Mark Noll, *The Rise of Evangelicalism: The Age of Edwards, Whitefield and the Wesleys* (Downers Grove, IL: InterVarsity, 2003), 60–65.

11. See James D. Hunter, *To Change the World: The Irony, Tragedy, and*

Possibility of Christianity in the Late Modern World (New York: Oxford University Press, 2010), 90.

12. Quoted in William McLoughlin, *Modern Revivalism: Charles Grandison Finney to Billy Graham* (Eugene, OR: Wipf & Stock, 2005), 257.

13. The story is told in Owen D. Strachan, "Reenchanting the Evangelical Mind: Park Street Church's Harold Ockenga, the Boston Scholars, and the Mid-Century Intellectual Surge" (unpublished PhD diss., Trinity Evangelical Divinity School, 2011).

14. Carl F. H. Henry, *The Uneasy Conscience of Modern Fundamentalism* (Grand Rapids: Eerdmans, 1947).

15. See Barry Hankins, *Francis Schaeffer and the Shaping of Evangelical America* (Grand Rapids: Eerdmans, 2008), 63. Hankins helpfully shows that Schaeffer's legacy was twofold. When he was in Europe (in the 1950s and 1960s), Schaeffer popularized to a generation of younger evangelicals the ideas of worldview and of moving out into public culture to speak and work in a society-influencing, distinctively Christian manner (see Hankins's ch. 5: "Progressive Prophet of Culture"). Later, when he returned to the United States (in the 1970s and 1980s), he laid the foundation for the Christian Right (see Hankins's ch. 8: "A Manifesto for Christian Right Activism"). In other words, Schaeffer was what we will later call a "Transformationist," operating at different stages in his life as neo-Calvinist thinker and Christian Right activist.

16. I would not call the pietistic stance a model for relating Christ to culture. It would be clearer to see it as the *absence* of a Christ and culture model, or even an "anti-model." Even Christ and culture models that advise deliberate withdrawal have particular (negative) views of human culture derived from reflection on Scripture and culture. The pietistic stance is more of a mind-set that ignores culture or sees it as mainly irrelevant.

17. Abraham Kuyper, "Sphere Sovereignty," in *Abraham Kuyper: A Centennial Reader*, ed. James D. Bratt (Grand Rapids: Eerdmans, 1998), 488. The entire address is found on pp. 463–90.

18. In his essay "Common Grace in Science," Kuyper wrote, "A thought of God forms the core of the essence of things; God's thinking prescribes their form of existence, their appearance, their law for life, their destiny." He likens this to a pocket watch. A child may see "the golden case, the face, and the moving hands" but will understand neither what lies within the watch to make it tick nor the purpose of the ticking—not just to make sounds but also to measure time. Until you know what a watch is for, you don't understand it, and you can't evaluate whether it is a good or bad watch. Kuyper then says that the non-Christian looks at the world the way a child looks at a watch. Only the person with the Word of God knows why things are and why they operate in the world as they do. What then is education and work done from a Christian worldview? It is to use "an ability imparted to man to unwrap the thoughts of God that lie embodied in creation" (Bratt, *Abraham Kuyper: A Centennial Reader*, 444).

19. The thinkers usually associated with neo-Calvinism include Abraham Kuyper, Herman Dooyeweerd, Herman Bavinck, Albert Wolters, Richard Mouw, Alvin Plantinga, Nicholas Wolterstorff, Cornelius Plantinga, George Marsden, Evan Runner, Calvin Seerveld, Craig Bartholomew, Michael Goheen, and James Skillen. Institutions include Calvin College and Calvin Theological Seminary in Grand Rapids, Michigan; Dordt College in Sioux Center, Iowa; the CCO (Coalition for Christian Outreach) and its annual Jubilee Conference; Redeemer University College in Ancaster, Ontario, Canada; the Institute for Christian Studies in Toronto, Ontario, Canada; the Center for Public Justice in Washington, D.C.; and Trinity Christian College in Palos Heights, Illinois. For an introductory sketch of the movement, see Derek Melleby, "Neo-Calvinism 101."

20. For a comprehensive but accessible survey, see David K. Naugle, *Worldview: The History of a Concept* (Grand Rapids: Eerdmans, 2002). Naugle lists those who pioneered the concept with Protestant evangelicals: Abraham Kuyper, Gordon Clark, Carl F. H. Henry, and Francis Schaeffer. For a brief, helpful introduction to the concept, see James W. Sire, *Naming the Elephant: Worldview as a Concept* (Downers Grove, IL: InterVarsity, 2004), and his classic, *The Universe Next Door: A Basic Worldview Catalog*, 5th ed. (Downers Grove, IL: InterVarsity, 2009).

21. Joel Carpenter ("The Perils of Prosperity: Neo-Calvinism and the Future of Religious Colleges," in *The Future of Religious Colleges*, ed. Paul J. Dovre [Grand Rapids: Eerdmans, 2002], 183) points out that older bases for Christian higher education "such as the Renaissance Christian humanism practiced at the early Harvard, or the Scottish Enlightenment's Common Sense philosophy, as propagated for a century out of Princeton, have largely disappeared from the American scene."

22. In the last part of his life, Francis Schaeffer, who originally promoted worldview as an inspiration for Christians to enter the arts, the academy, business, and the media, lent his support to Falwell and the growth of the Christian Right (see Hankin, *Francis Schaeffer*, 200–204). Kuyper's contemporary legacy is therefore quite politically mixed. On the one hand, the movement of neo-Calvinism based on Kuyper's thought is marked by thinkers whose political views tend to be centrist or center-left. On the other hand, Kuyper has been the hero of the Religious Right and to some degree to the followers of Rousas Rushdoony and those in the camp called Christian Reconstructionism or theonomy.

23. Ronald Reagan, in his presidential inaugural address, January 20, 1981, famously said, "Government is not the solution to our problem; government is the problem."

24. Lynne and Bill Hybels wrote an "autobiography" of Willow Creek under the title *Rediscovering Church: The Story and Vision of Willow Creek Community Church* (Grand Rapids: Zondervan, 1997).

25. G. A. Pritchard (*Willow Creek Seeker Services: Evaluating a New Way of*

Doing Church [Grand Rapids: Baker, 1995]) wrote an early critique of Willow Creek. Pritchard found that seeker services drew a greater percentage of believers than seekers. Kimon Sargeant (*Seeker Churches: Promoting Traditional Religion in a Nontraditional Way* [New Brunswick, NJ: Rutgers University Press, 2000]) provided another critique of the seeker movement. Sargeant and others argue that by adapting ministry to techniques drawn from the secular business and therapy worlds, churches unwittingly bring in the underlying values embodied in those techniques and subtly change the Christian message.

26. So much has been written about the emerging church that I won't even try to compile a bibliographic footnote!

27. See Lesslie Newbigin, "Can the West Be Converted?" *Princeton Seminary Bulletin* 6.1 (1985): 25–37, www.newbigin.net/assets/pdf/85cwbc.pdf (accessed January 30, 2012).

28. Darrell L. Guder, ed., *Missional Church: A Vision for the Sending of the Church in North America* (Grand Rapids: Eerdmans, 1998).

29. The forerunners of this stream of influence were Richard Foster, *A Celebration of Discipline: The Path to Spiritual Growth*, 3rd ed. (New York: HarperCollins, 1988), and Dallas Willard, *The Spirit of the Disciplines: Understanding How God Changes Lives* (New York: HarperCollins, 1988).

30. See Kent Carlson and Mike Lueken, *Renovation of the Church: What Happens When a Seeker Church Discovers Spiritual Formation* (Downers Grove, IL: InterVarsity, 2011).

31. D. A. Carson, *Christ and Culture Revisited* (Grand Rapids: Eerdmans, 2008), 224.

Chapter 10: The Cultural Responses of the Church

1. I know many of my readers are not ministering in the United States. However, because of its reach, the U.S. church's struggles have ripple effects everywhere. Those ministering in other countries may uncritically adopt materials forged in the United States because they don't know the background debates and perspectives the material represents. So I hope this description helps readers understand not only the U.S. situation but their own as well. For example, while there is no exact analogy to the Religious Right in the UK, other forms of the "Transformationist" category are present. I expect, therefore, that most of this chapter will be of some help to those who minister in cities around the world.

2. H. Richard Niebuhr, *Christ and Culture* (New York: Harper, 1956). This summary is based on that of George Hunsinger as outlined in R. Michael Allen, *Reformed Theology* (Edinburgh: T&T Clark, 2010), 168.

3. Niebuhr, *Christ and Culture*, 44.

4. Ibid.

5. Indeed, I'll go so far as to say that whenever a thinker (such as Newbigin) doesn't fit well into one model, it is a sign of strength.

6. Nicholas Wolterstorff, "In Reply," *Perspectives: A Journal of Reformed Thought* (February 2008), www.rca.org/page.aspx?pid=3772 (accessed January 31, 2012).

7. Steve Mathonnet-VanderWell, "Reformed Intramurals: What Neo-Calvinists Get Wrong," in *Perspectives* (February 2008), www.rca.org/page .aspx?pid=3771 (accessed January 31, 2012). *Perspectives* was previously titled *The Reformed Journal*, and in the 1970s and 1980s it was the main forum for Kuyperian neo-Calvinist writers such as Nicholas Wolterstorff, Alvin Plantinga, Richard Mouw, George Marsden, and others. See Barry Hankins, *Francis Schaeffer and the Shaping of Evangelical America* (Grand Rapids: Eerdmans, 2008), which shows the links between Kuyper, Schaeffer, and Colson (pp. 121, 139) and Schaeffer's role in the early formation of the Christian Right (pp. 192–227).

8. See Jeff Sharlet, *The Family: The Secret Fundamentalism at the Heart of American Power* (New York: HarperCollins, 2008), 342–50, 429; see also Hankins, *Francis Schaeffer*, 192–227, for the connections between the thought of Rousas Rushdoony, John Whitehead, and Francis Schaeffer as it helped influence the beginnings of the Christian Right.

9. See Rousas John Rushdoony, *The Institutes of Biblical Law* (Phillipsburg, NJ: P&R, 1990); Gary North and Gary DeMar, *Christian Reconstructionism: What It Is, What It Isn't* (Tyler, TX: Institute for Christian Economics, 1991). Reconstructionists have not called for a Christian minority to take power and impose biblical moral law on the majority but instead believe that Christianity will grow among the population in the future until there is a Christian consensus, and then biblical law—including execution for idolatry, adultery, homosexuality, etc.—will be put into effect.

10. Rushdoony, *Institutes of Biblical Law*, 100, 214, 747.

11. See David Field, "Samuel Rutherford and the Confessionally Christian State," http://davidpfield.com/other/RutherfordCCS.pdf (accessed January 31, 2012).

12. For a conservative Transformationist critique of the neo-Calvinist idea of "principled pluralism," see Field, "Samuel Rutherford and the Confessionally Christian State," 27–32.

13. This is, of course, a generalized statement. There are those within the Christian Right who use an educational strategy. Chuck Colson employs a predominantly educational strategy—worldview education—for cultural transformation, though clear political overtones often come through in his training and publications. And, by the same token, I understand there have been political movements, particularly within Canada, associated with neo-Calvinism.

14. See Albert M. Wolters, *Creation Regained: Biblical Basics for a Reformational Worldview*, 2nd ed. (Grand Rapids: Eerdmans, 2005), 27–39.

15. Herman Bavinck, "Common Grace," trans. R. C. Van Leeuwen, *Calvin Theological Journal* 24 (1989): 59–61.

16. Geerhardus Vos, *The Teaching of Jesus Concerning the Kingdom of God and the Church* (Eugene, OR: Wipf & Stock, 1998), 163. As soon as he says this, however, Vos goes on to make it clear that this does not mean the institutional church should have political power or control society through the state. Rather, the kingdom of God manifests itself in society outside the church as regenerate individual Christians do their work and live their lives to God's glory. Here he honors the important "sphere sovereignty" teaching of Kuyper. Vos defines the kingdom in this way: "The kingdom means the renewal of the world through the introduction of supernatural forces" (p. 192). By this he means it is not just a subjective experience of God in the heart, but the power of God that has come into the world through a great series of "objective ... facts and transactions" purposed to eventually overcome all sin, evil, suffering, and death in the world.

17. While many who hold to the Two Kingdoms model encourage Christians to excel in their vocations and see this as serving God in general, most strongly disagree that such work is *kingdom* work or that it furthers Christ's saving purposes. So, ultimately, I believe "Two Kingdoms" will in practice be less celebrative of Christians in secular vocations than will the Transformationists.

18. For a good, brief overview of the importance of institutions, see Hugh Heclo, *On Thinking Institutionally* (Boulder, CO: Paradigm, 2008).

19. For a book that provides something of this kind of self-examination and correction for the Christian Right, see Michael Gerson and Peter Wehner, *City of Man: Religion and Politics in a New Era* (Chicago: Moody, 2010). Gerson and Wehner are political conservatives who are critical of the Religious Right, warning of the danger of identifying the city of God with any particular political agenda. The book calls Christian readers to a much more measured and chastened—but still moderately conservative—political engagement.

20. James K. A. Smith, *Desiring the Kingdom: Worship, Worldview, and Cultural Formation* (Grand Rapids: Baker, 2009). Smith, citing Canadian philosopher Charles Taylor, proposes that the term *social imaginaries* would be a better term than *worldviews*.

21. Mathonnet-VanderWell, "Reformed Intramurals." This article lists a series of criticisms of Transformationism from within the neo-Calvinist movement.

22. I do not have room here to review Smith's important book. In brief, I believe his thesis is largely correct, especially in his dependence on Augustine, who argues that worldviews are the product of "the order of our loves," not merely our doctrine. However, I think the book tends to buy too deeply into Aristotle over Plato. Plato taught that right action follows from right thinking—"as we think so we are," while Aristotle taught that right thinking follows from right action and behavior—"we become what we do." I think Christians should be careful not to lift up either thinking or behavior as the key. An overly Platonic

view will indeed see teaching and preaching as the main way we change lives, while an overly Aristotelian view will tend to see liturgy and the sacraments as the main way. But the key is the heart. The heart's commitments are changed through repentance—which involves both thinking and behavior. As Thomas Cranmer taught us to pray, "Grant ... that our hearts, and all our members, being mortified from all worldly and carnal lusts, may in all things obey thy blessed will; through the same thy son Jesus Christ our Lord" (C. Frederick Barbee and Paul F. M. Zahl, *The Collects of Thomas Cranmer* [Grand Rapids: Eerdmans, 1999], 12).

23. Mathonnet-VanderWell, "Reformed Intramurals."

24. "The Christian way to eat your peas," as one anti-Transformationist wag once put it to me.

25. Quoted in Mathonnet-VanderWell, "Reformed Intramurals."

26. See James D. Hunter, *To Change the World: The Irony, Tragedy, and Possibility of Christianity in the Late Modern World* (New York: Oxford University Press, 2010), 3–98.

27. Ibid.

28. As we will see, while many Counterculturalists are too afraid of exercising power in society, many Transformationists are not afraid enough.

29. Hunter, *To Change the World*, 35.

30. See D. A. Carson, *Christ and Culture Revisited* (Grand Rapids: Eerdmans, 2008), 145–204. For a defense of Christendom, see Peter Leithart, *Defending Constantine: The Twilight of an Empire and the Dawn of Christendom* (Downers Grove, IL: InterVarsity, 2010). For a strong critique of Christendom—and how wielding political power corrupts the church—see the works of John Howard Yoder.

31. Miroslav Volf, *A Public Faith: How Followers of Christ Should Serve the Common Good* (Grand Rapids: Baker, 2011), 79.

32. Ibid., 17–21, 37–54.

33. See Mathonnet-VanderWell, "Reformed Intramurals."

34. Here I remain close to the terminology of James Hunter, who names this approach "Relevant To."

35. H. Richard Niebuhr, *Christ and Culture* (New York: Harper, 1956), 80.

36. Ibid., 106.

37. See ibid., 84, 90.

38. See the movement's most seminal book, written by the Peruvian priest Gustavo Gutierrez (*A Theology of Liberation: History, Politics and Salvation* [Maryknoll, NY: Orbis, 1971]).

39. Harvie Conn, "The Mission of the Church," in *Evangelicals and Liberation*, ed. Carl Amerding (Phillipsburg, NJ: P&R, 1977), 81. Conn brilliantly points out that liberation theology is indeed too "worldly"—too willing to "baptize" historical/cultural trends as the redemptive work of God. But, he

argues, conservative evangelicals who accept an unjust social status quo (and enjoy its benefits) instead of fighting against it are ironically doing just what the liberationists are doing, though in reverse. They are baptizing the historical/ cultural order as God's work. Conn writes (p. 82), "In spite of the apparent differences between the revolutionary and the conservative, there is basically one essential agreement—both identify the purpose of God with the present historical situation. In one there is conformity to the status quo; in the other a conformity with the revolution."

40. This is the way George Hunsinger summarizes this model. Hunsinger's useful summary of Niebuhr's models is found in R. Michael Allen, *Reformed Theology* (Edinburgh: T&T Clark, 2010), 168. Hunsinger adds that Niebuhr found the "Christ above culture" model "at one and the same time too credulous about culture and too conciliatory about Christ, lacking an adequate sense of divine judgment."

41. Niebuhr, *Christ and Culture*, 130; see D. A. Carson's treatment of the "Christ above culture" pattern in *Christ and Culture Revisited*, 20–22.

42. While the Two Kingdoms also has a positive view of God's activity in the world, it makes a very sharp distinction between what God does in the world and in the church; it would never say that God's work in the world, apart from the church and the preaching of the Word, is redemptive or something the church must adapt to and join with.

43. Robert Schuller, *Your Church Has Real Possibilities* (Glendale, CA: Regal, 1975).

44. Robert Schuller, *Self-Esteem: The New Reformation* (Waco, TX: Word, 1982), 14.

45. Bill Hybels and Rick Warren are friends of mine, and I can vouch for the fact that, despite a deluge of withering criticism of their churches from across the spectrum, they have not simply recoiled or responded harshly. They have listened to their critics, even the severest, with humility and appreciation and have continually made adjustments to their ministries. For example, see the self-critique by Bill Hybels and Greg Hawkins, *Reveal: Where Are You?* (South Barrington, IL: Willow Creek Association, 2007).

46. Gary Pritchard's PhD dissertation provided one of the first major critiques of the seeker church movement. A popular version of his Northwestern University doctoral thesis was published later as *Willow Creek Seeker Services: Evaluating a New Way of Doing Church* (Grand Rapids: Baker, 1996).

47. As we will see below, many emerging churches fit better into the Counterculturalist model than they do into this one.

48. Ultimately, this is the same path that seeker churches and liberal churches follow; they are simply adapting to a different dominant culture.

49. Darrell L. Guder, ed., *Missional Church: A Vision for the Sending of the Church in North America* (Grand Rapids: Eerdmans, 1998).

50. See ibid.

51. See J. C. Hoekendijk, *The Church Inside Out* (Philadelphia: Westminster, 1967), 19–20. See *The Church for Others and the Church for the World: A Quest for Structures for Missionary Congregations* (Geneva: World Council of Churches, 1967). For a good discussion of the recent history of the *missio Dei* concept and of how it grew out of new theological understandings of the Trinity and the kingdom of God, see Craig Van Gelder and Dwight J. Zscheile, *The Missional Church in Perspective: Mapping Trends and Shaping the Conversation* (Grand Rapids: Baker, 2011), 17–40.

52. This effect was predicted by J. Gresham Machen in *Christianity and Liberalism*, new ed. (1923; repr., Grand Rapids: Eerdmans, 2009).

53. See Kent Carlson and Mike Luekin, *Renovation of the Church: What Happens When a Seeker Church Discovers Spiritual Formation* (Downers Grove, IL: InterVarsity, 2011).

54. Van Gelder and Zscheile, *Missional Church in Perspective*, 70.

55. As we will see, the Two Kingdoms model also teaches that Christians should not try to transform culture along Christian lines, but it is much more sanguine about society as a whole and about the goodness of Christian participation in secular callings.

56. Stanley Hauerwas and William Willimon, *Resident Aliens: Life in the Christian Colony* (Nashville: Abingdon, 1989), 47.

57. James Hunter calls adherents of this model "Neo-Anabaptists" and gives a particularly insightful critique in *To Change the World: The Irony, Tragedy, and Possibility of Christianity in the Late Modern World* (New York: Oxford University Press, 2010), 150–66.

58. John Howard Yoder, *The Politics of Jesus* (Grand Rapids: Eerdmans, 1972).

59. Radical Orthodoxy at first glance may seem to have little to do with Anabaptists, since it is a contemporary movement of largely High Church Anglicans. Yet it levels a similar critique at modern secular thought and culture as that offered by Hauerwas (see James K. A. Smith, *Radical Orthodoxy: Mapping a Post-Secular Theology* [Grand Rapids: Baker, 2004]).

60. See Shane Claiborne, *Jesus for President: Politics for Ordinary Radicals* (Grand Rapids: Zondervan, 2008). Claiborne is known for his "litany of resistance": "With governments that kill … we will not comply. With the theology of empire … we will not comply. With the hoarding of riches … we will not comply. To the peace that is not like Rome's … we pledge allegiance" (quoted in Ron Cole, "The Subversive Alternative Language of the Kingdom" [October 11, 2007], http://thewearypilgrim.typepad.com/the_weary_pilgrim/2007/10/the -subversive-.html [accessed February 1, 2012)]).

61. For more on the new monasticism, see Jonathan Wilson, *Living Faithfully in a Fragmented World: Lessons for the Church from MacIntyre's After*

Virtue (Harrisburg, PA: Trinity Press, 1998); Shane Claiborne, *The Irresistible Revolution: Living as an Ordinary Radical* (Grand Rapids: Zondervan, 2006); Jonathan Wilson-Hartgrove, *New Monasticism: What It Has to Say to Today's Church* (Grand Rapids: Brazos, 2008).

62. It is worth observing that Wilberforce, who himself could be put in the "Christ transforming culture" model, was nonetheless helped immensely by Quakers and other Protestants from an Anabaptist tradition on how to relate to culture.

63. Carson, *Christ and Culture Revisited*, 218.

64. Hunter, *To Change the World*, 164.

65. Van Gelder and Zscheile, *Missional Church in Perspective*, 142.

66. David VanDrunen (*Living in God's Two Kingdoms: A Biblical Vision for Christianity and Culture* [Wheaton, IL: Crossway, 2010]) provides an accessible exposition of the Two Kingdoms model from the perspective of Reformed covenant theology. For summaries of the positions and arguments on both sides of this controversy within the conservative Reformed world (particularly in the U.S.), see the article by British scholar Dan Strange, "Not Ashamed! The Sufficiency of Scripture for Public Theology," *Themelios* 36.2 (July 2011): 238–60, http://tgc-documents.s3.amazonaws.com/journal-issues/36.2/ Themelios_36.2.pdf (accessed January 30, 2012).

67. See VanDrunen, *Living in God's Two Kingdoms*, 75–76.

68. VanDrunen, *Living in God's Two Kingdoms*, 27.

69. Ibid., 62.

70. Quoting VanDrunen, *Living in God's Two Kingdoms*, 26, and Strange, "Not Ashamed!" 244, respectively.

71. See Strange, "Not Ashamed!" 245. "[For the Two Kingdoms view] the secular state is ... one of the triumphs of the West."

72. VanDrunen, *Living in God's Two Kingdoms*, 27.

73. David VanDrunen, *A Biblical Case for Natural Law* (Grand Rapids: Acton Institute, 2006), 40.

74. See William Wright, *Martin Luther's Understanding of God's Two Kingdoms* (Grand Rapids: Baker, 2010).

75. T. David Gordon, "The Insufficiency of Scripture," *Modern Reformation* 11 (January–February 2002): 19. Gordon writes, "The Bible is sufficient to guide the human-as-covenanter, but not sufficient to guide the human-as-mechanic, the human-as-physician, the human-as-businessman, the human-as-parent, the human-as-husband, the human-as-wife, or the human-as-legislator." See also his response brought about by criticism of his original article ("Response from T. David Gordon," *Modern Reformation* 11 [May–June 2002]: 46).

76. See Gordon, "Insufficiency of Scripture," 11. I am also basing this statement on hundreds of comments and posts on Two Kingdoms websites.

77. VanDrunen, *Living in God's Two Kingdoms*, 168.

78. See Michael Horton, "Christ and Culture Once More," *White Horse Inn*

Blog (December 17, 2011), www.whitehorseinn.org/blog/2011/12/17/christ-and
-culture-once-more/ (accessed February 2, 2012).

79. Here is another example of differences within a model or category. Many
proponents of the Two Kingdoms approach teach that this material world will
burn up completely, and so nothing we do here—other than the spiritual work of
evangelism and building up the church—will transfer over into the new heaven
and new earth. However, Michael Horton (*The Christian Faith: A Systematic
Theology for Pilgrims on the Way* [Grand Rapids: Zondervan, 2011], 348, 989–90)
seems to follow Herman Bavinck and others in saying that this material world
will not be completely annihilated and replaced by a new one, but rather the
present one will be "transitioned" and renewed, along with our bodies. David
VanDrunen (*Living in God's Two Kingdoms*, 65–66) takes the position that our
bodies will be resurrected and renewed, but nothing else in creation will be
renewed—it will all be burned up and replaced.

80. Horton, "Christ and Culture Once More"; Horton's blog post was written in response to my post on Christ and culture in which I had summarized the
Two Kingdoms position. Horton states (quoting my post), "Nothing in the 2K
[Two Kingdoms] view entails that 'Christians do not, then, pursue their vocation
in a distinctively Christian way' or 'that neither the church nor individual Christians should be in the business of changing the world or society.'" As I've shown,
many Two Kingdoms proponents—including VanDrunen—say the opposite.
Horton also writes that, while the church as an institution should not be trying
to reform society, Christian individuals should be (as "salt") and can be part of
major movements such as the abolition of slavery.

81. A good place to start for a Two Kingdoms critique is Daniel Strange,
"Not Ashamed!" 238–60. While Strange focuses on recent exchanges within the
Reformed world, the broad outlines of his summaries and criticisms hold for the
broader conversation between models as well. For a general critique of the Two
Kingdoms model, both Lutheran and Reformed, see Carson, *Christ and Culture
Revisited*, 210–18.

82. John Calvin, *Institutes of the Christian Religion*, ed. John T. McNeill
(Philadelphia: Westminster, 1960), 1:273–75.

83. Ibid., 1:270–71.

84. See Nicholas Wolterstorff, *Justice: Rights and Wrongs* (Princeton, NJ:
Princeton University Press, 2008), 44–64; see also Brian Tierney, *The Idea of
Natural Rights: Studies on Natural Rights, Natural Law, and Church Law 1150 to
1625* (Grand Rapids: Eerdmans, 1997). In chapter 1, Wolterstorff points out that
before the Christian idea of *imago Dei*, no society thought of every single human
being as equal in dignity and worth. Human beings were judged by various "capacities," and any group that lacked, say, rationality or some other virtue was considered
worthy of being slaves. Even Aristotle said some people were born to be slaves.

85. See Samuel Moyn, *The Last Utopia: Human Rights in History* (Cambridge,
MA: Harvard University Press, 2010).

86. See David Bentley Hart, *Atheist Delusions: The Christian Revolution and Its Fashionable Enemies* (New Haven, CT: Yale University Press, 2009). Hart makes a case for these and many other "givens" of modern life coming from biblical understandings of things.

87. Quoted in Strange, "Not Ashamed!" 255–56.

88. See Rodney Stark, *For the Glory of God: How Monotheism Led to Reformations, Science, Witch-Hunts, and the End of Slavery* (Princeton, NJ: Princeton University Press, 2004), 291–366.

89. See Strange, "Not Ashamed!" 248.

90. Michael Sandel, *Justice: What's the Right Thing to Do?* (New York: Farrar, Straus and Giroux, 2009), 261.

91. Gordon, "Insufficiency of Scripture," 19.

92. Michael S. Horton, "How the Kingdom Comes," *Christianity Today* 50.1 (January 2006): 42, www.christianvisionproject.com/2006/01/how_the_kingdom_comes.html (accessed February 2, 2012).

93. See C. John Sommerville, *The Decline of the Secular University* (New York: Oxford University Press, 2007), 69–70.

94. Allen, *Reformed Theology*, 174. For example, justification by faith alone undergirds ethnic harmony within the people of God (see Gal 2–3). Similarly, the doctrine of Christ's resurrection threatens to undo various economic and political practices that developed around idol worship in Asia Minor (Acts 17; 19).

95. See Stark, *For the Glory of God*; Diogenes Allen, *Christian Belief in a Postmodern World: The Full Wealth of Conviction* (Philadelphia: Westminster, 1989).

96. Douglas Moo, *The Letters to the Colossians and to Philemon* (Pillar New Testament Commentary; Grand Rapids: Eerdmans, 2008), 422.

97. Ibid.

98. Volf, *A Public Faith*, 92.

99. Kevin DeYoung, "Two Kingdom Theology and Neo-Kuyperians," http://thegospelcoalition.org/blogs/kevindeyoung/2009/08/14/two-kingdom-theology-and-neo-kuyperians/ (accessed February 6, 2012).

100. Quoted in Allen, *Reformed Theology*, 170–71.

101. Allen, *Reformed Theology*, 172.

102. See p. 229 for Geerhardus Vos's argument that this is not the case, that laypeople doing work that honors Christ in the world is a sign of God's redemptive kingdom. David VanDrunen (*Living in God's Two Kingdoms*, 190) comments, "The gospel ministry is not just one profession among many. The Lord Jesus and his apostles never lamented the lack of good engineers or gave instructions for training electricians, but Christ did say, 'The harvest is plentiful, but the laborers are few.'" VanDrunen goes on to make clear he believes that when Jesus speaks of "laborers," he is referring to ordained ministers.

103. DeYoung, "Two Kingdom Theology and Neo-Kuyperians."

104. Timothy Keller, "Coming Together on Culture, Part 1: Theological

Issues," www.redeemercitytocity.com/blog/2011/12/15/coming-together-on
-culture-part-1-theological-issues (accessed November 30, 2015).

105. Ibid. See Mike Goheen's comment on the blog.

106. Horton, "How the Kingdom Comes."

107. Horton, "Christ and Culture Once More."

Chapter 11: Why All the Models Are Right ... and Wrong

1. See especially Daniel Strange, "Evangelical Public Theology? What on Earth? Why on Earth? How on Earth?" in *A Higher Throne: Evangelicals and Public Theology*, ed. Chris Green (Nottingham: Inter-Varsity, 2008).

2. Lesslie Newbigin, *The Gospel in a Pluralist Society* (Grand Rapids: Eerdmans, 1989), 222–33.

3. Lesslie Newbigin, *Foolishness to the Greeks* (Grand Rapids: Eerdmans, 1986), 143–44. Here Newbigin cites Herman Dooyeweerd and seems conversant with and supportive of themes associated with neo-Calvinism.

4. See Lesslie Newbigin, Lamin Sanneh, Jenny Taylor, *Faith and Power: Christianity and Islam in "Secular" Britain* (London: SPCK, 1998), 20–24, 144–61. The father of Christian Reconstructionism, Rousas Rushdoony, calls democracy a "heresy" (*The Institutes of Biblical Law* [Phillipsburg, NJ: P&R, 1980], 100, 214, 747).

5. Jim Wallis, *God's Politics: Why the Right Gets It Wrong and the Left Doesn't Get It* (SanFrancisco: HarperSanFrancisco, 2005).

6. See James K. A. Smith, "Constantinianism of the Left?" http://forsclavigera .blogspot.com/2005/05/constantinianism-of-left.html (accessed February 6, 2012).

7. N. T. Wright, *What Saint Paul Really Said* (Grand Rapids: Eerdmans, 1997). Wright argues (p. 119) that justification isn't "so much about soteriology as about ecclesiology; not so much about salvation as about the church." He writes, "The gospel creates, not a bunch of individual Christians, but a community. If you take the old route of putting justification, in its traditional meaning, at the centre of your theology, you will always be in danger of sustaining some sort of individualism" (pp. 157–58).

8. N. T. Wright, *Simply Christian: Why Christianity Makes Sense* (San Francisco: HarperSanFrancisco, 2006), 226.

9. Ibid., 235–36.

10. Ibid. See Wright's articulation of a "Christian worldview" using the traditional neo-Calvinist categories of creation-fall-redemption-restoration (*The New Testament and the People of God* [Minneapolis: Fortress, 1992], 132).

11. See Mark Noll, *The Civil War as a Theological Crisis* (Chapel Hill: University of North Carolina Press, 2006).

12. James D. Hunter, *To Change the World: The Irony, Tragedy, and Possibility*

of Christianity in the Late Modern World (New York: Oxford University Press, 2010), 41–42.

13. Ibid., 42–43.

14. Ibid., 37–38, 43–44.

15. See D. A. Carson, *Christ and Culture Revisited* (Grand Rapids: Eerdmans, 2008), 44–58.

16. Ibid., 60.

17. Ibid., 59, emphasis his.

18. Another, shorter survey of these biblical-theological points is found in R. Michael Allen, *Reformed Theology* (Edinburgh: T&T Clark, 2010), 157–69.

19. Ibid., 159.

20. Ibid., 160.

21. Francis A. Schaeffer, *Pollution and the Death of Man: The Christian View of Ecology* (Wheaton, IL: Tyndale House, 1970), 65–66. Schaeffer expands on this idea of substantial healing from the results of sin in *True Spirituality* (Wheaton, IL: Tyndale House, 1971).

22. For a short but comprehensive list of biblical examples of common grace, see Allen, *Reformed Theology*, 162.

23. John Murray, *Collected Writings of John Murray* (Edinburgh: Banner of Truth, 1977), 2:96.

24. Isaac Watts, "Joy to the World," emphasis mine.

25. See, e.g., Herman Bavinck, *Reformed Dogmatics, Volume 2: God and Creation*, ed. J. Bolt (Grand Rapids: Baker, 2004). The editor writes that "the teaching that 'grace restores nature' is seen as one of the key elements in Bavinck's theology" (p. 19).

26. A good summary of the teaching on the "present (yet) coming kingdom" is found in Bavinck, *Reformed Dogmatics, Volume 3: Sin and Salvation in Christ*, ed. J. Bolt (Grand Rapids: Baker, 2006).

27. Allen, *Reformed Theology*, 164; see Douglas Moo, "Nature in the New Creation: New Testament Eschatology and the Environment," *Journal of the Evangelical Theological Society* 49 (2006): 449–88.

28. See D. A. Carson, *The God Who Is There: Finding Your Place in God's Story* (Grand Rapids: Baker, 2010), 82. Some people read the parable of the weeds in Matthew 13 as being about true and false Christians within the church, but in the parable the kingdom is a field, and in Jesus' explanation he says, "the field is the world" (v. 38), not the church. Louis Berkhof (*Systematic Theology* [Grand Rapids: Eerdmans, 1996], 570) writes, "The visible church may certainly be said to belong to the kingdom, to be a part of the kingdom, and even to be the most important visible embodiment of the forces of the kingdom … [But] the kingdom may be said to be a broader concept than the church, because it aims at nothing less than the complete control of all the manifestations of life. It represents the dominion of God in every sphere of human endeavor." Berkhof represents the views of Abraham Kuyper, Herman Bavinck, and Geerhardus Vos as well.

Chapter 12: Cultural Engagement through Blended Insights

1. For more on this subject, see Timothy Keller, *Generous Justice: How God's Grace Makes Us Just* (New York: Dutton, 2010).

2. D. Michael Lindsay, *Faith in the Halls of Power: How Evangelicals Joined the American Elite* (New York: Oxford University Press, 2007).

3. See James K. A. Smith, *Desiring the Kingdom: Worship, Worldview, and Cultural Formation* (Grand Rapids: Baker, 2009). Smith believes that liturgy, corporate worship, and community practices such as radical hospitality, forgiveness and reconciliation, and shared resources within a common life are far more powerful for shaping a Christian worldview than classes about worldviews. Christians will only be equipped to integrate faith and work and to operate out of a Christian worldview if they are deeply involved and embedded in a strong and "thick" Christian community.

4. Michael Horton ("How the Kingdom Comes," *Christianity Today* 50.1 [January 2006]: 42, www.christianvisionproject.com/2006/01/how_the_kingdom_comes.html) writes, "There are no calls in the New Testament either to withdraw into a private ghetto or to 'take back' the realms of cultural and political activity. Rather, we find exhortations, like Paul's, to the inauspicious yet crucial task of loving and serving our neighbors with excellence."

5. I consider my Center Church model of "blended insights" to be essentially the same approach as James Hunter's "faithful presence" described in *To Change the World: The Irony, Tragedy, and Possibility of Christianity in the Late Modern World* (New York: Oxford University Press, 2010).

6. Miroslav Volf, *A Public Faith: How Followers of Christ Should Serve the Common Good* (Grand Rapids: Baker, 2011), 93–94.

7. Ibid., 90–91.

8. Ibid., 91–92. Volf (p. 158 n.1) observes that his approach has affinities with the approach of James Hunter.

9. See ibid., ch. 4, "Human Flourishing," 55–74.

10. Thanks to Dr. Michael Wittmer for leading me to this essay by Niebuhr and proposing that the spiritual health of our culture may influence the Christ and culture model we choose.

11. See H. Richard Niebuhr, "Toward the Independence of the Church," in *The Church Against the World*, ed. H. Richard Niebuhr, Wilhelm Pauck, and Francis P. Miller (Chicago: Willett, 1935), www.religion-online.org/showchapter.asp?title=412&C=194 (accessed February 7, 2012).

12. Niebuhr was evidently thinking that the first cycle occurred when the early church grew until it became a virtual state religion under Constantine and later had to be renewed by the rise of monasticism. The second cycle took place when the monastic orders evangelized pagan Europe, which led to the corruption

of the medieval church, which had to be renewed by the Protestant Reformation. The third cycle was the rise of Protestant and Catholic Christendom in Europe and North America and then the current decline under the rise of secularism. The right "renewal" mode is still being debated.

13. David Bentley Hart, *Atheist Delusions: The Christian Revolution and Its Fashionable Enemies* (New Haven, CT: Yale University Press, 2009); Nicholas Wolterstorff, *Justice: Rights and Wrongs* (Princeton, NJ: Princeton University Press, 2008).

14. See, e.g., Kevin DeYoung and Greg Gilbert, *What Is the Mission of the Church? Making Sense of Social Justice, Shalom, and the Great Commission* (Wheaton, IL: Crossway, 2011). DeYoung and Gilbert take what seems to be a moderately Two Kingdoms approach to culture. They rightly warn that some of the other models — like Transformationism, the liberal end of what we are calling the Relevance model, and the neo-Anabaptists undermine a strong emphasis on ecclesiastical evangelism.

15. Thanks to Michael Wittmer for the concept of each model as a tool kit.

16. Ephesians 4:11 speaks of God giving some the gift and calling of "evangelist," and Romans 12:7–8 speaks of the gifts of serving (*diakonia*) and mercy. First Peter 4:11 mentions "speaking" gifts and "serving" gifts, which many commentators believe refers to categories of gifts — gifts that have to do with preaching and teaching and gifts that have to do with deeds, administration, and service.

17. See Michael Goheen, *As the Father Sent Me, I Am Sending You: Lesslie Newbigin's Missionary Ecclesiology* (Zoetermeer, Netherlands: Boekencentrum, 2000), for an argument that the missional ecclesiology of Newbigin is not incompatible with a Kuyperian understanding. See Michael Goheen and Craig Bartholomew, *Living at the Crossroads: An Introduction to Christian Worldview* (Grand Rapids: Baker, 2008), for an excellent, accessible presentation of a Transformationist approach that is shorn of triumphalism and lifts up the importance of the church as contrast community.

18. Kevin DeYoung, "Two Kingdom Theology and Neo-Kuyperians," http://thegospelcoalition.org/blogs/kevindeyoung/2009/08/14/two-kingdom-theology-and-neo-kuyperians/ (accessed February 8, 2012).

19. Kevin DeYoung, "You Can Get There from Here," http://thegospel coalition.org/blogs/kevindeyoung/2011/12/22/you-can-get-there-from-here/ (accessed February 8, 2012).

20. See Andy Crouch, *Culture Making: Recovering Our Creative Calling* (Downers Grove, IL: InterVarsity, 2008), 90–96. Thanks to Michael Wittmer for reminding me of this chapter in Andy's book.

21. For a good traditional exposition of the Great Commission, see DeYoung and Gilbert, *What Is the Mission of the Church?*, 15–66.

22. John Bolt, *A Free Church, A Holy Nation: Abraham Kuyper's American Public Theology* (Grand Rapids: Eerdmans, 2000), 428–29.

23. R. Michael Allen, *Reformed Theology* (Edinburgh: T&T Clark, 2010), 174.

24. See ibid., 175.

Reflections on Cultural Engagement

1. Peter Berger, *The Sacred Canopy* (Garden City, NY: Doubleday, 1967).

Response to Andy Crouch

1. Louis Berkhof, *Systematic Theology* (Grand Rapids: Eerdmans, 1949), 205.

ABOUT THE CONTRIBUTORS

Daniel Strange (PhD, University of Bristol) is academic vice president and lecturer in culture, religion, and public theology at Oak Hill College, London. He is the author or coauthor of several books, including *Their Rock Is Not Like Our Rock* and *The Possibility of Salvation Among the Unevangelized*.

Gabriel Salguero is the president of the National Latino Evangelical Coalition and co-lead pastor of The Lamb's Church in New York with his wife, Rev. Jeanette Salguero. He serves on the board of Sojourners and has been named as one of the most prominent Latino evangelical leaders by the *Huffington Post*, the Center for American Progress, *El Diario*, and Jorge Ramos's *Al Punto*.

Andy Crouch is the author of *Playing God: Redeeming the Gift of Power*. His book *Culture Making: Recovering Our Creative Calling* won *Christianity Today*'s 2009 Book Award for Christianity and Culture. In December 2012, he became executive editor of *Christianity Today*, where he is also executive producer of *This Is Our City*, a multiyear project featuring documentary video, reporting, and essays about Christians seeking the flourishing of their cities. Crouch is also a senior fellow of the International Justice Mission's IJM Institute. His writings have appeared in *The Wall Street Journal* and in several editions of *Best Christian Writing* and *Best Spiritual Writing*. He lives with his family in Swarthmore, Pennsylvania.

Shaped by the Gospel
Doing Balanced, Gospel-Centered Ministry in Your City

Timothy Keller, with new contributions by Michael Horton and Dane Ortlund

It is easy to assume that if we understand the gospel and preach it faithfully, our ministry will necessarily be shaped by it — but this is not true. Many churches claim to be gospel-centered but do not have a ministry that is shaped by, centered on, and empowered through the gospel. The implications of the gospel have not yet worked their way into the fabric of how that church does ministry.

Gospel-centered ministry is more theologically driven than program driven. To pursue it, we must spend time reflecting on the essence, the truths, and the very patterns of the gospel itself. The gospel is neither religion nor irreligion, but something else entirely — a third way of relating to God through grace. In *Shaped by the Gospel*, bestselling author and pastor Timothy Keller addresses several current discussion and conflicts about the nature of the gospel and shows how faithful preaching of the gospel leads to individual and corporate renewal.

This new edition contains the first section of *Center Church* in an easy-to-read format with new reflections and additional essays from Timothy Keller and several other contributors.

Serving a Movement
Doing Balanced, Gospel-Centered Ministry in Your City

Timothy Keller, with new contributions by Tim Chester, Daniel Montgomery and Mike Cosper, and Alan Hirsch

In *Serving a Movement*, bestselling author and pastor Timothy Keller looks at the nature of the church's mission and its relationship to the work of individual Christians in the world. He examines what it means to be a "missional" church today and how churches can practically equip people for missional living. Churches need to intentionally cultivate an integrative ministry that connects people to God, to one another, to the needs of the city, and to the culture around us. Finally, he highlights the need for intentional movements of churches planting new churches that faithfully proclaim God's truth and serve their communities.

Serving a Movement contains the third section of *Center Church* in an easy-to-read format with new essays from several other contributors and Tim Keller's responses to the essays.

REDEEMER CITY to CITY

Any reader of *Center Church* might be interested to know that Timothy Keller founded an organization called Redeemer City to City.

Redeemer City to City carries out the ministry principles you've read about in this book around the world. Coaching and training urban church planters and starting gospel movements in global cities are at the core of CTC's mission.

If you'd like to know more about Redeemer City to City's work, write to us at hello@redeemercitytocity.com.

May Jesus Christ be known in cities.